'I have read the proposal for this book, and I really look forward to reading the whole work. It is very exciting to have a new volume highlighting the voices of individuals with learning differences which impede their participation in mainstream culture, showcasing their unique perspectives and experiences which is of tremendous value. I am particularly excited about the emphasis on community engagement and representation.'

Professor Susan Hogan, *PhD, DLitt, is Professor of Arts & Health at the University of Derby and a Professorial Fellow of the Institute of Mental Health at the University of Nottingham*

'*Art Therapy with People with Learning Disabilities: Authentic Voices in Clinical Practice and Research* is a groundbreaking anthology that rightly provides an important positionality, revealed through authentic co-production and sensitivity with individuals with learning disabilities at the heart of art therapy practice and research. Providing broad scope and depth of inquiry, the contexts range from the UK, Canada, the USA, China and Australia. Important themes of justice, agency, advocacy and relationality are integral to the chapters co-authored with individuals who have learning disabilities, offering unfiltered insights that challenge traditional power dynamics in therapeutic literature. With practical insights, evidence-based approaches, and innovative practices like community-based partnerships, this book pushes the boundaries of traditional art therapy. It's a must-have for practitioners, educators, and healthcare professionals seeking to deepen their understanding of inclusive art therapy practices, serving as both a valuable resource and a catalyst for change in engaging with individuals with learning disabilities.'

Dominik Havsteen-Franklin, *Professor of Practice – Arts Therapies, Brunel University, London*

I0121585

'Congratulations to Simon Hackett and Nicki Power and the fine international group of pioneers they have brought together from America, Australia, Canada, China and the UK. Art therapists were at the forefront of the first respectful work with people with ID and this book continues the proud tradition with a 21st century understanding, unpacking politics, stigma, inclusion, ableism, neurodiversity, justice, dignity, self-advocacy. Whilst acknowledging and calling out the external inequalities, the book provides inspiration over the transforming power of art and attachment. This book is relevant for all professionals working with disability.'

Valerie Sinason, *PhD, President, Institute of Psychotherapy and Disability*

'An important and groundbreaking book which should be essential reading for anyone working with people with learning disabilities. The voices of people with learning disabilities come through loud and clear. This accessible book engages the reader noting not only the challenges faced, but showing how well art therapy engages and empowers marginalised experiences allowing people with learning disabilities to express themselves and communicate in innovative ways. The authors are convincing that this work is able to enact social change by challenging inequalities. In short art therapy is shown to be a disruptive and revolutionary process.'

Professor Jill Maben OBE, *Professor of Health Services Research and Nursing and parent to a son with autism and learning disabilities*

'As the parent of a son with severe Learning Disabilities, and as a Patient and Public Voice partner with National Health Service England (NHSE), I have seen the transformative power of Art Therapy in both children's and adults' hospices and with working on a co-production project with Niki Power. I really welcome this new book and its view through an empowering and positive lens.'

Anna Gill OBE, *Member of Peoples' Advisory Forum at NHS England & Vice-Chair Cambridgeshire Community Services NHS Trust*

'This truly innovative book not only gathers international perspectives on art therapy with people with learning disabilities but also includes their voices and experiences in all its aspects. As such, it is a masterclass on how to conduct genuine co-production, and an inspiration to practitioners in all fields. It is a seminal publication which I will recommend to trainees and qualified art therapists.'

Dr Val Huet, *PhD, is a Visiting Professor at the University of Hertfordshire and Ulster University. She served as Chief Executive Officer of the British Association of Art Therapists from 2003 to 2021*

'The book moves beyond the often standardised inclusion of a few quotes or images to represent participant or client "voice": it addresses the complexities of how power, relationship, art, expression and meaning making interact within the creation of art therapy involving people with learning disabilities and with autism. Here are careful considerations of difference, divergence and the ways that othering and silencing can be reproduced within the apparently "free" or idealised "expressions" of creativity and art. The chapters explore routes to address how different voices can be facilitated in the face of societal forces that oppress within life outside, and inside, the art therapy space. This includes a rethinking of the relationships between professionals and participants to see how factors such as language, time, identity and role can be worked with differently to develop 'voice' and to enable change in research, and in practice, involving people with learning disabilities. The different chapters avoid the trap of essentialising one approach or set of methods and carefully acknowledge how varied contexts and situations enable nuanced opportunities and responses to emerge.'

Phil Jones *is Emeritus Professor of Children's Rights and Wellbeing, IOE, UCL's Faculty of Education and Society, co-author of* Child Agency and Voice in Therapy *(with Cedar, Haythorne, Mercieca and Ramsden, Routledge, 2020)*

'A label of learning disability can impose multiple constrictions for members of society, not only in the realm of interpersonal relationships, but in denying the full human rights we all need. This book shows the power of art therapy to change lives even in these most difficult circumstances. Skilled art therapist practitioner-researchers from around the world show us that building communication through art is key to unlocking psychological and social health. The progressive approaches shown here will be of relevance to both the learning disability field and more widely to all practitioners seeking a credible biopsychosocial model of practice.'

Dr Neil Springham, *Chief Therapies Officer of Oxleas NHS Foundation Trust, London. Consultant Art Therapist*

'This book offers a sensitive, insightful and very much needed text that makes the multiple uses of art therapy with clients with disabilities accessible to a wide readership. Themes such as justice, agency, advocacy and connections are explored. Unlike other publications, the voices of the clients are at the centre of this book, making this an exemplar text for co-creation that needs to become accessible widely.'

Professor Vicky Karkou *is the Director of the Research Centre for Arts and Wellbeing at Edge Hill University*

Art Therapy with People with Learning Disabilities

Art Therapy with People with Learning Disabilities brings together diverse, international contributions from practitioners, researchers and clients within the field of art therapy to inform best practice when working with people with learning disabilities. Focusing on four core themes – justice, agency, advocacy and connection – this engaging volume invites readers into the transformative world of art therapy, where creativity serves as a powerful tool for self-expression and positive change.

Emphasising the voices and experiences of individuals with learning disabilities, many chapters are co-authored with clients who bring invaluable lived experience, which offers readers a fresh perspective on art therapy in practice. These insights are woven together in a rich tapestry of case studies, intervention descriptions and consideration of therapist positionality to illustrate how art therapy can empower people with learning disabilities.

Readers will gain practical insights, evidence-based approaches and a variety of creative techniques that can be applied to both clinical and research settings. This book demonstrates how art therapy facilitates self-expression and fosters personal agency, making it a compelling read for both new and seasoned art therapists alike. It will also resonate with educators and healthcare professionals seeking to enhance their understanding and application of inclusive art therapy practices across a range of health, social care and educational settings.

Nicki Power is Strategic Lead for Arts Therapies (Learning Disability) at East London NHS Foundation Trust and a Doctoral Researcher at Queen Mary University, London, supported by Barts Charity. She specialises in inclusive arts-based research with people with learning disabilities and using arts for system change in healthcare.

Dr Simon Hackett is a Consultant Art Psychotherapist with over 20 years of experience working with people with learning disabilities. He is a Senior Clinical Lecturer in Applied Mental Health Research at Newcastle University and a UK National Institute for Health and Care Research Advanced Clinical Academic Fellow.

Art Therapy with People with Learning Disabilities

Authentic Voices in Clinical Practice and Research

Edited by Nicki Power
and Simon Hackett

Routledge
Taylor & Francis Group
LONDON AND NEW YORK

First published 2026
by Routledge
4 Park Square, Milton Park, Abingdon, Oxon OX14 4RN

and by Routledge
605 Third Avenue, New York, NY 10158

Routledge is an imprint of the Taylor & Francis Group, an informa business

© 2026 selection and editorial matter, Nicki Power and Simon Hackett; individual chapters, the contributors

British Library Cataloguing-in-Publication Data
A catalogue record for this book is available from the British Library

ISBN: 978-1-032-39651-4 (hbk)
ISBN: 978-1-032-39650-7 (pbk)
ISBN: 978-1-003-35073-6 (ebk)

DOI: 10.4324/9781003350736

Typeset in Times New Roman
by codeMantra

Access the Support Material: www.routledge.com/9781032396507

This book is dedicated to the people with learning disabilities whose resilience and creativity inspired this work. We honour the many individuals who have shaped both our clinical and research practice over the years. We hold in deep respect those whose stories we cannot tell – the voices silenced by time, circumstance or the inability to give consent. May these stories – told and untold – continue to shape the field of art therapy.

We hope this volume will contribute to the ongoing journey towards a more inclusive, equitable and accessible society, where the voices and rights of people with learning disabilities not only heard but championed. To the next generation of art therapists and advocates with lived experience, who will carry this work forward with passion, creativity and a clear commitment to social justice.

Contents

Figures

Tables

Contributors

Shehnoor Ahmed is an Art Therapist who has worked in a Community Learning Disabilities Team for seven years and is currently working in Forensic Services. Her experience of working in learning disabilities from the start of her career has shaped her practice into one that is able to adapt to the needs of the person and their environment. She is particularly curious about extending her practice into spaces outside of traditional clinical settings such as nature-based art therapy as well as museums and galleries.

Gemma Allen is an experienced Palliative Care Inclusion and Community Partnerships lead for The Mary Stevens Hospice and has worked in the hospice sector for over ten years. She is a co-founder of the award-winning *No Barriers Here* programme, an independent consultant and was a former Chair of the Palliative Care for People with Learning Disabilities Charity (PCPLD). She champions for equity of marginalised communities, working in co-production and adopting a public health approach to palliative care.

Dr Elizabeth (Liz) Ashby has worked in learning disability services in the NHS for over 25 years and loves her work as an Art Therapist. Liz gained a PhD in 2018 and enjoys research and writing, as well as making art. Liz is passionate about supporting people with learning disabilities and addressing health inequalities, as well as other issues that people suffer from experiencing in the wider world. Liz is also passionate about her relationship with God and is delighted that her NHS Trust now requires respect, excellence, integrity, collaboration and compassion to be the values that its employees hold.

Jane Batt is a mother and a grandmother, and these roles are the most special to her. A native of Bristol, England, Jane has many memories of the city and of all the places she has lived in. Jane can be recognised easily with her striking blonde and red hair and the beautiful colourful clothes that she enjoys wearing. Writing has provided an unexpected enjoyment for Jane.

Mairi Benton is an Art Therapist who has been practising in the Southwest of England in a Learning Disability Community Health Team for the past 20 years. She has developed a specialist interest in trauma and in working with people who have 'learning disability', in particular, exploring collaboration and co-production within creative therapies. Mairi is passionate about open-water marathon swimming and can usually be found splashing around in a local lake or swimming pool.

Siobhán Burns qualified as an Art Therapist at the University of Sheffield in 2000. After working with Looked After Children in Yorkshire and Lincolnshire and in NHS Adult Mental Health Services in Bradford, Siobhán has been working in an NHS Adult Learning Disability Service in Rotherham since 2005. She is also a Co-Director of a Community Interest Company and, through this, has been involved in providing art therapy groups in the community in Sheffield. Siobhán enjoys working collaboratively with clients and appreciates the opportunity for learning from each new person she meets.

Tomas Calhoun is a prolific artist, practising for as long as he can remember. Tomas agreed to be a co-author because he likes being involved in artistic pursuits and enjoys the recognition he receives for his artistic talents. Tomas attends social events in the regional town where he lives and enjoys creating and dancing. He has a Down syndrome diagnosis and works with other neurodivergent artists in art studios or on his own at home.

Dr Emma Gentle is an Art Therapist and researcher working with neurodiverse and neurotypical people. She completed her PhD (USyd) on group artmaking processes, MA in Art Therapy (UWS), MA in Applied Anthropology, Community and Youth Work (GU) and Diplomas in psychology and applied psychology (BU). Emma's research and practice centres on the capacity of creativity to improve mental health. In her practice, she utilises art processes to cultivate unencumbered expression of feelings, tell story, increase connection, reduce stigma and as a creative recovery tool. Her arts practice includes sculpting, multimedia and photography.

Toni Leigh Harrison is an Art Psychotherapist working within the National Health Service (NHS) in the North East of England. Toni has completed a Master's degree in Art Psychotherapy Practice and an undergraduate Bachelor's degree in Psychology. Toni qualified as an Art Psychotherapist in 2017, having worked as an arts Psychotherapies team assistant prior to this. Toni is currently undertaking a part-time PhD exploring the benefits of manualised art psychotherapy for individuals with intellectual disabilities within secure care (forensic) settings in the UK.

Sandra Hewitt-Parsons is a registered Art Therapist and PhD student in the Faculty of Education at Memorial University of Newfoundland and Labrador. As one of the first Art Therapists in her region, Sandra is passionate about supporting mental health in her province. A survivor of a major childhood stroke, Sandra truly believes in the healing power of artmaking. Drawing on a person-centred, disability-sensitive and trauma-informed framework, she invites clients to participate in various expressive multimodal techniques designed to promote their potential.

Dr Jed Jerwood is an Art Psychotherapist and Clinical Academic Researcher. Jed's current clinical practice is in adult mental health. His research interests lie in addressing inequity in health care, particularly palliative and end-of-life care. His doctoral research focused on improving palliative care for people with serious mental illness (SMI). Jed is passionate about the use of arts-based methods in both clinical practice and research. He is co-founder of the *No Barriers Here* programme.

Elizabeth King is an Art Psychotherapist (MA) who has worked in a variety of professional settings since qualifying 20 years ago and has a particular interest in working with adults and children with learning disabilities. For the last 13 years, she has worked in a specialist support primary school in the north-west of England. She is an avid supporter of enabling people to achieve their full potential within their relationships and occupations through Art Therapy. Her work, which is generally done in a group environment, aims to bring people together and enable them to tolerate each other's differences and support one another. Elizabeth is also a strong believer in the healing powers of nature and spends a lot of her spare time walking in woodland climbing hills and wild swimming.

Mizuho Koizumi is an UK Health and Care Professions Council (HCPC)-registered Art Psychotherapist. She has worked in the Forensic Directorate as part of the Learning Disabilities and Autism Service in East London NHS Foundation Trust since 2015. Recently, she presented her work at the 30th International Association for Forensic Psychotherapy Conference in London and the 14th European Congress of Mental Health in Intellectual Disabilities in Helsinki. She is a committee member of the Institute of Psychotherapy and Disability (IPD). She grew up in Japan and moved to the UK in her early adulthood. She graduated from the Royal College of Arts with a master's in metalwork and has exhibited her artwork both nationally and internationally.

Professor Chi Kin Kwan is an Assistant Professor at the City University of Hong Kong, specialising in the fields of diversity, equity, inclusion and mental health. Although he nurtured a passion for drawing in his youth, he has since directed his creative energies towards conducting research in these areas.

Lizzy chose not to enter an author biography.

Joey Mander is a young man with a passion for activism in the disabled community to right the wrongs that they face. Joey has autism and SPG10 Spastic Paraplegia which affects both his brain and body, and experiences pain most of the time, but does not allow these problems to limit what he can do. He has a particular ability to communicate with people whose communication is a problem, and he is fluent in Makaton. He is also an excellent artist and gives articulate talks at events. Joey is Chair of the Coventry Youth Activists group, which is supported by Coventry Grapevine.

Hazel Meakin qualified as an Art Therapist at Leeds Beckett University in 2017. After offering long-term Art Therapy to adults with mental health needs, many of whom had experienced early relational trauma and societal trauma. Hazel has been working in an NHS Adult Learning Disability Service in Rotherham since 2020 and more recently an NHS Adult Learning Disability Service in Doncaster since 2023. She is also a Co-Director of a Community Interest Company providing art therapy groups in the community in Sheffield. Before qualifying as an art therapist, Hazel had a background in mental health advocacy that informs the value she places on collaborative working.

Dr Connie Newcombe gained a Doctorate in Clinical Psychology from The University of Sheffield in 2023. She is currently working in an NHS Adult Learning Disability Service in Rotherham. Connie has co-facilitated Art Therapy group sessions, including collecting outcome measures. She is enthusiastic about the role of creative therapies within the psychological therapies team.

Tsz Yan Yana NG is an Art Therapist and supervisor. She has worked in a wide range of healthcare and educational settings, predominantly with children and adolescents with learning disabilities, and their parents. She is currently exploring Ebru Art and Korean Minhwa, which she finds solace and inspiration in.

Sarah Offley is the Chief Officer for the self-advocacy charity Dudley Voices for Choice, a founder partner of the *No Barriers Here* programme. Her role involves supporting experts with lived experience of learning disabilities and/or autism across a range of services including advocacy, employment, training and health programmes. Sarah has worked in the health and care sector for 30 years.

Vince Peters is an expert with lived experience and a strong advocate, employed by Dudley Voices for Choice as a lead trainer delivering Autism Awareness training. Vince is a member of The Grassroots Group, which is national end-of-life care research group. Vince is a member of the co-production group for the *No Barriers Here* programme.

Samantha Reeves (Sam) is a strong advocate, using her lived experience to address inequalities. Sam is employed by Dudley Voices for Choice as a lead trainer delivering Learning Disability Awareness training. Sam is a member of the co-production group for the *No Barriers Here* programme.

Tania J. Rose is a neurodiversity-affirming arts psychotherapy practitioner, clinical supervisor and educator dedicated to advancing inclusive practices within therapeutic and creative professional development spaces. With extensive experience in working with individuals with cognitive differences, Tania's work is informed by a deep commitment to evidence-based research and alternative models of disability. In addition to facilitating impactful workshops, Tania is an accomplished creative and content creator, focusing on professional development and audio designed to foster well-being and educate practitioners on inclusive neurodiversity-affirming practice. Tania's approach is rooted in the principles of 'nothing about us without us', ensuring that the voices of neurodivergent individuals are central to their work. As a creative practitioner, Tania integrates mindfulness into her practice, fostering a holistic approach to well-being. As a researcher, Tania's enquiries include the creative practitioner experience in the disability space, arts-for-arts-sake, and accessibility and workplace well-being. Tania's ongoing work is aimed at providing resources for therapists and educators, with a focus on ethical considerations and practical applications in working with neurodivergent clients.

Claudia Rossi, MA(AT) AThR PACFA. Reg. Clinical, is an artist, Art Psychotherapist and counsellor living and working in Bunurong Country in Naarm, Melbourne, Australia. Claudia has a Bachelor of Fine Art and in 1997 and completed a Master of Art Therapy degree. Claudia works in the disability field, with clients experiencing mental health challenges and addiction and those seeking personal development. Claudia uses a psychodynamic, psychoanalytic and trauma-informed approach. Claudia's influences include Jungian psychology. She has trained at the CG Jung-Institut Zurich and will soon train in Internal Family Systems at the Australia & New Zealand International Partner of the IFS Institute (US).

Rochele Royster, PhD, ATR-BC, is an Assistant Professor of Art Therapy at Syracuse University. With 20 years of experience, she has integrated Art Therapy into educational settings, working with youth and young adults with learning differences. Her trans-disciplinary approach encompasses community and school-based Art Therapy, race, power and policy in education, multi-sensory methods in reading and literacy, trauma-informed classrooms, environmental justice, black disability and special education within the context of decolonisation in institutional and public settings. Royster's PhD in Community Psychology, completed in 2017 at National Louis University in Chicago, reflects her grassroots approach to arts-based social change, focusing on gun violence, death and grief through memorials of resistance. She has contributed to transformative art-based social justice curriculum development for various organisations and conducted workshops for teaching artists. Royster is also a practising artist, infusing her work with printmaking, quilting and meditative stitching, creating evocative portraits and paintings that explore the profound interplay of individuals lost in intricate patterns.

Kayleigh Sage is the proud owner of two dachshund puppies who keep her active and busy every single day. She enjoys a close relationship with her Mum, and together they are inseparable. Kayleigh's varying health conditions and life experiences have given her a strength and energy to face anything that comes in her way. Writing has been a cathartic and empowering experience for Kayleigh.

Joanne Vallance is an expert with lived experience who empowers others to have their voices heard using her own personal experiences to help professionals get it right for others. Joanne is a member of the co-production group for the *No Barriers Here* programme.

Acknowledgements

We extend our deepest gratitude to all the people with learning disabilities whose resilience, creativity and voices are at the heart of this work – both those named and pseudonymised. The lived experiences of our co-authors with learning disabilities have shaped the authenticity and depth of this volume. Without these diverse contributions, this book would not have been possible.

We also thank all those involved in the case studies and research featured anonymously here, whose real-world insights and stories highlight the transformative potential of art therapy.

Our heartfelt thanks go to the art therapists who wrote from near and far, sharing their passion and expertise. We are deeply proud of their combined dedication to social justice, which will continue to shape the field of art therapy with people with learning disabilities. We are especially grateful to our co-authors – both by training and through lived experience – for their collegiate and collaborative spirit.

We are especially grateful to our colleague Arman Iranpour for his support in developing the index, ensuring the book is as accessible and useful as possible.

We also wish to acknowledge the families, carers and support networks who tirelessly advocate for and empower people with learning disabilities, often in challenging circumstances. Of course, we must thank our loved ones, families and pets, whose support has sustained us through many late nights of writing and editing.

Finally, our sincere thanks go to the editorial and publishing team at Taylor & Francis for their unwavering patience and invaluable support in bringing this book to life.

Introduction

Chapter 1

Disrupting Narratives

The Role of Diverse Voices in Co-Creating Change in Art Therapy

Nicki Power and Simon Hackett

Introduction

This book arose from our recognition of the lack of a comprehensive volume focused on contemporary art therapy practice for adults and children with learning disabilities in the 21st century. As editors, we were keenly aware of the slow systemic changes in socio-political contexts for people with learning disabilities through legislation and activism, juxtaposed with the rapid transformation of social life (and clinical practice) precipitated by, and continuing after, the global COVID-19 pandemic (Power, Dolby & Thorne, 2021). This led us to consider how we could capture and reflect the current cultural context for art therapy with people with learning disabilities in a fresh and authentic edited volume.

Together, we dreamed of a book that would be fully co-produced with people with learning disabilities, would represent global practice in all its diverse richness and challenges, and would present a broad range of cutting-edge practice in the field. When we began gathering the chapters for this volume, we found incredibly sensitive, social justice-orientated, and collaborative work that was occurring in the parts of the world we could reach, whilst also recognising many barriers and gaps.

This seemed to mirror our understanding of the lived lives of people with learning disabilities in the 'here-and-now' within our clinical and research practices, which highlighted entrenched health inequalities and social stigma. This view was strengthened through our discussions with the art therapists from across the world who contributed to this book, despite the diverse contexts, people with learning disabilities continue to be one of the most marginalised in our global society.

At this point, it's important to clarify who we mean when we refer to people with learning disabilities. Throughout this book, we define learning disabilities using the World Health Organization's (2018) classification. This refers to a diverse group of people who, due to a cognitive impairment, have lifelong difficulties with thinking, understanding, and processing information, typically identified during childhood development. Globally, an estimated 1% - 3% of the population has learning disabilities (Harris, 2006), with high prevalence in low- and middle-income countries (Maulik, et al, 2011).

DOI: 10.4324/9781003350736-2

Learning disabilities are distinct from 'learning difficulties', such as dyspraxia or dyslexia, which affect specific aspects of learning but do not involve broader cognitive impairment. Autism, though a life-long neurodevelopmental condition, which impacts a varied group of individuals, does not inherently affect intellectual ability, but there is a higher prevalence of autism among people with learning disabilities than in the general population (Brugha, et al., 2016). Understanding who we mean by 'people with learning disabilities' is crucial, not just for clarity in this book, but also to recognise the wider structural disadvantages faced by this population. Beyond diagnostic definitions, their lived experiences are shaped by wider social determinants of health, which significantly impact their quality of life and life expectancy. Social determinants, such as inadequate housing, barriers to education, and lower income, exacerbate their lower quality of life (Wigham & Emerson, 2015). On average, where analysis of records has taken place, women with learning disabilities die 23 years younger, and men die 19 years younger than the general population (Glover et al., 2017). In some countries, people with learning disabilities from an ethnic minority background have an average age of death of 34 years, which is half the life expectancy of their white counterparts (NHS Race & Health Observatory, 2023).

Limited social networks contribute to increased feelings of loneliness and isolation (Mencap, 2020; *Sense*, n.d.). Additionally, mental health issues are prevalent, with estimates of psychiatric illness among people with learning disabilities ranging from 30% to 50%, significantly higher than in the general population (Buckles et al., 2013; Cooper et al., 2007; Einfield et al., 2011). Complications in addressing mental health needs include co-morbid health conditions, a focus on behavioural interventions, and delays in diagnosis, all of which can lead to further deterioration and prolonged suffering (Beail, 2016; Joint Commission for Mental Health, 2013; Einfield et al., 2011).

We acknowledge this stark picture of inequality and offer a vision for an equitable and accessible society. This book presents examples of the 'real world' impact that art therapy can have as an accessible therapy for many children and adults with learning disabilities. We present this volume as part of that ongoing journey towards greater inclusion.

Telling the Story about Art Therapy with People with Learning Disabilities

We view this volume as part of an evolving narrative centred on art therapy practice with people with learning disabilities, which charts the development of the profession, changing clinical approaches and, ultimately, better lives for people with learning disabilities. This work serves as a companion to two instrumental texts: Mair Rees' (1998) *'Drawing on Difference'* and Stephanie Bull & Kevin O'Farrell's (2012) *'Don't Guess my Happiness!'*, both books made an important contribution to art therapy practice when they were published.

Drawing on Difference was the first collected chapter edition in this field. Published in the same decade as Valerie Sinason's seminal work *Mental Handicap and the Human Condition (1992)*, which validated the role of psychotherapy with people with learning disabilities, Rees' book was a landmark publication in itself marking a significant milestone. It compiled clinical case studies alongside reflective accounts from practitioners. It emphasised the importance of creativity as a vital means of communication for people with learning disabilities with sections covering 'art therapy at work', 'allied approaches', and 'professional issues'.

Fourteen years later, *Don't Guess my Happiness!* sought to map the themes common across practice with this client group. Interspersed between chapters are excerpts from clients themselves, illustrating their perspectives in snapshots. The chapters underscore the importance of understanding each person's unique context and utilising tailored approaches to facilitate meaningful engagement in the therapeutic process. Themes of client empowerment and the value of collaborative or cross-disciplinary working are threaded through the text. It addressed key topics on 'personalisation', 'having a learning disability', 'loss', 'attachment and separation', 'infantilisation', 'powerlessness', and 'self-identity'.

Both volumes are situated within the specific socio-cultural contexts of their respective eras. During the 1990s, as Mair was writing for example, the United Kingdom (UK) witnessed the closure of long-stay hospitals that had housed individuals with learning disabilities for decades (Hackett et al., 2017).

Despite their significant contributions, both texts have limitations when viewed through the critical lens of the 21st century. These texts describe UK-based art therapy practice which is a Western-based practice, linked to the evolution of art therapy as a profession in both the United States (US) and the UK. Alongside the absence of other global cultural paradigms, the diversity of culture within the West is largely unexplored nor is there a focus on post-colonial issues in art therapy. This means that consideration of culturally sensitive practices is much needed within the field of art therapy with people with learning disabilities. Additionally, given the varied group of people which constitutes this client group, these texts may not clearly describe, or may lack, sufficient representation of diverse backgrounds and identities within the learning disability community (and their art therapists), including cultural and socio-economic factors that affect access to art therapy. Furthermore, people with severe and profound learning disabilities, who are often the least visible in society and face significant barriers to accessing and using art therapy, appear largely absent from these books, as they are in the wider literature.

Both texts have strongly shaped the conversation around art therapy for people with learning disabilities. This volume, a further 15 years on, we see as a bridge connecting past insights with contemporary practices and perspectives through the inclusion of co-authors with lived experience.

Privilege and Critical Allyship

There is an inherent contradiction between those who hold expertise and those who hold power related to exclusion, health inequalities, and disparities, and this can be sustained by people being unaware about their own positions of privilege (Nixon, 2019). We therefore start this first chapter of the book with a positionality statement by the editors, and you will find that positionality statements have been made by all of the chapter authors. We have also sought to include people with learning disabilities, the experts, as co-authors in the writing of chapters, thus challenging the presumption of art therapists being 'experts' about the experiences of the people they work with and for. We also acknowledge and give detailed accounts of the expertise of art therapists in their roles and skills.

In this sense, we wanted to assuage and mitigate against any naivety about power imbalances that are inherent in describing the experiences of others, from a privileged position (Eastwood, 2021).

With this in mind, we overtly name the context of some of the social structures, experiences, and the responses to them by people with learning disabilities in relation to 'justice', 'agency', 'advocacy', and 'connections', all explored within art therapy. We hope that a key outcome for the reader will be 'insight' into the lives of people with learning disabilities, their voices, priorities, and experiences. You will find this articulated through their own words or images, and the voices of art therapists who are working towards a 'practical critical allyship', that is, being aware of their own position in relation to understanding societal inequalities experienced by others (Nixon, 2019). You will discover many examples of art therapists becoming 'allies' and operating in 'solidarity' with people with learning disabilities, whilst understanding their own roles as professionals within the power differentials that are inherent in both healthcare settings and communities.

Editorial Positionality Statements

Nicki Power is a white woman with a hidden disability who is an immigrant to the UK from Ireland. She does not have learning disabilities. She is a firm advocate and ally alongside people with learning disabilities, having worked in this field since 2010. Before her art therapy training, she had very limited experience or knowledge of people with learning disabilities. She acknowledges that her social status, level of educational attainment, and professional qualification imbue her with significant power and privilege.

Simon Hackett is a white man without learning disabilities who is working as an art psychotherapist in the UK. Simon's involvement and work with people with learning disabilities pre-date's his art therapy career, going back over 30 years. A member of his extended family has learning disabilities. Simon is aware of his personal highly privileged position and social advantage, being in fulltime employment, having a PhD, owning a home, being married, and having a family, in fact, fitting in with many of the historical and traditional 'social norms' that are inherently valued in Western cultures.

Core Principles

Throughout this book, you will find practice descriptions and evaluations of interventions which seek to include people with learning disabilities as explicit partners in the work, rather than passive subjects to be observed. To achieve this, we employed four core principles, as follows

i **Positive Disruption**

From our first conversations about his book, we wanted to intentionally challenge traditional discourses within art therapy with people with learning disabilities. We saw this as a positive disruption. A term we later learned originated in business (Elasser, 2020). In this context, we consider positive disruption as a deliberate and constructive challenge to established norms and practices which fosters innovative thinking and drives meaningful change. In art therapy, this involves questioning traditional narratives that prioritise behaviour-focused or verbally led approaches and instead advocating for practices that centre on accessible ways to prioritise lived experiences of our clients. Where their unique knowledge and expertise are valued in the therapy and therapists employ a range of adaptive techniques informed by trauma-informed approaches and with an awareness of the impact of wider socio-cultural movements. By embracing positive disruption, we aim to create an environment where voices that have been historically marginalised are amplified, allowing for a richer and more nuanced understanding of individual needs and experiences.

This book intends to initiate such a shift by encouraging practitioners to rethink their methodologies and consider the broader socio-cultural factors that impact people with learning disabilities. Readers are invited to engage deeply with clients' stories and the facilitative therapeutic process which art therapists drive, one that acknowledges the complexities of their lives. We emphasise the importance of involving clients as active participants in this discourse, ensuring that their insights and perspectives shape the therapeutic journey. This collaborative approach not only empowers clients but also enriches the practice of art therapy, fostering a more inclusive and responsive therapeutic environment.

In promoting positive disruption, we acknowledge that change involves transforming the underlying philosophies that guide our practice. By prioritising social justice, we can challenge the established norms, paving the way for a more equitable art therapy landscape that genuinely reflects the diverse experiences of all individuals. Ultimately, this approach seeks to cultivate a profession that is not only aware of but actively works against the systemic inequalities that have long affected people with learning disabilities.

ii **Power and Positionality**

Within our society, invisible norms dominate our cultural practices. Thus, all social systems have groups who are privileged and groups who are not. Although the exclusionary practice of ableism may be particularly relevant for people with learning disabilities, given the diversity of this population, a range of other intersectional aspects of a person's identity must also be considered. Protected characteristics, such as ethnicity, gender, or sexuality, are likely to increase the experience of stigma and inequality for certain groups, whether they also hold a learning disability or not. The impact on health, in its broadest sense, of unequal and unjust social systems is profound, and as we have seen is linked to early mortality and poorer quality of life overall.

Further to us highlighting issues of 'privilege and critical allyship', Stephanie Nixon's (2019) *coin model of privilege* is definitive in illustrating the dynamics of unearned advantages and disadvantages within societal structures, highlighting that inequity is relational and shaped by the intersectional identities people hold. We found this model particularly valuable in conceptualising this book, as it encourages us to critically examine how privilege manifests in our practice and to address oppression within the therapeutic setting. By advocating for both interpersonal interventions and structural change, Nixon emphasises the importance of individual accountability among those in privileged positions, while also striving for cultural safety that acknowledges and respects the lived experiences of those facing inequity.

Given the intersections of marginalisation which people with learning disabilities experience, we wanted to acknowledge the complexities of power and privilege in the roles that we as editors and our authors hold. We asked each author to explicitly consider the intersecting aspects of their identities in order to forefront our inherent and actual power as clinical art therapists and lived experience co-authors. We have also sought to name the potential power and privilege at every stage in both writing and editing this book, in recognition of the discrimination, inequalities, and stigma that people with learning disabilities continue to face globally. Each chapter presents a positional statement at the outset.

iii **Language and Labels**

The term *learning disability* was not chosen by the people whom it defines. Valerie Sinason (1992) drew our attention to the uncomfortableness society had in naming this group of people, leading to successive re-naming by others. Throughout this book, we have tried to remain consistent in our use of people with learning disabilities (Power et al., 2022), but you will see some of the authors' preferences which are linked to their specific cultural context, such as 'neurodivergent' and 'cognitive-differability'. In the National Health Service (NHS) in the UK, where Simon and Nicki are based, the term 'people with a learning disability' is used. Internationally and in the field of psychiatry, the term 'intellectual disability' or 'developmental disability' is widely used. We have not chosen to use this term, because the lived-experience researchers with learning disabilities we work alongside don't like it. Their preference was learning disabilities (Power et al., 2022). Some people with learning disabilities have been given other labels, like having 'challenging behaviour' (behaviour that challenges). We think it important to state that outward 'behaviour' should be seen as a sign of what is being communicated. It is also important to recognise that places where people live or visit can increase behaviours that challenge. Especially if people experience limited social interaction, a lack of meaningful occupation, lack of choice, excessive noise, crowding, and under or over-stimulation, for example (Power et al., 2023).

Language is powerful, and the labels we use can impact how individuals are perceived and treated. It is crucial to recognise the implications of our language, as terminology can shape societal attitudes and contribute to either empowerment or marginalisation. By prioritising language that reflects the preferences of those to whom we refer, we build a culture of respect and dignity. This book invites readers to engage critically with language, encouraging ongoing discussions about the labels we use in the field of art therapy. Additionally, as societal attitudes evolve, so too should our language; being open to change and willing to adapt our terminology is essential for fostering inclusivity and understanding within the therapeutic space. Ultimately, this approach highlights the importance of listening to the voices of those we aim to support and ensuring that their identities are valued through the language we choose.

iv **Practical Implementation**

As intervention developers in the field of applied research, we have been influenced by the Medical Research Council's *Guidance on Developing and Evaluating Complex Interventions* (Skivington et al., 2021). This guidance advocates for describing any intervention in terms of what, when, where, by whom, how often, how much, and expected outcomes. Although we'll revisit complexity in art therapy again in the conclusion of this book, for now we ask readers to hold in mind that the authors have sought to address these questions in their chapters.

Ensuring that the art therapy and art-based practices are outlined in sufficient detail enables readers both within art therapy and beyond to understand the techniques, components, and resources used when delivered art therapy. For practitioners, especially those new to the field, clear guidance on practical implementation reduces uncertainty. Clinicians can apply techniques effectively in a range of settings, as well as consider specific adaptation that may be required based on their unique context. This approach ensures that art therapists can translate theoretical knowledge into meaningful interventions that address the diverse needs of people with learning disabilities.

Through sharing what has been successfully delivered, we contribute to growing the existing evidence base for the use of art therapy for children and adults with learning disabilities. This is particularly important in promoting diverse practices that cater to the unique needs of different individuals, ensuring that art therapy remains relevant and effective across various contexts. Ultimately, a focus on practical implementation not only enhances the quality of care provided but also fosters a culture of continuous learning and improvement within the field of art therapy.

Overview of Book Sections in this Volume

This book is divided into four sections: Justice, Agency, Advocacy, and Connections. Each section includes several chapters which look at different aspects of the topic in relation to the lived lives of people with learning disabilities who have received art therapy.

In Section 1, we delve into the theme of *justice* through the lens of art therapy, exploring how this practice can challenge systemic inequalities and empower marginalised voices. The first three chapters weave a narrative of justice that not only highlights the challenges faced by people who have been marginalised but also emphasises the transformative power of art therapy in fostering empowerment and social change.

In Section 2, we consider the theme of *agency*, exploring how art therapy empowers individuals with learning disabilities to express themselves, make choices, and assert their identities. Chapters 4–7 underscore the central role of art therapy in fostering agency, enabling individuals with learning disabilities to assert their voices, engage in meaningful relationships, and take control of their narratives.

In Section 3, we explore the theme of *advocacy* within art therapy, highlighting the essential role it plays in empowering individuals with complex needs to assert their voices and navigate their care. Chapters 8–10 illuminate the critical intersection between advocacy and art therapy, showcasing how creative expression can empower individuals to reclaim their narratives, enhance their self-advocacy, and foster a more inclusive society.

In Section 4, we investigate the theme of *connections*, emphasising how art therapy can forge meaningful relationships among individuals, communities, and their environments. Chapters 11–14 illustrate the powerful impact of art therapy in forging connections that enhance individual well-being and community cohesion, offering valuable insights for practitioners dedicated to building inclusive and supportive environments.

Chapter Synopses

In Chapter 2, Rochele brings to light the intersection of blackness and disability in the US, revealing the pervasive discrimination and multiple levels of stigma faced by these communities, which is further compounded by social deprivation. By transforming educational spaces through community-oriented art initiatives, Rochele demonstrates, using three different projects, how sensitively delivered art therapy can serve as a catalyst for social justice, providing 'positive disruption' alongside more traditional educational approaches.

In Chapter 3, Mairi writes, along with her clients Jane and Kayleigh, about their experiences of navigating the UK legal system as they pursued justice as survivors of sexual trauma. Their shared but different journeys highlight both Jane and Kayleigh's individual resilience and the importance of therapeutic support as part of the justice-seeking process. Mairi shows how her trauma-informed approach to art therapy can facilitate healing and empower individuals to reclaim their narratives.

In Chapter 4, Liz and her client Joey address the everyday injustices encountered by individuals with learning disabilities and autism. Common interactions which could be overlooked, such as taking public transport, are brought into focus to highlight the impact that repeated 'micro-discrimination' can have. Liz emphasises that compassionate communication can support expression of these experiences in art therapy. Together, Liz and Joey, underscore the critical need for systemic change within healthcare advocating for the rights of this client group.

Chapter 5, by Jed and his co-authors, introduces the '*No Barriers Here*' approach, a pioneering arts-based intervention that enables individuals to engage in crucial discussions about end-of-life care. By emphasising the co-production process and integrating creative expression, the authors highlight how participants can find their voices and advocate for their needs, ultimately fostering dignity and self-advocacy within palliative settings.

Chapter 6, set in Australia, follows Claudia's individual therapy with Geoffrey, a composite character representing various clients' experiences. Using art, Geoffrey articulates his fragmented life story, showcasing the power of being heard and the deep connection between creativity and self-discovery. Claudia's reflections on the therapeutic relationship highlight the importance of patience and compassion, advocating for spaces where individuals can share their narratives and reclaim their agency.

In Chapter 7, Elizabeth explores group art therapy with children who have severe learning difficulties. She illustrates how artmaking fosters communication, emotional expression, and a sense of belonging among participants. By creating a safe and supportive environment, the children are empowered to express themselves and navigate their interactions, highlighting the significance of group cohesion in developing their agency. The children also consider what being part of a chapter in a book will be like!

Chapter 8 takes us to Australia, where Emma and Tomas discuss the impact of inclusive art workshops on neurodivergent individuals. By showcasing collaborative artmaking as a means of enhancing self-expression and community connection, they advocate for practices that prioritise autonomy and creativity. This chapter illustrates how empowering individuals through participatory art can promote agency and belonging in diverse contexts.

In Chapter 9, by Toni and her client Lizzy, advocacy becomes a central tenet of their therapeutic journey. Following a life-changing accident, Lizzy utilises art therapy to create a visual timeline, articulating her questions and emotions. Toni's adaptive practices extend beyond traditional therapy, as she collaborates with a multi-agency team to amplify Lizzy's voice, ensuring her needs and feelings are visually represented in care plans and supporting her in pursuing a formal complaint about her care. This chapter underscores the transformative potential of art therapy as a medium for self-advocacy and communication.

Chapter 10 shifts the focus to Mizuho's work with Jayden in a secure care setting, where she navigates cultural barriers and the challenges of trauma-informed care in this context. Mizuho emphasises the importance of establishing psychological safety within therapeutic relationships for both the client (often called patient in inpatient settings) and the care team. She illustrates how art therapy can illuminate the impact of trauma and support the wider multi-disciplinary team in understanding some of the most complex clients in high-stress environments.

In Chapter 11, we find Tania in Australia, as she introduces the concept of a 'creative corridor', blending therapeutic and educational practices to enhance self-expression for individuals with cognitive differences (learning disabilities). Through the narrative of Paul, a creative artist with learning disabilities, Tania advocates for a societal shift in how disabilities are perceived, urging recognition of people's rich experiences and creative potential. She calls for interdisciplinary approaches that celebrate diverse expressions, promoting dignity and respect for all individuals.

In Chapter 12, Shehnoor shares her experience in co-developing a gallery-based art therapy group, where themes of belonging and identity come to the forefront. Shehnoor highlights the significance of creating a democratic and accessible space that encourages personal exploration and strengthens group bonds. Through engaging vignettes and participant feedback, she illustrates how art can serve as a powerful medium for fostering both community and personal growth, showcasing the collaborative nature of the therapeutic process in a public setting.

In Chapter 13, Yana and Ricky introduce an innovative short-term intervention combining art therapy, reminiscence, and bookmaking with young adults with Down Syndrome in China. This approach not only enhances communication using less-verbal means but also strengthens the connections between participants and their carers. Yana's art-based reflections on the intervention reveal key themes of understanding, well-being, and improved relationships, emphasising the critical role of the wider community in therapeutic settings.

Chapter 14, by Hazel, Siobhan, and Connie, revisits the impactful experiences of participants in an art therapy group during the COVID-19 pandemic, highlighting their insights a year later. Through activities that symbolise hope and connection, such as planting flower bulbs, participants articulate their emotions surrounding loss and relationships. The authors draw attention to adaptive communication strategies, demonstrating how art therapy creates a safe space for emotional expression and connection among individuals navigating grief and hope.

Chapter 15 takes us to Canada, where Sandra shares her journey of establishing 'Art Hives', community arts studios that foster inclusivity and connection. By intertwining her personal identity with broader societal issues, Sandra reflects on the biases within therapeutic relationships and demonstrates how to rebuild trust with people with learning disabilities. Her insights into creating inclusive art spaces and engaging support staff underscore the importance of genuine connections in promoting empowerment and community engagement.

Finally, we conclude the book by drawing together the diverse approaches and experiences of Art Therapy described in the previous chapters and summarise them for comparison. We end this book with a 'manifesto' for change in art therapy, to collectively facilitate greater representation, to explore innovative ways to increase accessibility, to widen the global diversity of practice being shared, and to champion the development of art therapists as leaders who can influence the improvements in wider practice, services, and organisations that are needed to benefit people with learning disabilities.

Conclusion

Before you savour the art therapy practices described in the next 15 chapters, we encourage you to engage critically with the ideas presented and consider how they can be applied in your contexts. The case studies and evaluations within these pages offer a rich tapestry of experiences that underscore the potential of art therapy to challenge systemic inequalities and improve the quality of life of people with learning disabilities.

By foregrounding the voices of people with learning disabilities as co-authors, we aim to enrich this text with diverse experiences and insights. This collaborative approach not only enhances the authenticity of the content but also serves as a vital reminder of the importance of inclusion in our field. The contributions throughout the book highlight practical descriptions of art therapy interventions, showcasing real-world applications and the transformative potential of inclusive art therapy practices.

The four core principles that underpin this volume—Positive Disruption, Power and Positionality, Language and Labels, and Practical Implementation—guide our exploration of art therapy's role in fostering justice, agency, advocacy, and connections. These principles are not merely theoretical; they are woven into the fabric of each chapter, inviting practitioners to reflect on their practices and embrace a more inclusive and empowering approach.

Ultimately, this volume is a call to action for all of us engaged in this vital work. It acknowledges both the progress made and the challenges that persist. However, by embracing diverse voices and fostering inclusive practices, we can contribute to the ongoing journey towards a more equitable and compassionate society. We invite you to join us in this exploration, as we collectively seek to disrupt narratives, co-create change, and improve the lives of people with learning disabilities.

References

Beail, N. 2016. *Psychological Therapies and people who have intellectual disabilities.* British Psycholgical Society.

Brugha, T., Spiers, N., Bankart, J., et al. (2016) Epidemiology of autism in adults across age groups and ability levels. *British Journal of Psychiatry* 209(6): 498–503.

Buckles, J., R. Luckasson, and E. Keefe. 2013. "A systematic review of the Prevalence of psychiatric disorders in Adults with intellectual disability, 2003-2010." *Journal of Mental Health Research in Intellectual Disabilities* 6 (3): 181–207.

Cooper, S., E. Smiley, J. Morrison, A. Williamson, and L. Allan. 2007. "Mental ill-health in adults with intellectual disabilities: Prevalence and associated factors." *British Journal of Psychiatry* 190: 27–35.

Eastwood, C. 2021. "White privilege and art therapy in the UK: Are we doing the work?" *International Journal of Art Therapy* 26 (3): 75–83. https://doi.org/10.1080/17454832.2020.1856159.

Einfield, S., L. Ellis, and E. Emerson. 2011. "Comorbidity of intellectual disability and mental disorder in children and adolescents: A systematic review." *Journal of Intellectual & Developmental Disability* 36 (2): 137–143.

Elasser, J. 2020. *The power of positive disruption.* November. https://www.prsa.org/article/the-power-of-positive-disruption.

Emerson, E., S. Baines, L. Allerton, and V. Welch. 2011. "Health inequalities & people with learning disabilities in the UK 2011." *Improving Health & Lives: Learning Disability Observatory.* https://pureportal.strath.ac.uk/files-asset/7402206/vid_7479_IHaL2010_3HealthInequality2010.pdf

Glover, G., R. Williams, P. Heslop, J. Oyinlola, and J. Grey. 2017. "Mortality in people with intellectual disabilities in England." *Journal of Intellectual Disability Research* 61 (1): 62–74.

Hackett, S., E. Ashby, K. Parker, S. Goody, and N. Power. 2017. "UK art therapy practice-based guidelines for children and adults with learning disabilities." *International Journal of Art Therapy* 22 (2): 84–94.

Harris, J. (2006) *Intellectual disability: Understanding its development, causes, classification, evaluation, and treatment.* New York: Oxford University Press.

Joint Commission for Mental Health. 2013. *Guidance for commissioners of mental health services for people with learning disabilities.* Rafferty's.

Mencap. 2020. *"I don't know what day it is or what the weather is like outside": Social care cuts for people with a learning disability leaves families stuck in lockdown.* 10 August. Accessed March 13, 2022. https://www.mencap.org.uk/press-release/idont-know-what-day-it-or-what-weather-outside-soical-care-cuts-people-learning.

NHS Race & Health Observatory. 2023. *New review identifies poorer care and lower life expectancy for ethnic minorities with a learning disability.* NHS Race & Health Observatory. Accessed June 29, 2024. https://www.nhsrho.org/news/new-review-identifies-poorer-care-and-lower-life-expectancy-for-ethnic-minorities-with-a-learning-disability/.

Nixon, S. A. 2019. "The coin model of privilege and critical allyship: Implications for health." *BMC Public Health* 19 (1637). https://doi.org/10.1186/s12889-019-7884-9.

Maulik, P., Mascarenhas, M., Mathers, C., et al. 2011. Prevalence of intellectual disability: A meta-analysis of population-based studies. *Research in Developmental Disabilities.* 32 (2): 419–436. https://doi.org/10.1016/j.ridd.2010.12.018.

Power, N., E. Millard. 2022. The Lawnmowers Independent Theatre Company, and C. Carr. 2022. "Un-Labelling the language: Exploring labels, Jargon and power through Participatory arts research with arts therapists and people with learning disabilities." *Voices: A World Forum for Music Therapy* 22 (3). https://doi.org/10.15845/voices.v22i3.3391.

Power, N., R. Dolby, and D. Thorne. 2021. ""Reflecting or frozen?" The impact of Covid-19 on art therapists working with people with a learning disability." *International Journal of Artelor Therapy* 26 (3): 84–95. https://doi.org/10.1080/17454832.2020.1871388.

Power, N., T. Harrison, S. Hackett, and C. Carr. 2023. "Art therapy as a treatment for adults with learning disabilities who are experiencing mental distress: A configurative systematic review with narrative synthesis." *The Arts in Psychotherapy* 86 (102088). https://doi.org/10.1016/j.aip.2023.102088

Sense. n.d. *"Someone cares if I'm not there": Addressing loneliness in disabled people. Jo Cox commission on Loneliness: Disabled people.* Accessed March 13, 2022. www.sense.org.uk/support-us/campaign/loneliness/.

Sinason, V. 1992. *Mental handicap and the human condition: An analytic approach to intellectual disability.* Edited by 3rd. Free Association Books.

Skivington, K., L. Matthews, S. Simpson, P. Craig, J. Baird, J. Blazeby, K. Boyd et al. 2021. "A new framework for developing and evaluating complex interventions: Update of Medical Research Council guidance." *BMJ (Medical Research Council: MRC)* 374 (n2061). https://doi.org/10.1136/bmj.n2061. PMID: 34593508; PMCID: PMC8482308

Wigham, S., and E. Emerson. 2015. "Trauma and life events in adults with." *Current Developmental Disorders Reports* 2 (2): 93–99.

World Health Organization. 2018. International statistical classification of diseases and related health problems (11th revision). Retrieved from, 2018. Available: https://icd.who.int/browse11/l-m/en.

Section 1

Justice

Chapter 2

Deconstructing Blackness in Disability

Co-Creating Freedom Spaces in Schools & Community

Rochele Royster

Positionality Statement

I, Rochele Royster, authored this chapter as a Black woman without a learning disability. I have worked as an Art Therapist, special education teacher, and community psychologist in public schools within a large urban city in the United State of America. As a Black Art Therapist in a predominantly white profession, teaching and working in black and brown spaces, I am viscerally aware of my blackness and the juxtaposition of my role as teacher and university academic in community art settings. The individuals mentioned in my narrative have not been named to preserve their privacy, although they have granted me permission to share our collective experiences.

Introduction

As Ally Henny states: "Part of laying down your privilege is listening to oppressed people without arguing, interrogating, minimizing or gaslighting them" (2019). This idea underpins the importance of acknowledging the lived experiences of Black disabled individuals. To be Black and disabled in the United States reveals a troubling reality shaped by historical oppression and systemic discrimination. More than half of disabled African Americans face arrest by the age of 28 (Thompson, 2021). Understanding the policing and education of Black disabled individuals requires recognizing the entrenched dogma and propaganda used to justify the subjugation of African people. The elitist class of European perpetuated systems, laws, and policies that marginalized the poor, Black, and disabled, thereby protecting their own privilege. These linkages between racism and ableism trace back to the arrival of enslaved people on American shores, where they were coerced to labor in fields, homes, and bedrooms. Shockingly, in the United States, half of those killed by police are disabled, with African Americans facing twice the risk compared to their white disabled peers (Thompson, 2021).

Anti-literacy laws prohibited Blacks from learning to read and write due to fears that educated slaves might resist and rebel (Woodson, 2023; Clarke, 2014). Historically, the Black psyche was depicted as immoral, criminal, and inferior, often

DOI: 10.4324/9781003350736-4

resulting in unjust incarceration in prisons or mental institutions (Peterson, 2021). Additionally, the intertwining of slavery and Christianity was used as a complex means of both purported salvation and a tool for oppression and discrimination. Regrettably, psychology and education fields have embraced racist and ableist opinions as science, relying on biased assumptions and weak evidence (APA, 2021). Discriminatory laws, policies, and theories in psychology, education, and social sciences perpetuate racist ideology, manifesting explicit and implicit bias in teaching and practice (Rothstein, 2018). This chapter delves into how race, class, and disability ideologies impact the classroom and the people in them.

Narratives abound of Black individuals, predominantly children, facing harm or fatality at the hands of officers responding to calls, often initiated by citizens (primarily white women) reporting perceived suspicious behavior. Numerous victims in these stories shared the intersectionality of being both Black and disabled. The following cases spotlight just two instances, among numerous others, where the heavy-handed response of the state resulted in aggression toward Black and disabled youth.

In 2010, Reginald Latson, a Black 18-year-old high school student with autism was sitting outside a library when a stranger called police reporting his behavior as suspicious (Vargas, 2020). When the police confronted Reginald, who had committed no crime, he responded with a fight or flight response and was arrested. Despite his disability, Latson was convicted and sent to jail where he spent over 100 days in solitary confinement (Vargas, 2020). Latson was given a full pardon in 2021 but continues to suffer trauma from the police encounter and his subsequent incarceration. Once a perfect candidate for independent living, Latson is now unable to take a walk unassisted. His life will never be the same.

In 2014, Laquan McDonald, a 17-year-old special education student in the tenth grade, tragically lost his life in an encounter with a Chicago police officer. Laquan's brief life was marred by involvement in systems that failed him (Gutowski et al., 2019). Removed from his mother's home and placed in foster care, he faced abuse and neglect. His last year was marked by suspensions and altercations, leading to time in psychiatric hospitals. The circumstances surrounding Laquan's death prompt questions about whether the police that night perceived his disability, his race, or both. His story underscores systemic shortcomings in educational and social service systems, which inadequately addressed his emotional, intellectual, and housing needs.

Recognizing and accepting signs of mental illness and disability are special challenges for first responders (Watson, 2021). Training may address this, but the reality is that our society has historically encouraged intersectional discrimination and oppression centered in racism, ableism, and classism with laws, policies, and ideology that continue to harm and isolate.

In specific contexts, disability can stem from structural racism or historical systems designed to perpetuate racial and ableist inequities. This requires an exploration of social determinants of health, prioritizing factors such as healthcare and education accessibility, exposure to police violence, environmental injustice, housing insecurity, limited political power, and low employment. Despite evidence underscoring the detrimental health effects of racism, oppression, and discrimination, research frequently neglects these constructs and their impact on individuals and communities (Harris, 2023). What is the cultural relativity and positionality of blackness and disability? Blackness alone, of course, is not a disability but blackness as a trait in a socially constructed white-dominant world is understood as disabling with inherent disadvantages.

In the United States, Black children are disproportionately placed in special education and experience harsher disciplinary measures compared to their white counterparts. Research suggests that factors like test bias, poverty, inadequate instruction, and a lack of Black and Brown teachers contribute to this overrepresentation (Harry and Klingner, 2014). The system has historically wielded both race and disability as tools for subordination. The individuals most marginalized often find themselves at the crossroads of race, disability, and socio-economic class.

Crenshaw (2018) emphasizes that intersectionality explores the convergence of all identities, forming a distinct and multifaceted experience of discrimination. In the special education classroom, as a Black teacher teaching Black children, I understood race and disability through this intersectional lens. In this complex interplay of race and disability, race is often the dominant lens. As the prior examples show, Blackness coupled with disability and poverty place folks at risk for extreme marginalization, discrimination, and potential pawns in systems of structural oppression.

Standards for Whom? A Look at Standardized Tests, Race & Disability

Schools use two ways of diagnosing children with a learning disability. Historically a psychologist will use a psycho-educational assessment that tests a child's intelligence in comparison to other children his or her same age. Recently, many schools in the United States have also adopted the Response to Intervention Model which considers how children are responding to academic interventions. Teachers identify students struggling with the general curriculum and then create a specialized instructional plan to support that child's learning. Screening for learning disabilities can be complicated and too often choices are guided by misperceptions and bias.

In third grade, I moved to a small, conservative, rural town. Upon entering class, I was immediately placed in a Reading Lab for struggling readers. My black skin must have been the indicator for my teacher since I was never given a placement test or asked to read. I remember sitting in Reading Lab and being instructed to read silently. I, along with three other students, sat silently reading for an hour. When the other students realized that I could read, they would ask me to read the words they did not know. I often think about the reading group and why the teacher had struggling readers reading silently. I also think about the time I spent reading silently when I should have been receiving instruction in the general education curriculum. Unfortunately, this story is not unusual. Reading instruction can be political, dictated by trends and popular education celebrities that make millions selling trendy reading curriculum not always evidence based (Hanford, 2019).

Fast forward 30 years, as a special educator, trained to teach older students struggling to read, I was told by administrators not to teach decoding or phonics but instead focus on cues and guessing strategies to teach reading. Black children are often stigmatized within the educational system and when given instructional support, although well intentioned, it is often inferior or subpar. Many children have been harmed by schools adopting reading programs that had many bells and whistles but with further inspection revealed smoke and mirrors.

Ibram X. Kendi's observation that: "The tests have failed time and again to achieve their intended purposes: measuring intelligence and predicting future academic and professional success. The tests, not the black test-takers, have been underachieving" (NEA, 2020) resonates deeply within this context. Standardized tests, assumed to enhance educational attainment and earnings by narrowing score gaps, have consistently proven unreliable for measuring student learning. The focus on closing achievement gaps began in the early 21st century, with schools mandated to test and analyze performance data. Despite improvements for Black and Hispanic students, the achievement gap persisted (Ansell, 2011). The gap, apparent in academic performance indicators and assessments, is expected to decrease through targeted instruction, exposure to rigorous curriculum, and periodic standardized testing. Over time, test scores were employed to evaluate teacher performance and rank schools. In Chicago, parents and students were greeted in each entryway with the school's passing or failing status. Imagine being greeted with a sign each morning that says your school is failing. You are failing. You are not enough.

The No Child Left Behind Act (NCLB), enacted in January 2003 by President George Bush, aimed to address the achievement gap among students based on ability, race, and class. In response to perceived low expectations among teachers, the act mandated higher standards, rigorous testing, and accountability. However, this approach posed challenges for students facing various difficulties, such as those struggling with reading or English, dealing with trauma, or having specific learning disorders. The policy led to stress, shame, and emotional distress for my students, as they were forced to take standardized tests based on age and grade rather than their actual performance level. As an educator, I sensed that the progress I had achieved in fostering my students' reading confidence and self-esteem was being undermined. Many of them had endured years of humiliation, embarrassment, and anxiety related to reading, and the standardized tests only intensified these feelings of failure. The excessive focus on testing and preparation reinforced notions of inadequacy, fostering a sense of not being good enough, smart enough, or being perceived as different and marginalized. Moreover, the shift toward prioritizing reading and math test preparation resulted in the removal of music and art classes, which were areas where many of my students excelled. Losing these creative outlets felt like a punitive measure.

Teacher grade level meetings began to change. Meetings consisted of reading stacks of xeroxed copies of student scores arranged by various categories including grade, teacher, gender, and race. Sitting in a dim room staring at test score data converted to colorful graphs projected on a screen, teachers would have to volley questions and answers back and forth on trial for all to judge. Teachers lucky enough to see an increase in test scores were championed and cheered. Those whose scores were less than lack luster were faced with embarrassment and shame forced to explain and answer for the scores of their students.

In a heated meeting with the administration and the district CEO, I was asked why a student was failing to make gains on his benchmark assessments. Years of test scores were highlighted in yellow ink before me. It was true, his scores were dismal. His reading and math scores had stayed the same for three years. He was working three grades below grade level. I shared my student's story. I told the team about the death of his grandmother, his primary care giver, and his transition into another home and then into foster care. I tried to explain that a few months later, my student had been hit by a car and was in the hospital for three months recuperating from his injuries. I tried to share with them his emotional trauma and social challenges and his stay in the psychiatric hospital after threatening to hurt himself. I explained that despite these challenges, my student had persevered and still showed up to class each day. I relayed that I was proud of the work he had completed in class and although he was not reading fluently, he had made significant gains that the standardized test failed to capture. I was met with uncomfortable gazes from my colleagues and a blank stare from the administration. The new Chief Officer of my district adjusted her gold watch and pushed the ends of her bob behind her ears. She clicked her pen and began to explain to me that all those factors I mentioned were horrible, but outside of my control. She was interested in the components I did have control over, his instruction. She continued to state that my mindset and low expectations were the problem, and the reason this students' scores were stagnant. As a trained therapist, I was in disbelief, but I remained silent, heat rushed to my face, and my heart quickened. Despite my years of experience, skills, numerous degrees in education, special education, and therapy, my internal child sat quiet holding in her hands the humiliation, embarrassment, and shame. My feelings mirrored my students. I had witnessed those feelings as they mustered up enough courage to take a test they could barely read. I now carried their feelings of inadequacy for all to witness. The Chief Officer, fixated on control, failed to acknowledge the systemic issues contributing to the challenges faced by both students and educators. Rendered speechless, I realized the battle extended beyond me – it was a systemic flaw, reducing individuals to mere numbers, statistics, and financial considerations.

Historical Context: Standardized Testing in the United States

In the early 19th century, concerns about increasing diversity in U.S. schools prompted psychologists and scientists, influenced by the eugenics movement, to create aptitude and IQ tests like the Scholastic Aptitude Test and the Stanford Binet

Intelligence Test. Originally used to justify racism, these tests persist today for assessing students for special education and gauging college readiness.

Accountability is important. Every child should have a teacher that is qualified and effective in raising student achievement, but the measurement tools used to define and judge achievement should not replicate racial and economic inequality tools that were formulated and used to affirm the horrors of eugenics. If there is a problem, if you look deep enough you will find people who are making money off that problem. In this instance, test prep, testing companies, test prep coaches reading curriculums, and textbook companies were making millions selling reading curriculum to school districts and my students were still struggling.

Integrating Art Therapy into the Classroom: Community-Based Art Studios in Schools

As a novice student teacher, I was caught off guard by the emotional and social challenges my students were grappling with. Teaching reading, writing, and math became a struggle as they faced issues like depression, anxiety, and complex trauma. Recognizing the need for additional skills to address emotional and social aspects before academic challenges, I made the decision to pursue a graduate degree in art therapy.

As a child, I loved Mr. Rogers' Neighborhood. There I learned the importance of relationships in what felt like a uniquely personalized learning environment just for me. It was his expression of care and his naming of emotions and feelings, his ability to have deep and small conversations and spark wonder and joy in learning which nurtured my creativity and imagination. Could I create a therapeutic classroom that addressed both academic, social-emotional learning and wellness in a public-school setting? Could the ideas around an open classroom using an art-based studio approach spark creativity and joy in learning for my neurodiverse students? I was about to find out.

I needed to reimagine special education. Instead of seeing my students' deficits, I focused on their strengths. All students had specific learning needs and it was my job to empower my students to utilize their learning strengths to gain knowledge and excel academically and in life. How could I make learning relevant and meaningful? Can learning be also fun, magical, joyful, and playful? Could an open art studio, a creative workshop for learning through doing, working, and experimenting, encourage autonomy and agency in my neurodiverse students? I wanted to create a liberating place that functioned like a workshop or a studio and encouraged critical thinking, conversation and creativity. I removed the rows of desks and replaced them with large round conference tables. I put art materials and found objects in crates around the room. I led each lesson with a question and encouraged my students to create authentic artifacts to exhibit and publish. The classroom became a gallery, a studio, a dojo, a church. Soon other students in the school wanted to come to the "art room" and it became an inclusive AND exclusive place for collective minds to meet and gather.

Open Art Studios

In an open art studio, the emphasis is on freedom and self-expression (Allen, 1995; Moon, 2015). This environment encourages students to experiment with various materials and techniques, nurturing their self-esteem and self-confidence. Unlike conventional classroom settings that often prioritize conformity and rigid structures, open art studios celebrate innovation and creativity. In such spaces, students with learning disabilities can discover their strengths, building resilience and a positive self-image. Engaging in artistic activities can help students reduce stress, manage anxiety, and process complex emotions. It provides students with a constructive outlet for their frustrations and allows them to gain a sense of control over their lives, which is especially empowering for those who struggle with learning difficulties. Open art studios in school settings are also conducive to social interaction and the development of essential life skills. The artmaking process encourages collaboration, communication, and cooperation amongst the collective, fostering a sense of belonging and camaraderie.

All students, regardless of their learning differences, deserve access to the benefits of art therapy, open art studios, and inclusive freedom spaces that allow students to create, collaborate, and problem-solve. Teachers and art therapists can work together to adapt activities and materials to suit the diverse needs of each student. This approach not only enhances the educational experience but also helps to break down the stigma associated with learning disabilities, promoting a culture of acceptance and understanding within the school community.

Creating a special education classroom that integrated art therapy and functioned as an open art studio contributed to a more vibrant and dynamic classroom community that empowered my students to dream, imagine, and take risks (Royster, 2024). By recognizing the transformative potential of art, my classroom created a nurturing and enriching environment that addressed student's social-emotional learning, academics, increased resiliency, and prepared them for a brighter future.

Roots & Resilience: The Vital Role of Supervision in Balancing Roles

While recounting and summarizing this journey may seem neat and concise, the reality was a prolonged and challenging process marked by both successes and failures. I navigated through a school closure, two pregnancies that hindered my tenure, frequent changes in administrators, and three strikes followed by another mass school closure. Administrative responses fluctuated based on external pressures and political dynamics. Teachers' reactions varied, with some embracing arts integration and collaboration, while others viewed the special education room negatively or overlooked it all together.

Amidst this, many teachers sought art therapy for self-care, recognizing the need for reflection to combat compassion fatigue in under-resourced schools. Feeling isolated and misunderstood, I constantly faced the burden of explaining and justifying art therapy to administrators and staff. Teacher evaluations often reflected confusion about whether I was teaching art or academics, emphasizing the ongoing challenge of prioritizing safety, connection, and a sense of belonging for effective learning.

Through both challenges and triumphs, I discovered the crucial role of effective supervision in maintaining my overall well-being while juggling the responsibilities of a professional, therapist, educator, and new mother. It served as my sounding board, a sanctuary for honest and unapologetic expression, and a space for creative exploration. However, securing such supervision came at a personal cost, as I had to pay for it out of pocket. As the sole art therapist in a school, navigating uncharted waters, I realized that investing in supervision was an essential aspect of my professional journey.

While I developed partnerships and sought mentorship from other service professionals within the schools, art-based supervision with an experienced art therapist proved to be particularly vital for my practice and growth. I later took on the role of supervising graduate art therapy students, inviting them into the classroom to delve into the world of art therapy in school settings. The lessons I gleaned from these experiences, coupled with the positive energy of my students, became a source of strength during challenging days. These relationships and learning communities played a pivotal role in shaping my professional path.

I may not have changed all views or opinions, but the perseverance of the children and their families inspired me to "keep on keeping on." Their ability to endure adversity highlighted the importance of valuing small victories in the face of challenges.

The following section will look at two projects that happened organically in schools as a response to specific needs within the community and empowered my students to think, engage, and find innovative solutions to problems and heal collective trauma.

Art Therapy in Praxis

In this section, I present two challenges and the solutions which I implemented through an art therapy intervention.

Challenge: Budget Cuts Lead to the Removal of Arts Education in Public Schools

"I don't know how to use scissors," he said with a slight attitude. I was taken aback, trying to gauge his mood. Was he joking? It seemed inconceivable that the student before me could not use scissors, given my observations of his fine and gross motor skills.

"What do you mean?" I asked.

"I've never had to cut anything before," he replied, pushing the paper I handed him back to my side of the table.

"Not even in art class?" I inquired, still unsure if he was being truthful.

"We don't have art class," he explained.

After a series of questions and exploring the school's enrichment class schedule, I discovered that the school only offered music, physical education, and computer during a 45-minute teacher preparation time. Art-centered activities like coloring, cutting, handwriting, or drawing were removed, seen as a waste of valuable instruction time due to budget constraints and pressure for standardized test scores. This resulted in a school full of students who had never been given the space to creatively explore, problem-solve, dream, and imagine.

Many of my students struggled academically, and the arts presented opportunities for them to shine, build self-esteem, find connections, and express themselves.

This realization prompted me to initiate an after-school art therapy program, emphasizing social-emotional intelligence, mindfulness, and creativity for interested students in grades K-5. The program provided a space for exploration of art materials and engagement in the artistic process, fostering self-discovery and understanding of others (see Figure 2.1). It became an inclusive environment for all learners to take risks, grow together, and acquire new art skills.

In one project, students crafted puppets from cardboard, wrote stories about the puppets, and then read and performed the stories to each other. Through activities like painting and maintaining the studio space, students learned problem-solving, preparation, and gained confidence in themselves and their communities.

Initially voluntary, the after-school art therapy program operated without charge. I initially opened my classroom to students, supplying art materials like construction paper, glue, crayons, markers, and found objects. After the first year, I secured funding from the public schools' after-school tutoring and enrichment program, allowing an expansion of the program's focus to include reading instruction through the arts. It further evolved to highlight social-emotional learning and extended into the summer months. Additionally, I collaborated with a community program near public housing projects, a non-profit receiving government grant funding, to create STEAM programs for children and families in the vicinity, many of whom were also part of the food voucher program.

Responding to a bullying incident at the school, our group initiated a project creating a community map. Students identified safe and problematic areas, engaging in collaborative problem-solving. Using a bulletin board paper, we discussed safety and consent, mapping out these areas. After completing the map, students requested to share their findings with the principal. Choosing a peer with a strong rapport, they approached the principal, who visited our classroom the following evening. The visual data astonished her, and she shared it with the staff and faculty at the next faculty meeting.

This activity provided teachers and administration with an honest depiction of how school culture impacted students. Unsafe spaces, particularly the playground and lunchroom, were identified. In response, a recess coordinator was hired, and parents began patrolling the playground. A peer mentor program addressing lunchroom bullying was initiated, focusing on positive behavior and intervention systems to build positive peer relationships.

The success of the community mapping project led to its extension beyond the school to the surrounding community. Identifying safe and problem areas, students

Figure 2.1 A photograph of two students painting a wooden play-house during the after-school community art enrichment program.

engaged stakeholders and community leaders, addressing issues like gentrification, school closings, and gun violence through community art therapy. The initiative aimed to create safer neighborhood spaces and foster a sense of belonging for all community members.

Challenge: Closure of Schools Exacerbate Inter-Neighborhood Tensions

The mass closure of schools in Chicago created a complex environment for students from rival neighborhoods, exacerbated by gentrification and the erasure of historical Black figures. In 2013, Mayor Rahm Emanuel's decision to close 50 schools in Chicago's Black and Brown communities evoked grief-like emotions. The school grappled with a gentrifying community, further complicated by the consolidation of two campuses and a name change. Originally dedicated to a beloved local doctor, the school now bore the name of a white hotelier, effectively silencing the close-knit Black and Brown community.

Additionally, students from rival blocks and schools faced navigating gang territorial lines to reach the school, leading to increased conflict and mistrust among teachers, students, and parents. The pressing question arose: How could art play a role in healing these wounds?

Participating in community talks and gatherings, I witnessed profound hurt and anger as people mourned the loss of a crucial part of their history embodied in the school's original name. The challenge ahead was clear: How could we reclaim that history and unite to form a collective voice for the revitalization of both the school and the community?

This realization prompted me to initiate a Community Mural and Storytelling Project. The school desperately needed maintenance as paint peeled and plaster fell from the old walls, contributing to the physical uprooting and emotional sense of upset and confusion felt among students. Vandalism and frequent fights in dim hallways added to the challenges. With approval from the principal, the after-school art therapy program initiated a plan to create murals that would beautify and uplift the school. Targeting areas that were vandalized and neglected, we started with a dark hallway leading to the lunchroom.

Students from diverse classrooms, spanning general and special education, were chosen to participate in the mural project. Initially, students from the after-school program were tasked with selecting peer leaders from their classrooms to join the painting sessions. Simultaneously, during school hours, I engaged students who had been involved in conflicts or infractions, inviting them to contribute to the mural. This approach allowed for individual painting sessions which allowed me to build connections with these students, emphasizing their essential role in completing specific parts of the mural and being stewards of their artwork (see Figure 2.2).

Throughout the painting sessions, conversations flowed – sometimes filled with laughter, other times in companionable silence. Together, we adorned the walls with vibrant flowers and faces, successfully bringing an end to the vandalism. A particularly proud moment arose when a student, once involved in vandalizing the walls, proudly declared, "Don't mess up my wall! I painted that!" This transformation underscored the positive impact of the project on student attitudes and ownership of the shared artistic space.

Another mural depicted the Black icon that had been erased from the school's history. Painting this mural became a family affair, with my husband working on the portrait while I painted the background. Our children were running back and forth, contributing to the artistic process. As we painted, a sense of community emerged, with mothers, grandparents, kids, and new parents gathering each weekend to share stories about the school and the neighborhood. The mural program became a healing force for the community, combining art and storytelling. It provided a space for work and play, where witnessing and testimony allowed us to find our collective voice, heal, and grow into a new school family.

Painting community heroes on the school walls became a powerful act of reclaiming our community's history, telling our stories, and defining our space. It symbolized a new beginning where both schools found a sense of belonging and allegiance to our shared history and the present that we were actively shaping.

Figure 2.2 A photograph showing the hallway leading to the lunchroom during the initial stages of painting the mural.

Conclusion

"Work is love made visible." *Kahlil Gibran,* from *The Prophet* (Gibran, 1923). This poem is in the public domain.

Artwork is work, a struggle for creative actualization, involving both physical and mental engagement to achieve results. The praxis and pedagogy of art encompass both mind and body, drawing inspiration from life stories. In the art studio, we serve as artists, builders, creators, shapers, and stewards of culture and change, utilizing both mental and physical capacities. The studio becomes a space that sparks imaginations, holding room for dreams, fears, joy, and beauty.

Community arts, created intentionally together, establish connections among individuals through the act of creating. Open art studios offer a space for communities to unite through artmaking and storytelling, fostering engagement, problem-solving, mobilization, and organization for collective social action, community care, and aid. The central question arises: How do we empower communities and liberate ourselves? How can we transition from fear and scarcity to love and abundance?

Open art studios facilitate creative, student/community-centered artmaking and expression by forging positive connections between schools, communities, and cultural institutions. Community art therapy within open art studios engages communities to address collective harm and trauma through participatory artmaking, dialogue, and joy making. This approach aims to provide care, repair harm, and achieve freedom, autonomy, restoration, and reconciliation.

This chapter delves into how special education, art therapy, and community psychology integrate in pedagogy and praxis to instigate change in communities. The author examines social determinants of health, public policies, and local events impacting the social and emotional well-being of children within the community, illustrating how community art therapy is employed to address these challenges.

References

Allen, Pat B. *Art Is a Way of Knowing*. Shambhala, 1995.

Ansell, Susan. "Achievement Gap." *Education Week*, 7 Jul. 2011, www.edweek.org/ew/issues/achievement-gap/index.html?r=2581321064.

"Apology to People of Color for APA's Role in Promoting, Perpetuating, and Failing to Challenge Racism, Racial Discrimination, and Human Hierarchy in U.S." *American Psychological Association*, 29 Oct. 2021, www.apa.org/about/policy/racism-apology.

Clarke, John Henrik. *Christopher Columbus and the Afrikan Holocaust Slavery and the Rise of European Capitalism*. Lushena Books, 2014.

Crenshaw, Kimberle. "Demarginalizing the Intersection of Race and Sex: A Black Feminist Critique of Antidiscrimination Doctrine, Feminist theory, and Antiracist Politics [1989]." *Feminist Legal Theory*, 19 Feb. 2018, pp. 57–80, https://doi.org/10.4324/9780429500480-5.

Gibran, Kahlil. *The Prophet*. 1923. https://www.kahlilgibran.com/images/The%20Prophet%20Ebook%20by%20Kahlil%20Gibran.pdf. Accessed 2 Dec. 2024.

Gutowski, Christy, and Jeremy Gorner. "The Complicated, Short Life of Laquan McDonald." *Chicago Tribune*, 23 May 2019, www.chicagotribune.com/2015/12/11/the-complicated-short-life-of-laquan-mcdonald/.

Hanford, Emily. "At a Loss for Words: How a Flawed Idea is Teaching Millions of Kids to be Poor Readers." *APM Reports*, 2019, 1–35. https://www.apmreports.org/episode/2019/08/22/whats-wrong-how-schools-teach-reading

Harris, Jasmine E. "Reckoning with Race and Disability." *The Yale Law Journal – Home*, 30 June 2021, 130, pp. 916–958. www.yalelawjournal.org/forum/reckoning-with-race-and-disability.

Harry, Beth, and Janette K. Klingner. "Ethnic Disproportionality in Special Education." In *Why Are so Many Minority Students in Special Education?: Understanding Race & Disability in Schools*, Teachers College Press, 2014, pp. 1–29.

Henny, Ally. *Part of laying down your privilege is listening to oppressed people without arguing, interrogating, minimizing or gaslighting them*. 18 June 2019. https://www.facebook.com/allyhenny. Accessed 2 Dec. 2024.

Moon, Catherine Hyland. "Open Studio Approach to Art Therapy." *The Wiley Handbook of Art Therapy*, 6 Nov. 2015, pp. 112–121, https://doi.org/10.1002/9781118306543.ch11.

National Education Association (NEA). *Racist Beginnings of Standardized Testing*. 2020. https://www.nea.org/nea-today/all-news-articles/racist-beginnings-standardized-testing. Accessed 2 Dec. 2024.

Peterson, B. "A Virginia Mental Institution for Black Patients, Opened after the Civil War, Yields a Trove of Disturbing Records" *The Washington Post*, 6 Apr. 2021, www. washingtonpost.com/lifestyle/magazine/black-asylum-files-reveal-racism/2021/03/26/ ebfb2eda-6d78-11eb-9ead-673168d5b874_story.html.

Rogers, Fred. *You Are Special: Words of Wisdom from Mister Rogers*. Penguin Books, New York, 1995.

Rothstein, Richard. *The Color of Law: A Forgotten History of How Our Government Segregated America*. Liveright Publishing Corporation, a Division of W. W. Norton & Company, 2018.

Royster, Rochele, and Emily Nolan. "Making Something Out of Nothing: The Intersection of Art Therapy and Education: Creating Liberatory Practices Within Public Schools." In Emily Goldstein Nolan, ed., *Community Art Therapy: Theory and Practice*, Routledge, 2024, pp. 34–38.

Thompson, Villissa. "Understanding the Policing of Black, Disabled Bodies." *American Progress*, 10 Feb. 2021, https://www.americanprogress.org/article/understanding-policing-black-disabled-bodies/. Accessed 5 Nov. 2023.

Vargas, Theresa. "Perspective|Remember Neli Latson, the Black Teen with Autism Who Seemed 'suspicious' Sitting Outside a Library? Ten Years after His Arrest, He Still Isn't Fully Free." *The Washington Post*, WP Company, 11 June 2020.

Watson, Amy. "Redefining Police Interactions with People Experiencing Mental Health Crises: Models of Response." *Social Work*, 23 Nov. 2021, https://www.oxfordbibliographies.com/display/document/obo-9780195389678/obo-9780195389678-0308.xml.

Woodson, Carter Godwin, et al. *The Mis-Education of the Negro*. Penguin Books, an Imprint of Penguin Random House LLC, 2023.

Chapter 3

Justice

Art Therapy, Power, and Change

Mairi Benton, Jane Batt and Kayleigh Sage

Positionality

I (Mairi Benton) have written this chapter as a white woman without learning disabilities who is working as an Art Psychotherapist. When I have included the words of people with learning disabilities in my writing, I have used direct quotes. The people I have written about gave their permission for me to use their words and they let me know that they were happy for people to read their words. Jane was able to go through this chapter with me as I read it to her and consent to the words chosen. Kayleigh and her Mum were able to read this chapter together and consent to the words chosen.

Introduction

What is art therapy? What exactly is it that you do? These are questions that have followed me throughout my career. It is not always easy to describe in words what happens in art therapy as each client and situation can be very different. At times working within the field of learning disabilities can be largely non-verbal and rely on creative and bodily based expression. Often the work can be intensive, emotional, and challenging, both for the client and for the therapist. However, what becomes clear is that within this creative process comes change, an experience of shared meaning-making and a freedom that can be empowering. The art therapy that myself, Jane, and Kayleigh will tell you about took place in a Community Learning Disability Team (CLDT) in the National Health Service (NHS) in England. The setting for our work together crossed two localities, the first a space in a supported housing tenancy in a suburb of a large city and the second a local community hub in a small coastal town.

Jane and Kayleigh are two strong women who came to art therapy and found their voices. They both worked hard to process trauma, relating to significant sexual abuse, and instinctively and bravely sought justice at different times in their life. Our experiences together inspired us, and it felt like a natural step for each of us to embark on writing this chapter together. In doing so, Jane, Kayleigh, and I wanted to shine a light on the difficulties that they had faced individually, to explore what helped them to keep going, and to give hope to other survivors of sexual abuse.

DOI: 10.4324/9781003350736-5

Reflecting on the work that we have undertaken together, I am aware of a bright, connecting thread that runs through each of our lives and our circumstances, a thread that seeks out justice for the things that have happened to us and makes us experts of our own lived experiences.

- prior to becoming an art therapist, I experienced a violent and traumatic event that introduced me to police interviews, line-ups, and being a survivor. I never received justice, but I often think about how difficult the process of going to court would have felt for me at that time.
- after a lifetime of abuse and being controlled by her family, Jane decided to bring historical charges against a family member. This was a difficult decision for her to make and the outcome was painful to process. The case never made it to court and Jane never received the justice she sought.
- as a young woman, Kayleigh brought her perpetrator to court in another country where he received a significant custodial sentence. She was required to attend two separate court cases after the perpetrator appealed the initial charge, he later died in prison. Kayleigh fought hard to receive justice for the crimes that had been committed against her

This chapter will not go into detail about the historical events that Jane or Kayleigh experienced, rather it will seek to explore their individual experiences of art therapy with me, their therapist. We hope to highlight the collaborative nature of our work together, making sense of and attending to the often complex and everyday trauma that resulted from Jane and Kayleigh's painful experiences. In choosing to tell their stories in their own way, at their own pace, they have been able to share their wisdom and insights and have regained a sense of control over their own healing process. This has led to Jane and Kayleigh reaching a place today where they both feel safe, well, and able to live more fully.

Seeking Justice after a Hidden Crime

Hidden crime, a crime that we are oblivious to, and that is often unreported, is especially relevant at this time. Access to justice for many women who have been victims is difficult, but with learning disabilities it can often be insurmountable. As a nation, we are becoming more able to talk openly about sexual crime and violence, but learning disability is still not part of the discussion yet. Sometimes people with learning disabilities may not be listened to or believed. Simply having learning disabilities may make someone's story not credible. Gaps in their information or not being able to articulate a cohesive account often equates to something being believable or not (Rape Crisis 2020). When a learning disability is recognised, there can often be a lack of awareness of the spectrum of learning disabilities. Even with the support of witness intermediaries and appropriate adults, most rape cases currently do not make it to court, and the process itself can be re-traumatising for many survivors (Victims' Commissioner 2022).

Justice, in its broadest sense, can be described as *fairness* and *equality* in the way that people are treated. Legal justice can provide a starting point for many survivors to begin therapy, but in reality, this is currently unattainable for many people with learning disabilities. The term *survivor* is used here instead of *victim* in order to focus on the experiences of the survivors, rather than the acts of violence perpetrated against them. As Jane and Kayleigh's stories highlight, the trauma still remains with the survivor, whether the perpetrator has been convicted or not. Art therapy can support survivors when they feel powerless, helping to reduce the barriers that they face in day-to-day life. Treating survivors with compassion and allowing their voices to be heard can help to reduce the shame that is imposed on them by others, that is not theirs to carry (Dana 2023; Sinason 2020).

Art Therapy with a Trauma Focus

My art therapy practice can incorporate a psychodynamic approach. In my practice, I often focus on using myself as a resource in the therapy. With my supervisor, I explore my own unconscious responses to help provide an insight into the person that I am working with. I have found this, alongside art-making and creative play, to be particularly useful in working with people with learning disabilities whose primary expressions are not always verbal. Exploring my own transferential and counter-transferential responses within regular supervision can help me to unpick complex narratives and experiences of trauma that are held tightly within the body, sometimes only coming to light for the first time in therapy (Van der Kolk 2014; Rothschild 2017). Relationship becomes key within the therapy and often, how that relationship plays out during the therapy, can give me clues about other relationships and ways of relating in the client's life. As an art therapist, I am continually developing my skills in understanding my own responses and feelings and knowing what belongs to me and what belongs to my client. In my approach to working with Jane and Kayleigh, I also found it helpful to incorporate a trauma-focused therapy framework within my creative practice.

Many trauma-focused therapies recognise that there are phases in therapy that a client will experience on the path to recovery: safety, remembrance and mourning, and reconnection (Herman 1992). Whilst these stages are commonly observed, it is accepted that not everyone reaches these stages at the same time and that the pacing of therapy looks different for different people. Trauma therapy requires a careful and intricate approach over a longer period of time. It aims to better situate clients in their body and to co-create and find meaning together after trauma. The trauma doesn't go away, but the client becomes more able to live alongside it, connecting with the loss and sadness, but not being overwhelmed by it, and therefore more able to engage with the process of living.

Art therapy for Jane and Kayleigh was provided by a CLDT, a specialist health service commissioned by the NHS. It consists of a range of specialist learning disability health professions: Arts Therapies (Art, Music, Drama), Occupational Therapy, Physiotherapy, Speech and Language Therapy, Psychology, Community

Nursing, Positive Behaviour Specialists, and Psychiatry. Jane and Kayleigh's art therapy was carried out at a regular time and place each week in the community. Art therapy supervision was provided fortnightly by an art therapist in the CLDT.

Jane and Kayleigh Share Some of their Story

Jane

"I wish I had never been born".

Jane was 69 years old when she was referred to psychological therapies in the CLDT by a local charity specialising in support for rape and sexual abuse survivors. Jane had been seen briefly by a psychologist within our team who told her about art therapy, and they had begun a genogram of her family. Jane had been held by our specialist health service for most of her adult life but had chosen to come to art therapy to tell her story and to process deep and painful feelings relating to her past that were overwhelming her. Jane was diagnosed with cancer during the time that we worked together, and this prompted her to act, later reporting a family member to the police for historical abuse.

Jane presented as mischievous and playful, and often appeared with a twinkle in her eye and would pat me gently on the shoulder or arm. At times she shared a large, infectious smile and chatted animatedly. At other times Jane looked very serious and spoke with a low voice and with a sense of urgency, "*I need to talk to you*". Jane appeared tall and physically able, presenting with beautifully coloured blonde hair with red underneath, which she enjoyed getting done regularly at the hairdressers at her supported housing tenancy. She usually wore colourful outfits and had an incredible collection of footwear. Our therapy sessions took place in the Memory Room at the complex where Jane lived, just across from her flat. The Memory Room was a space that lent itself to going back in time. It had a mural on the wall of the city and its landmarks, memories of residents were written on a timeline, and there were many comfortable sofas and chairs. This room especially, as with the whole building, was kept warm throughout the year for the many elderly and frail residents that lived there.

Jane experienced a complex and abusive childhood, and this continued throughout her early adulthood where she described being controlled and abused by her family. Jane's parents met during the Second World War, and she remembers hearing that her Mum made bombs during the war years. Jane is aware that her Mum and Dad had 16 children but lost 10 of them. Jane was the only girl, alongside her Mum, in a family of men. She recalls vividly the violence that she witnessed between her Mum and Dad at an early age and the family having regular contact with the police and social services. Her Dad left the family home and stayed in a psychiatric institution before he died. Jane said that her Mum later died of "*too many beatings*" due to the violence that continued within the family home. When Jane was five years old, she was able to attend a residential boarding school for children with additional needs. Jane loved this experience away from her family, between the ages of 5 and 18 years, and described the dread and fear she felt returning home for the holidays. She made a friend at school and often reflects that "*I should have run away with her*". Jane recalls eventually running away from school one holiday with another friend but was found and returned home to her family by the police. Jane continued to live with her family and extended family members, going on to marry and have a child, before planning and escaping from family control with the help of a new friend. He later became her partner and her biggest support. She had a second child with him and was able to settle down, only moving to her current accommodation when her partner later died. At the time of referral to art therapy, Jane had very few visitors and would wait for her son to phone her each day.

During our art therapy assessment, Jane seemed to instinctively know why she was meeting with me. She had a watchful gaze and she said to me "*I wish I hadn't been born into this family. I didn't choose to be in this family. I wish I had never been born*". We were sitting at a table with a large sheet of white paper, drawing out her family tree with a pencil. Jane seemed to engage fully from the first moment we met. I became aware that Jane was starting to open up, stirring up a sense of dependency and vulnerability in me, in a rush to show me her trauma. We spent many sessions writing details together on paper with pencil, fragmented dates, addresses, names, and places were carefully scribed near the centre of each page with large, flowing writing. Jane engaged me in helping her to spell out the words correctly and showed me that it was important for her to record the facts accurately. Slowing the process down by using grounding strategies and anchoring to the present moment helped us to develop a sense of safety and containment within the sessions. Sometimes looking through the pens and pencils together, touching them and selecting them, was enough to connect us to the here and now. Slowing the pace of the work also helped to reduce feelings of shame and humiliation that can often accompany opening up too soon. Naming Jane's experiences for what they were, taking her suffering seriously, and validating her trauma became an important part of honouring the telling of her story. A strong theme, family secrecy, emerged in the verbal narrative and written words. Jane showed me in many different ways that she was a survivor of generations of trauma. Secrecy in Jane's family protected others from knowing the truth, and family loyalty helped maintain an image of the outside world that kept the status quo. Jane's family felt much bigger than her, truth became dangerous, and secrecy suppressed each family member's individual experiences of trauma (Figure 3.1).

Responding to Trauma as a Therapist

Familiar responses that I experience when I begin an intensive piece of work with a client who is the victim of sexual abuse include "*Will I manage to bear the extent of their pain? How long will this piece of work last?*" "*Will I be able to tolerate knowing the details of what has happened to my client?*" "*What happens if it becomes too painful for my client to come to therapy?*" I have described a common

Figure 3.1 Photograph of Jane's image of her house made in art therapy.

feeling in supervision many times, as it appears to me like an approaching black tsunami wave that there is no escape from. Physical responses that I have had in relation to these narratives include nausea, tearfulness, feeling hot and flushed, and feeling claustrophobic and panicky. I am able to rely on these transferential clues in supervision to help me to understand and connect to the raw, unprocessed, re-telling of trauma. What I have learned experientially over the years is that feelings don't stay the same, they change, and we change. Painful experiences, with the right support at the right time, can often transform into healing experiences that leave us with a renewed energy and purpose in life. But the work itself, between client and therapist, can be intense and harrowing.

Slowly, over time, Jane peeled back the layers to reveal uncomfortable and deeply difficult experiences that she had kept hidden away. The therapy space began to feel like a re-enactment of where the abuse took place. Jane would meet me at the front door, take me to the Memory Room, and then lock the door. She was now in the role of protector and keeping me safe, yet the room was locked, and we were quite hidden away. Often, I could arrive and leave unnoticed by staff, but I was always seen by other residents. Powerful feelings began to arise in the sessions, and I engaged in a parallel process with Jane, not cognitively, but through attunement at an unconscious level. Attunement can be described as a way of responding that shows clients that their feelings are seen, heard, and understood (Cottis 2009).

During many of the sessions when Jane verbalised her experiences from the past, I felt extremely tired and struggled to keep my eyes open. I felt like I was going under. I was aware that I did not feel like this before the session started or when the session ended, only during it. I experienced incredible shame and guilt for shutting down and being unable to stay present at the most crucial time. I spoke of this regularly in supervision and explored various practical attempts to adjust my response. I drank strong coffee before the session, ate my lunch after the session, chewed gum, and ate sweets under my face mask (Personal Protective Equipment (PPE) required during the COVID-19 pandemic), and I even held a range of small, sharp objects in my hands at different times to help prompt me to be alert. It was only when Jane's narrative began to shift into the present day that I recognised that I was beginning to feel like myself again. I now understand that in those terrifying moments of being abused, Jane's survival mechanism was to shut down, to dissociate. This was not a choice for her, but her body's response to overwhelming threat and fear. My body was mirroring this response. Reflecting on the space that we were in together, I imagined that if the Memory Room could have words it would say to us, "*trust that your body is doing the best it can, give it kindness and compassion. Forgive and praise your body for how it was in that moment*". Our experience together of attunement at an unconscious level helped Jane to process her unconscious feelings, supporting her to co-regulate her trauma responses with another person, leading to self-regulation, consciously making her own choices, and eventually towards taking action.

Jane and I gradually moved to a larger communal area where Jane still locked the doors, but we could see out at other residents. Often the doors would spring open by themselves, but this was tolerated and then became something we laughed about. Some sessions were held in Jane's flat as our created space together became more relational and flexible. Staff became an identifiable part of our routine and were very mindful and supportive of Jane's sessions. I began to experience Jane as maternal and caregiving towards me as she talked about important experiences with her son and grandson, who continue to be the light in her life. Jane's social relationships increased within her care home, and she took time to smile and thank me after each session. In one of our last sessions, Jane was really mischievous and playful, initiating a game of hide and seek with me in the car park and enjoying watching me ask staff and residents where she had gone. It seemed that she was feeling and being exactly as she should be. Jane reflected that she liked me coming to visit her every week at the same time and that it helped her to have someone to talk to.

Kayleigh

"*I wanted to kill myself*".

Kayleigh was 31 years old when she was referred to the CLDT by her General Practitoner (GP or doctor) following an appointment at the doctor's surgery where she described "*breaking down*". Kayleigh had experienced traumatic abuse in another country where she had been living with her family. Following disclosure and investigation, Kayleigh took her perpetrator to court when she was 15 years old. At the time of referral, Kayleigh had been diagnosed with post-traumatic stress disorder and was experiencing flashbacks and night terrors. She was overwhelmed and wanted to talk to someone about what had happened to her. Kayleigh was referred to Arts Therapies by an Occupational Therapist in our team who had been supporting her with sensory-based exercises. At that time, Kayleigh was understandably quite mistrustful of services and presented with anxiety and frustration. Kayleigh chose art therapy and later told me that it was my face that she had selected from the accessible leaflet.

Kayleigh arrived for her art therapy assessment a few months before the start of the COVID-19 pandemic (2020) a time when we were unaware of the immense changes ahead. Kayleigh's therapy sessions took place at a local community hub which housed a café, a library, a GP surgery, and spaces for community groups and local services. We had a comfortable room upstairs with a sink, a table with art materials, and several large windows that looked out over a garden. Sessions were booked in at the same time each week and our routine gradually became predictable and safe. Kayleigh arrived with her Mum and Stepdad, and I saw her waiting nervously for me to approach her. She followed me up to the room and asked for my arm to help her to walk up the stairs. Kayleigh seemed to instinctively know why she was there, and her expectations were clear, she wanted a "*new start*".

Figure 3.2 Photograph of Kayleigh's image of a chameleon made in art therapy.

During the first session, Kayleigh drew an image of a chameleon, her pet (see Figure 3.2). It seemed quite a gentle and unassuming image and similar to how she presented. She had short dark hair, was of average height and build, and held a soft, timid gaze. Kayleigh was able to describe the events that had happened to her abroad when she was a teenager and how this had impacted not only her but her family too. My sense at the time was of a young woman who was full up with lots of complex and painful feelings, her body working hard to contain them, and of someone desperate to be listened to. Our first session mirrored this and felt incredibly full. Important themes that Kayleigh shared related to a loss of innocence, a loss of part of herself, living on borrowed time, being a burden, being different from others, and having a voice but feeling silenced. These can be familiar themes in therapeutic work with clients who have learning disabilities and who have experienced trauma (Sinason 1992).

Kayleigh spent time at the beginning of her therapy educating me about some of her various diagnoses, including autism, learning disability, microcephaly, and auditory processing disorder. This reminded me that people with learning disabilities do not fit into neat little boxes, but have their own individual strengths, difficulties, and personal experiences of the world. Quite early on, I recognised that I had begun not to notice or even think about Kayleigh as having learning disabilities in our sessions. I learned that this was a familiar response to her and that it was important for me to slow down. Kayleigh was able to articulate her experiences well and showed incredible insight into her conditions and how these labels made her feel about herself. We slowly developed a means of interacting and a routine where Kayleigh would use the sensory objects and art-making (regularly drawing her house) as means of grounding herself, before moving into narratives that became emotive and increasingly difficult to hear. In supervision, I began to express the emotions that Kayleigh was unable to connect with yet, I felt sad, tearful, overwhelmed, and hopeless.

Reflecting on her life, Kayleigh said that her family had *"never had a break from anything"*. Her early experiences were impacted by domestic violence and being the only person in her family with learning disabilities. She attended various special schools from the age of six years old and, as a young teenager, she disliked school and was bullied, attempting to run away several times. When the opportunity arose, she chose to move abroad with her family and attended two different boarding schools. She spoke of enjoying the first school and then, at the second school after the abuse, feeling like she wanted to end her life. *"Why did it have to happen to me? What did I do so wrong?"* Kayleigh experienced many difficult times of not feeling like she was being listened to, authority figures not understanding that her behaviour was linked to trauma, and her increasing health needs not being believed. She returned home after her court cases and attended college in this country, experiencing various attempts at counselling, but found it difficult to engage. Kayleigh struggled for several years in pain with acute diverticulitis before she was diagnosed and had an operation to remove a badly damaged part of her intestine and a second appendix. She described feeling like she had hit rock bottom.

During the COVID-19 pandemic, as inside spaces became unsafe and risky, Kayleigh and I were able to maintain weekly sessions for an hour each week by telephone. We had lost the opportunity for art-making together but were grateful to be able to maintain our connection. I experienced Kayleigh as looking forward to the social contact, across our social distance, and enjoying the safe routine that we created together. She was able to speak for the whole session and this brought us into the present as we reflected together about the changes and difficulties that we were experiencing as a country (in the UK). Kayleigh was able to share her worries about her Mum, who was also vulnerable to infection due to additional health needs, and she began to share her worries and care for my safety too. When we returned to face-to-face sessions in the community, we changed room to one downstairs, next to the café. Kayleigh often became upset during these sessions and would ask that I place my hand on hers to help her to feel calmer. This helped to co-regulate her trauma responses before she was able to return to the sensory objects and begin to self-regulate and self-soothe. Kayleigh asked that we record all the events of her abuse in a letter that we kept in an envelope, in a box. Gradually Kayleigh did not require the box to come into our sessions. I noticed too that Kayleigh was beginning to develop her own friendships outside of the room, meeting in the café before and after our sessions.

"Don't ever think my life is perfect because it's not". Kayleigh came to art therapy to process her trauma and to reconnect with the world. We were able to grieve the loss of her innocence together and the loss of the person that she was before the abuse. Art therapy enabled Kayleigh to explore in depth her close relationship with her Mum and reflect on all the moments that she had experienced her unwavering care and loving attention. Kayleigh's Mum was trusting and supportive of our work together, further helping to make sense of the trauma that had impacted on both their lives. Kayleigh was also very well supported by an extended family who she regularly spent time with and enjoyed.

Kayleigh bounded into the room, dressed in a bright, colourful hoodie, leggings, and trainers, and smiled excitedly *"I've got some good news to tell you"*. Happy and chatting and keen to share her story, Kayleigh told me that she had two new dachshund puppies. She shared photos of them with me on her phone. She repeated her news and brimmed with joy as she took me out to the car to meet them.

I keep myself alive now for my Mum. I can't be a wreck anymore or have a nervous breakdown. I'm not happy every day and I still have nightmares. I have good days and bad days. I feel a lot happier now that I have my dogs. I care for them, and they look after me.

This chapter has also brought into focus my own self-care and the daily processes that I engage in to keep myself healthy and actively curious within my practice. Regular connection with my CLDT colleagues, arts therapies team and therapist friends, robust supervision, and protected clinical time are all incredibly important to me. Those who know me will also be aware that open water swimming is a big passion of mine. It offers me both a sense of belonging and adventure, a place to engage my mind and body simultaneously, together with others or alone, and, most importantly, time to connect with nature.

Conclusion

This chapter illustrates that we never lose the need to connect with others, as we continually seek safety in our bodies, our relationships, and our environment. Over the years, as psychotherapies have experienced a paradigm shift from *"them and us"* to *"us and us"*, we are now much more aware of ourselves (as therapists) as an important resource in art therapy and that we must look after the needs of ourselves to protect the work that we do. It has taken strength, courage, and determination for Jane and Kayleigh to tell their stories and to allow their stories to be heard by others. It has not been an easy journey for them as they live it and feel it every day. I continue to be impressed that Jane and Kayleigh took a stand to change the way of things, proving to be positive role models that young people with learning disabilities can look up to. Jane has stopped the trauma that has lived in her family for generations, protecting the future for her son and grandson. Kayleigh, whilst only a child at the time, has held her abuser accountable and spoken out against hidden crime. Jane, Kayleigh, and I came together by chance to carry out intensive and important work, but we have also experienced a lot of fun, enjoyed being in each other's company, respected each other, and listened carefully to one another. That which makes us all human.

References

Access to Justice Webinar (23/09/2020). Rape Crisis: Tyneside & Northumberland.

Cottis. T (2009). *Intellectual Disability Trauma and Psychotherapy*. East Sussex: Routledge.

Dana, D (2023). *Polyvagal Practices*. London: W.W. Norton & Company Ltd.

Herman, J. L. (1992). *Trauma and Recovery*. New York: Basic. Mencap. https://www.mencap. or.uk/learning-disability-explained/research-and-statistics. Accessed on 30/06/23.

Rothschild, B. (2017). *The Body Remembers. Volume 2: Revolutionizing Trauma Treatment.* London: W W Norton.

Sinason, V. (1992). *Mental Handicap and the Human Condition.* London: Free Association Books.

Sinason, V. (2020). *The Truth about Trauma and Dissociation.* London: Confer Books.

Van der Kolk, B. (2014). *The Body Keeps the Score.* Penguin: Random House, UK.

Victims' Commissioner Annual Report (2021/2022). London: HH Associates Ltd.

Chapter 4

Everyday Trauma

Elizabeth (Liz) Ashby and Joey Mander

Positionality Statement

Joey Mander is also a social activist who works with Grapevine, a group that supports people with learning disabilities and autism in various ways, including speaking about issues to members of the Leadership Board in my National Health Service (NHS) Trust (in the Midlands in England, UK) where he hopes that change will result from his intervention in terms of health inequalities being addressed, person-centred care established, and training in learning disability and autism awareness being established. I (Liz) have been working with Joey in art therapy sessions in an individual art therapy room in a health centre occupied by the Community Learning Disability Team (CLDT) on a weekly basis, for approximately four years. Our discussions about Joey's experiences have given rise to this chapter as they resonate with issues that many other people have discussed in both individual and group art therapy sessions.

I have written this chapter as a white woman without learning disabilities who is working as an Art Psychotherapist. My co-author, Joey, is a white man who does have learning disabilities and autism. This chapter has been written by Joey sending me his narratives by email. These were originally written as speeches which he has delivered in various contexts and also talked about in our individual art therapy sessions. I then added text within this chapter, which includes my own views too.

Joey's direct quotes are shown with double speech marks, and other people's words with single quote marks. He has consented to their use in the chapter which will be read by people who buy the book.

Introduction

Trauma is usually thought about in terms of big harmful events with a big impact on people's lives, and subsequent responses within the body that they become aware of (Van der Kolk, 2014; Porges, 2017). However, in my work as an art therapist, I have become aware of difficult issues that people with learning disabilities experience in the context of their everyday lives, which is what this chapter is about. These issues, such as the difficulties presented by travelling, attending medical

DOI: 10.4324/9781003350736-6

appointments, the experience of going online which is marred because of safe-guarding issues that emerge, and just general attitudes encountered out and about have often been discussed by service users in art therapy groups and in individual sessions, and Joey, as co-author, has experienced all of them and written about them for this chapter.

Oliver McGowan, who sadly died in care, resulted in mandatory training being offered to NHS professionals, to equip them to understand learning disability and autism. This came about as a result of pressure from Oliver McGowan's mother and LeDeR (Learning from lives and deaths – people with learning disability and autistic people) (Strydom, 2022). In England, there were also attempts to prevent unnecessary hospitalisation of people with learning disabilities, autism, and complex needs, including care, housing, mental health provision, substance misuse, and unemployment (Jacks et al., 2019). The Health and Care Act 2022 introduced a statutory requirement that regulated service providers must ensure their staff receive learning disability and autism training appropriate to their role.

As an art therapist working in the NHS, it is my hope that these initiatives will transform current practices in the NHS, Social Care, and other agencies that provide services to people with learning disabilities or autism, or who have other kinds of complex needs. In my psychology team, art therapy is one of our reasonable adjustments as an alternative to talking therapy which many people with learning disabilities really need, in addition to offering adaptations such as Easy Read information.

Bullying on Public Transport

In our art therapy sessions, Joey has often spoken about these issues, and Joey wrote:

As I am disabled, I've experienced a different perspective of public transport that has been going on for many years. I am physically disabled but I used to be able to walk and go out unaided back when I was at secondary school. I am autistic and seemed to stand out, which I didn't understand. Other people my age were also getting the same buses to school as me and there were two schools on that route.

I suffered from a lot of bullying from the other people my age, they would shout very bad words at me, and often called me discriminatory names such as 'here comes the sp*z again' (Joey asked for the full word to be obscured here) and worse. I couldn't respond verbally and always ignored it. I was too frightened to react anyway even if I could. That then turned into physical bullying, and every day people would throw things at me like pennies and bottles - I didn't respond to that either.

Then a person folded a piece of paper into a sharp point and every morning for months he would stand behind me just poking my back with it. I also never responded to this. It was hard, because with the shouting I knew everyone could hear (especially as so many people laughed), but a bus driver never once told them to stop (not that I really expected them to, is that even part of their job?). This eventually did stop because a lady, who had taken that same bus all the years I'd been taking it, one day said to the boy 'Why do you do that to him? He's never once spoken to you or reacted to you, and what you're doing is wrong - leave him alone'. I was very grateful for that, and he never did that to me again.

Joey's experiences with this kind of bullying relate to hate crime, which sadly he experienced week in and week out as a young person. Joey did not report any of this as hate crime but he could have done. Hate crime is defined as 'any criminal offence which is perceived, by the victim or any other person, to be motivated by hostility or prejudice towards someone based on a personal characteristic'. The statistics relate to people and race or religion, transgender identity, disability, and sexual orientation (UK Government Hate Crime, 2022 to 2023) and in 2023 there were 13,777 hate crimes related to disability reported to the police, but many more go unreported (Figure 4.1).

Joey wrote about his experiences with taxis next, which he had discussed in many sessions:

When I started work, I relied on taxis and by this point I was a wheelchair user. I had many very difficult incidents with taxis. Many drivers did not want to strap my chair in or said that they couldn't do it or that they didn't know how to. I had an occasion where a driver came to pick me up and when he saw my wheelchair, he told me to wait across the road and he'd turn around to get closer to the curb. When he turned around, he opened his window and waved and drove off. I was particularly upset as it was a late winter evening, and therefore it was dark, and in an area that I felt was unsafe.

Joey has written about the very difficult experiences he has had over many years with buses and taxis, and I hope that these difficulties will begin to be addressed in society in the future, with more acceptance of people who are disabled in various ways and more appropriate responses to their needs. Currently, society disables people more than is necessary through attitudes such as the ones Joey has been discussing. Social inclusion is reported to be negatively impacted by both onset and persistent disability, with poverty also being implicated (Gannon and Nolan, 2007). Quality of life is significantly impacted by intellectual and physical disability and a greater understanding of practices that support inclusion was said to be needed in 2012 (Bigby, 2012) and this is still the case 12 years later.

Harassment when Shopping

Joey also described to me experiences in shops, such as being laughed at by the owner of a shop, an experience that could be described as harassment. Joey wrote:

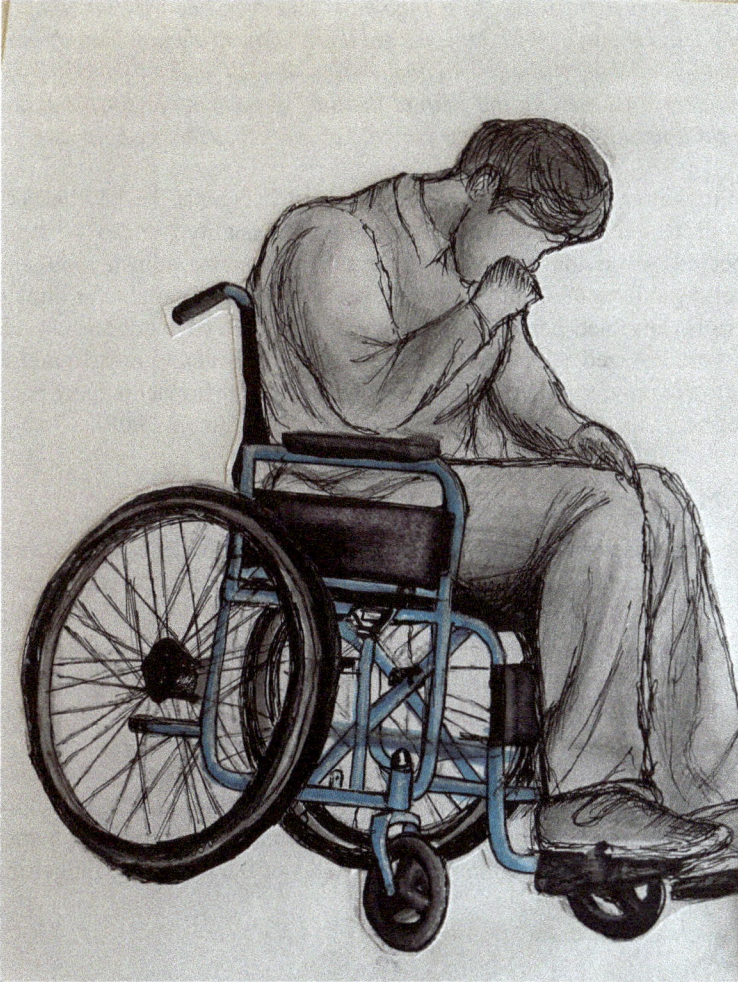

Figure 4.1 'People only see the wheelchair, not me' (2022) artwork by Joey.

On one occasion the elderly owner of a shop started to laugh at me when I entered. I think it was because people say I'm always looking scared in public. He said loudly: 'Are you lost? What have you even come in for?' And proceeded to laugh and did this in front of students from my school who all started to laugh too.

I didn't react or say anything. Then he walked over to me and said: 'Are you blind?' This time I said "no". But he laughed again, which everyone again joined in with. He then said: 'What do you want?' and I responded "Milk" - it's important to note I was fourteen years old when this happened, because what he then said next was 'Well, where does your mummy keep milk at home? Cupboard or fridge'. I went to the fridge to get the milk, and everyone was watching, he then laughed and shouted 'Well done, we got there'. Once I'd paid, I left the shop, and I didn't tell anyone. Nobody told him to stop, they all joined in and sadly some of the students that were in the shop at the time were in my lessons that day. They brought it up and joked about it and told all of their friends about it.

Discrimination against people who are disabled is against the law and is one of the nine protected characteristics covered by the Equality Act (2010). Employers are expected to provide disabled people with reasonable adjustments, and there is a useful guide to the rights of people with disability available at https://www.gov.uk/rights-disabled-person. Education, the provision of goods and services, and transport are covered by the Act. More powers are available now to address discrimination legally, and there is more recognition of the impact on people's mental health of being discriminated against (Sayce and Boardman, 2008).

Social Media and Hate Crime

In art therapy sessions Joey has discussed his many experiences of extreme hate, and awful comments made about him or his friends by people who seem to feel that they have some right to make the comments. In my view, they constitute hate crime. Joey has reported some of the most distasteful comments to Facebook, as he runs a big group on Facebook, but Meta refused to do anything about it, which is tantamount to condoning it. The comments all relate to people's views that disabled people should be aborted prior to birth or killed.

The image below, made by Joey, shows the hateful comments made by many people and which he could not get removed by Facebook (Figure 4.2). The blurred-out parts are the images and names of those who made the comments, which even include mothers of small children, and the sizes of the words are bigger the more times they have been said:

Joey told me that:

a big problem for me, is that I feel that laughing at, discrimination or being abusive towards people with learning difficulties, autism and additional needs, is normalised. I feel like it's acceptable in general, by society, and a lot of people don't see it with the same severity as other forms of discrimination.

Also a lot of people just say things like 'just don't be on social media'. The problem with that is, firstly, people with additional needs are already isolated and will struggle with things like going anywhere outside independently. Secondly, why should it be us taking the responsibility of removing ourselves when the responsibility should be taken by the people who are saying these things online? However, it is not just online, this happens both online and in the street.

Joey told me that all the comments were reported to Meta numerous times but were not considered a direct attack on disabled people. Even though they have a policy of 'removing de-humanising speech, which includes statements of inferiority,

put it back in its cage

burn it

breeding more defectives??

Just exterminate it

Kill it

another useless born disabled

just put her down

Throw her away

They should force sterilization on people who make defective humans

Damn.... whatever happened to good old fashioned natural selection?

useless disabled children.!!!!

Burn it

Kill it

just put her down

zombies

I want to kill it so bad

Used to be a time you'd pay a nickel to see something like this, now it's free.

I can't tell if it's human or dinosaur

The furnace is on throw them in

Kill it with fire 🔥🚒 🤣🤣🤣

Just a nuisance to everyone

just put her down

put her down

another mutant 💀

Yesterdays abortions

the world would be a better place and not so overpopulated if we didn't save every broken thing....... Some things are not meant to make it...

Should've never be born.

Not all life is valuable

Abort it (it's never too late)

alien

kill it

Still a monster 👊👊

that thing is ugly as hell should be in the garbage where it belongs

Just kill it already

When you decide to stop mid abortion 😏

Someone put it down

Kill it

I don't understand why they have to multiply.

What's the point in keeping it alive?

Throw it away,

row row row your spaz gently down the stream

abort her

Put her down

Figure 4.2 'Facebook hateful comments regarding people with learning disability' (2023) artwork by Joey.

disgust or contempt, or calls for exclusion or segregation' (Meta, 2018), Meta did not consider these comments needed to be taken off their platform, or that they were examples of de-humanising speech. People with learning disabilities and/or autism cannot live their lives with the freedom that most young people can, and social media should be accessible to them, but unfortunately there are both benefits and risks associated with social media use by people with learning disabilities (Anderson et al., 2023).

Medical Appointments

Joey has experienced numerous issues with medical professionals and has many physical issues related to his condition.

In an art therapy session, he told me that:

In the past I have had problems with doctors and other professionals not believing me, which impacted my thoughts about myself and made me doubt myself because it happened so often. There have been occasions where, when investigating degenerative physical symptoms, it was assumed that these symptoms were psychological, rather than that there was a physical problem. On multiple occasions that this has happened, it has been later discovered that in fact there were underlying physical causes, including brain damage, that was discovered four years after I was told that a symptom was psychological.

This was not only damaging psychologically, but from a physical perspective, attitudes like the ones I faced can be dangerous, as symptoms disregarded as being 'psychological', or as I've had said to me multiple times 'a product of anxiety', could be signs of a physical illness that may be missed and could have been treated.

I had an experience just around a year ago, where a Consultant wrote a pre-scription to increase an anti-depressant medication I was on. I told him I didn't want that increase, and that I believed it was dangerous, especially because that medication is prescribed by the psychiatry team. The opinion of the professional writing this prescription was that 'COVID is making everyone quite low and if you are anxious your physical struggles will get worse'. I again said I did not want that increase and I was very visibly upset, but he ignored what I said and said to the person with me 'I'll write it anyway, it would be good for him to try it'.

NHS England has addressed the overmedication of people with learning disabilities and/or autism in the STOMP (Stopping the overmedication of people with a learn-ing disability, autism or both) policy (Branford et al., 2018, 2019), which aims to stop this practice, and there is a STAMP (Supporting Treatment and Appropriate Medication in Paediatrics) policy too for children and adolescents. This policy is now adhered to by our psychiatrists in the CLDT, but it needs to be standard prac-tice in inpatient services as well.

Joey continued:

Often I notice, (and not just me, but many others I have spoken to) that when you have autism, a learning disability, additional needs and so on, particularly if you struggle to communicate in different ways, then assumptions are made about you, even by those in the medical field, particularly when it comes to physical illness. Assumptions are made about what you feel or whether your symptoms are even 'real'. Sometimes it feels like people do not want to put the effort into hearing you as a person. This causes long-lasting emotional damage, because once a person has experienced this over extended periods of time, it starts to feel as though there is no point in me trying to explain. It's so tiring, and very upsetting. It is scary to feel that people have power and authority over you, but they don't want to put the effort into listening.

Diagnostic overshadowing is what Joey has described here (Manohar et al., 2016; Javaid et al., 2019). This is where doctors fail to address or investigate the possi-bility of underlying physical conditions which they dismiss as part of the learning disability presentation or behaviour. This has now been recognised as an issue that needs to be addressed in the medical interventions offered in health care settings across the nation.

I have experienced that the values of the NHS Trust I work in have greatly changed and now in 2024 require their workers at all levels of practice to operate with compassion, respect, collaboration, integrity, and excellence. These changes are required to be represented in staff appraisals. This change in culture in our NHS Trust should result in these experiences, which for Joey have been so numerous, changing; doctors have not considered Joey to be able to tell them appropriately about what he instinctively knew about his own body and mind, and further to value his opinions on what treatment he would or would not accept. And with the inclusion of mandatory Oliver McGowan training, there should be some overall changes that we could expect to see in the attitudes of medical professionals.

Discussion

Third Class

Joey's opinion is that there is a class system in our society that plays itself out in various scenarios.

> *I often feel as though, when it comes to travel, there's a bit of a 'class system'. First class, second class and then, finally, third class. I often feel third class on public transport - it's feeling like a burden, and I see that in the attitudes from people too, so often people do not want to support you to get onto a bus or make people feel like they are 'lesser than most of society'. Sometimes I describe it to people by asking them to imagine society in the context of travelling by plane: we have first class, second class and third class… why do I say third class? Well, have you ever noticed that on planes even food and drink trolleys have more thought and access put into them to be able to have full unrestricted access to the entire plane?*

Passed Back and Forth

> *I was on waiting lists for years; I was passed back and forth. This is a repeated pattern we see, and it's degrading. I felt like a burden to the system, I did not feel seen as a person, I felt like a number or a statistic. I think for me a big part of the reason I experienced this pattern so intensely was due to my autism. I didn't fit into a perfect box that the system wanted me to fit into.*
> *I very rarely saw the same person more than twice due to constant team rotations and the already constricted amount of time you get in an appointment is diminished more, as you constantly have to start from the beginning, telling your story over and over again, revisiting trauma over and over again, even simply introducing yourself over and over again. This inevitably caused me to deteriorate after years of the same repetitive cycle, and ultimately led to life-threatening and life-altering situations.*

Little Things Make the Difference

> *But what is good support? When I think of the most impactful support I've received, it's the really small things that have made the biggest impact…*

relationships between professionals and service users is one of the key components of successful treatment (Chipidza et al, 2015).

Things like remembering my name, what I do or an activity I've taken part in for a long time. These are not huge things; in fact, these are things that can be found by quickly scanning over my notes before a meeting.

Trust Is Important

When it comes to mental health, trust is incredibly important. During mental health appointments people are sharing their most vulnerable thoughts and are expected to be able to do this with someone they have never met before, which is, as I've mentioned, a very common occurrence in the mental health service. Trust is needed to be built very quickly and this is a frightening situation to be in.

Trust is: 'The firm belief in the reliability, truth, or ability in someone or something'. However, we must acknowledge that trust is a lot more complex than this, particularly in terms of mental health treatment...

A uniquely deep degree of trust is required in a relationship between a person and a mental health professional, where a person can feel heard, receive empathy, kindness, honesty and consistency.

Mental Health

For people who struggle with their mental health, life can feel chaotic and unpredictable. For some people, being heard by a mental health professional might be the first time they've ever experienced being listened to or received empathy. It is so important to make that first experience the best it can be. We need to feel that people are committed to us, and that there are reliable people that genuinely care.

Joey has shown considerable insight into what should happen in different services that people come into contact with. I totally agree with Joey that medical professionals should approach people with additional needs – such as learning disabilities, autism, mobility issues, deaf and blindness, and other kinds of issues that affect their day-to-day functioning – as people who need their help, to be treated with dignity, respect, kindness, and compassion.

Art Therapy

Joey has always found art therapy his psychological intervention of choice because of his appreciation of the attitudes and values I have worked with in my contacts with him. Love and kindness are principles that I think are central to the way I work, and having a non-judgmental attitude as part of working with a person-centred approach is key to why it works so well. I believe that it is essential to tailor your approach to each individual, ensuring their needs and preferences are prioritised. This also means liaising with families and colleagues as necessary, both within and outside of the NHS – such as care providers, and social care colleagues and first and foremost we must consider what the person you are working with needs and wants.

Conclusion

Joey's thoughts on these issues are as follows:

> *We need to be seen as people, not a list of diagnoses. We need to feel equal and to be shown humility. We need active listening. We need professionals mirroring our language, so that conversations can happen using words that we understand, another small action that makes us feel heard.*

Joey has been able to speak to the issues that we have raised powerfully. We can see that there is a will to change attitudes within government, within the NHS, and in other settings. However, we can also see that within the population of any given place there are people who express hateful thoughts to people they experience as different, and no understanding that this is discrimination and is against the law.

So, it seems to me that there is still a long way to go in the hearts and minds of ordinary people and in the hearts and minds of professionals in all the various settings where people with learning disabilities and autism may see them.

Unfortunately, LeDeR reports (Strydom et al., 2022) show that big mistakes are still being made in NHS services and result in the deaths of people with learning disability and autism. Oliver McGowan training is beginning, in the NHS Trust that I work in, to tackle the very difficult attitudes that Joey has so often encountered, and I very much hope that if all the professionals in our Trust receive this training it will make them re-think how they approach patients.

All disabled people need protection from health inequalities that can result in their unfair incarceration in various services or in their deaths as a result of not being listened to by the very people who should be trying to assist them back to health.

We need to bless the people in our care in every possible way.

Art therapy has been extremely helpful to Joey, in enabling him to think about difficult and very stressful events in the context of making art; and he knows that I listen carefully to what he says and reflect that back in my replies. This has resulted in the development of a very trusting therapeutic relationship, and he has often told me this.

References

Anderson, S., Araten-Bergman, T., and Steel, G. (2023). Adults with intellectual disabilities as users of social media: A scoping review. *British Journal of Learning Disabilities*, *51*(4), pp. 544–564. https://doi.org/10.1111/bld.12534.

Bigby, C. (2012). Social inclusion and people with intellectual disability and challenging behaviour: A systematic review. *Journal of Intellectual & Developmental Disability*, *37*(4), pp. 360–374. December 2012.

Branford, D., Gerrard, D., Saleem, N., Shaw, C., and Webster, A., (2018). Stopping over-medication of people with intellectual disability, autism or both (STOMP) in England part 1–history and background of STOMP. *Advances in Mental Health and Intellectual Disabilities*, *13*(1), pp. 31–40.

Branford, D., Gerrard, D., Saleem, N., Shaw, C., and Webster, A., (2019). Stopping over-medication of people with an intellectual disability, autism or both (STOMP) in England part 2–the story so far. *Advances in Mental Health and Intellectual Disabilities*, *13*(1), pp. 41–51.

Chipidza, F. E., Wallwork, R. S., and Stern, T. A. (2015). Impact of the Doctor-patient relationship. *Primary Care Companion for CNS Disorders 2015*, *17*, p. 5. https://doi.org/10.4088/PCC.15f01840

Equality Act (2010). London: HMSO.

Gannon, B., and Nolan, B. (2007). The impact of disability transitions on social inclusion. *Social Science & Medicine*, *64*, pp. 1425–1437.

Jacks, A., Cooper, Y., Brown, M., and James, R. (2019). *Transforming Care: What Next?* All-Party Parliamentary Group Briefing.

Javaid, A., Nakata, V., and Michael, D., (2019). Diagnostic overshadowing in learning disability: think beyond the disability. *Progress in Neurology and Psychiatry*, *23*(2), pp. 8–10.

Manohar, H., Subramanian, K., Kandasamy, P., Penchilaiya, V., and Arun, A., (2016). Diagnostic masking and overshadowing in intellectual disability—How structured evaluation helps. *Journal of Child and Adolescent Psychiatric Nursing*, *29*(4), pp. 171–176.

Meta (2018). *Enforcing our Community Standards*, online at, https://about.fb.com/news/2018/08/enforcing-our-community-standards

Porges, S (2017). *The Pocket Guide to the Polyvagal Theory: The Transformative Power of Feeling Safe*. Ed. The Norton series on interpersonal neurobiology. W. W Norton & Company.

Sayce, L., and Boardman, J. (2008). Disability rights and mental health in the UK: recent developments of the disability discrimination act. *Advances in Advances in Psychiatric Treatment (2008)*, *14*, pp. 265–275. https://doi.org/10.1192/apt.bp.106.003103

Strydom, A., Sheehan, R., White, A., and Ding, J. (2022). *Learning from Lives and Deaths – People with a Learning Disability or Autistic People (LeDeR)*. King's College, London University.

The Oliver McGowan Mandatory Training on Learning Disability and Autism (NHS England) – can be, online at, https://www.hee.nhs.uk/our-work/learning-disability/current-projects/oliver-mcgowan-mandatory-training-learning-disability-autism

UK Government Hate Crime, England and Wales, (2022 to 2023). Second edition, online at, https://www.gov.uk/government/statistics/hate-crime-england-and-wales-2022-to-2023/hate-crime-england-and-wales-2022-to-2023

Van der Kolk, B. (2014). *The Body Keeps The Score: Mind, Brain and Body in the Transformation of Trauma*. Penguin UK.

Section 2

Agency

Chapter 5

Doing Things Differently

Working Together to Talk More about Death and Dying: The *No Barriers Here* Approach

*J. Jerwood, G. Allen, V. Peters, S. Reeves,
J. Vallance and S. Offley*

Positionality Statement of Authors

All authors worked together to co-author this chapter, each bringing their unique skills and expertise.

Jed is a middle-aged, middle-class man without learning disabilities or autism. I have a personal experience of marginalisation in relation to other aspects of my identity and a personal and professional interest in health inequalities and in finding ways for healthcare professionals to hear the voices of people who are marginalised in healthcare and wider society. I work clinically as an Art Psychotherapist. I am the lead researcher for the *No Barriers Here* project. I facilitated the planning and co-writing of this chapter with people with learning disabilities and/or autism.

Gemma is a white, cisgender woman without learning disabilities or neurodiversity. I work as a hospice Palliative Care Inclusion and Community Partnerships Lead and lead the *No Barriers Here* programme. I have professional experience of chairing a national learning disability charity and my interests lie in working with and alongside people who experience inequities accessing palliative and end-of-life care.

Samantha is a young woman with a learning disabilities. I co-designed some of the activities in the *No Barriers Here* project. This project was important to me as it helped me to understand and support my family when my nan died. I am an expert with lived experience who works as a self-advocate to reduce the inequalities that we have to face on every day.

Vince is a young(ish) man with a autism and learning difficulties. I co-designed some of the activities in the *No Barriers Here* project. This project has changed the way that I think about planning for the future. I thought it was going to be scary but felt confident when I had done the sessions. I am an expert with lived experience who works as a self-advocate to reduce the inequalities that we have to face on a daily basis.

Joanne is a young woman with learning disabilities. I worked on the *No Barriers Here* project from the beginning and co-designed the sessions with the team. I like

DOI: 10.4324/9781003350736-8

to do arts and crafts so enjoyed doing the project. I am an expert with lived experience who works as a self-advocate to make things better for my friends.

Sarah is a woman Sarah is a woman without a learning disability or autism. I am passionate about reducing inequalities in health and society for everyone. I am employed as Chief Officer of the self-advocacy charity Dudley Voices for Choice. My role includes supporting the experts with lived experience.

Box 1   Our Approach

This chapter is co-authored by people with learning disabilities and/or autism, an art therapist researcher, advocacy worker and a diversity and inclusion manager in a hospice. It discusses how the core elements of co-production, art therapy and arts-based research methods became the *No Barriers Here* approach to advance care planning (ACP). People with learning disabilities and/or autism have been at the centre of the development, implementation and evaluation of *No Barriers Here*, and we continue to be involved with the development of what has become a much larger project working with other underserved people and communities in palliative care.

Introduction

This chapter outlines the origins of *No Barriers Here* (No Barriers Here© www.nobarriershere.org), an ACP approach in palliative care, and explore the co-production process and the role of arts-based methods within the *No Barriers Here* approach. It highlights the benefits of working in co-production for people with learning disabilities and/or autism, for researchers and for health and social care organisations. Importantly, it explores the role of the art therapist in the development of the approach and explores how art therapy practice underpins it.

The project was first developed by a group of people with learning disabilities and/or autism, an art therapist researcher, advocacy organisation (Dudley Voices for Choice https://www.dudleyvoicesforchoice.org.uk/) and a hospice (Mary Stevens Hospice https://www.marystevenshospice.co.uk/) just prior to the COVID-19 global pandemic and was first delivered in the early months during the first UK lockdown. It was developed in response to a need expressed by people with learning disabilities and/or autism to be able to have more meaningful conversations about end-of-life care wishes. The negative impact of the pandemic on people with learning disabilities and/or autism heightened this need further (Public Health England, 2020; Kuper and Scherer, 2023).

Since then, *No Barriers Here* has evolved into an equity-oriented, arts-based approach to ACP. It has two aspects. Firstly, it is a tool for carrying out ACP conversations with people and groups who are underserved in palliative care. Secondly, it is a research method for understanding the expectations, barriers and experiences of those groups when accessing palliative care.

Box 2   What Is Advance Care Planning?

ACP is a key element in palliative care. It is a practice that involves communication and decision making to discuss and understand goals for care, what's important to people and their choices and preferences regarding future care (Sudore et al., 2017).

Why Do We Need to Talk More about Death and Dying with People with Learning Disabilities and/or Autism?

People with learning disabilities and/or autism are often excluded from decisions about their care, infantilised and not listened to by care and support agencies (Ferguson et al., 2011). Historically, people with learning disabilities and/or autism have been repeatedly prevented from having conversations about death and dying, with little consideration of personalised ACP (Heslop et al., 2013). Healthcare workers often fear that having ACP conversations with people with learning disabilities and/or autism will be too distressing and therefore these important discussions are often neglected.

Evidence shows that people with learning disabilities have a lower life expectancy than the general population and will often die from unjust and preventable deaths (White et al., 2022). Despite high mortality rates for this population than the general population, overall people with learning disabilities are living longer (Ryan, 2021). However, this means people are outliving their parents and living longer with additional health conditions. Both factors increase the need for effective ACP. People with learning disabilities can be at higher risk of a range of health conditions as highlighted during the pandemic with excess deaths estimated to be double that of the overall population and the most common cause of death recorded on death certificates being COVID-19 (White et al., 2022). Both during the pandemic, and generally in society, people with learning disabilities and/or autism are negatively impacted on through their experiences of bereavement. Many people have been excluded from funerals, from conversations about loss, death and dying and not expected to explore feelings and emotions associated with loss and grief (Read, 2011). Living longer increases the experiences of loss through bereavement and it is important for people with learning disabilities and/or autism to be able to have these conversations with people around them.

The Beginnings

As co-authors and co-production group members, we thought together about the importance of speaking with people with learning disabilities and/or autism about death and dying and expressed views about growing older, planning ahead and personalised ACP.

Talking about death and dying and the way we want to be cared for in the future is important to me because death is an eventuality that NO ONE with or without autism and learning disabilities can avoid. If we are in frail health in later life we want to be as happy, comfortable, and stay as independent as we can be with the time we have left so we still have a good quality of life.

(Co-author and co-production group member)

To help others understand us.

(Co-author and co-production group member)

Over recent years, more resources have become available to support people with learning disabilities and/or autism in conversations about death, dying and bereavement. These often form an easy-read or pictorial format to aid with communication and whilst they are suitable for some people, others may find it difficult to relate to images that are not about themselves and likewise may find it difficult to explore or think about their own wishes, choices and feelings.

The co-authors looked at some of the available resources together and thought about how we could create an approach that would move away from forms, cards and booklets and instead embrace personalised ACP. In thinking about a different approach, it was important to the co-authors to encourage healthcare professionals to engage in ACP either one-to-one or less traditionally in small groups alongside our peers. We wanted ACP to happen earlier, when we are well, to think about planning ahead, how we would like to be cared for and consider what would matter to us at the end of our lives.

What Is *No Barriers Here*?

The initial scope of *No Barriers Here* was to explore how ACP could be more inclusive and move away from thinking about accessibility in terms of easy-read literature. It became clear that it needed to be more than developing a way of learning about people's priorities for end-of-life care by translating existing forms and templates into accessible formats. It needed to offer space and time for people with learning disabilities and/or autism to both explore and express their wishes.

Co-production, art therapy principles and arts-based research methods form the key elements of *No Barriers Here*. Together we co-produced a series of three workshops, each focused on a different aspect of ACP, exploring our choices and preferences as we grow older, become unwell or are dying.

We used the art materials and found it was a lot easier because it explained everything in a simple form. I thought that I could explain the way I was feeling by doing it in an artistic way. When we started the No Barriers Here project, I didn't think I could explain my feelings. It was better when we did the creative sessions to explain everything so then we could understand better and communicate better.

(Workshop participant)

Figure 5.1 Co-production group members developing creative activities.

As a co-production group, we tested each workshop, thinking about language, art materials and accessibility issues, and used our lived experience to inform the development of the approach (see Figure 5.1).

When thinking about the workshops it was important for us to think about two aspects. Firstly, how it would feel for people with learning disabilities and/or autism to participate? We had to think about the length of the workshops, and how they would work online (due to COVID-19 restrictions) as well as face to face. Secondly, we wanted the stories and themes from the workshops to be used to help healthcare and other professionals to be curious and listen to what is important to us, our identity and our place in society.

> *It's not just about me dying, it's about what I want in life too.*
>
> (Co-author and co-production group member)

Figure 5.2 shows the phases in the development of the *No Barriers Here* Model.

Why Arts–Based Methods?

We know that many people find talking about their experiences and feelings difficult (Malchiodi, 2003). Traditionally, we have understood this in relation to disability, language difference, sensory impairment and other physical and physiological conditions. In recent years, greater understanding of the impact of trauma has developed and it is now more widely understood that for some people a less verbal, more body-based approach is more helpful in exploring and expressing experiences (Malchiodi, 2003; Elbrecht, 2019). Art-making and other creative expression is a useful tool in clinical practice and in research and relies less on verbal expression (Fraser and Al Sayah, 2011).

> *It was different to just talking because a picture says the words for us. If we can't find the strength to talk and express our emotions. A picture tells the story for*

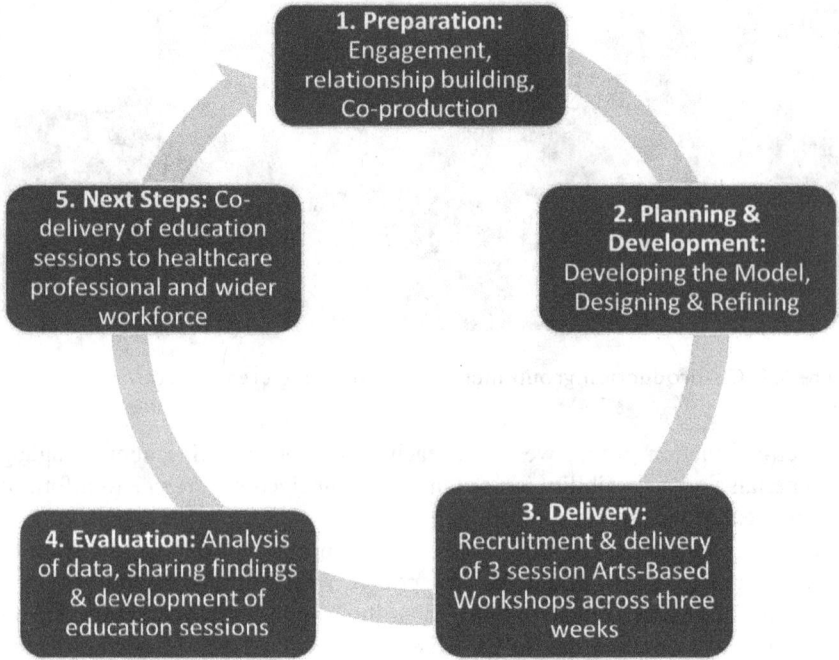

Figure 5.2 Diagram showing the phases in the development of the *No Barriers Here* Model.

us and sometimes you just don't need words for what you are presenting. Sometimes there simply aren't any words to say.

(Workshop participant)

Arts-based research methods are used widely when seeking to understand the views and experiences of people and communities underserved or marginalised in healthcare and wider society (Mannay, 2015; Kara, 2015).

For people with learning disabilities and/or autism, art-making offers the opportunity to express views and experiences differently. It also offers space to explore and understand topics which people might not have had a chance to think about before.

The arts and crafts brought me a sort of comforting feeling and because we were working together as a group, we were able to find similar emotions and thoughts. It just brought us all together and we were like a support and comfort to each other as we all have different stories and life journeys to share.

(Workshop participant)

Talking about death and dying can be difficult for people including people with learning disabilities and/or autism. Western society struggles to talk about dying and many rituals surrounding death and dying have been lost. It has become stigmatised in healthcare and staff fear upsetting patients and often avoid conversations about death and dying. This is especially so for groups deemed to be vulnerable. In thinking about a different approach to ACP conversations, we felt it was important to think about a less verbal approach and to make sure we offered space to slow down and encourage exploration of views. This was especially important in working with people with learning disabilities who are often given even less opportunity to think about their own care wishes for the end-of-life. Using art-making can allow people to regulate anxious feelings as well as offering a visual way of communicating something that might be hard to articulate in words (Gruber and Oepen, 2018).

It is important to think about how to use art-making and art materials safely and below are some things to consider when doing so.

Box 3   Things to Consider When Using Arts-Based Methods

- partner with an art therapist to ensure your project is offering psychological safety, particularly when using art-making
- think about accessibility of art materials, trial and pilot the activities with people with lived experience
- undertake the activities yourself, it is important not to offer activities you haven't experienced
- think about the space you need for art-based activities – do you need access to water, wet wipes, aprons or gloves, are the materials toxic, have you got hard floors, are wet materials appropriate?
- what will happen to the images? Who do they belong to? Has this been established when taking consent to participate?
- in research studies, if using art-making as a tool for data collection, how will this visual data be analysed?

Why Did We Work with an Art Therapist?

In the early planning stages of the project, when we began to think about a different way of having ACP conversations together, some people with learning disabilities and/or autism took part in a bereavement workshop using art-making (Allen, 2021). In the workshop, participants suggested that art-making felt a more familiar and safe way of expressing difficult feelings.

Sometimes we can't find the words to speak, the pictures we created together did the talking for us where talking was at its most sensitive time. It is hard to find the words we want to say sometimes as it is a very sensitive subject. drawing is another way of communication, a more informal way. A reasonable adjustment if we don't feel like talking.

(Co-author and co-production group member)

Art therapy is a form of psychological therapy which uses art-making to explore and express difficult feelings and emotions and art therapists are trained to carry out this work to help people understand, process and express emotions and distress.

Although art-making is used widely in services for people with learning disabilities and/or autism, and within hospice and palliative care services, it can open up complex feelings and we wanted to consider how to do this safely. The art-making aspects of *No Barriers Here* are different to art-making as vocation or occupation which many people with learning disabilities and/or autism are exposed to regularly. We also knew that the topic of death and dying is often avoided by families, carers and professionals when talking with people with learning disabilities and/or autism for fear of causing distress that can't be contained (Read, 2001).

In developing the approach, it was important to work with an art therapist who was skilled and experienced in designing arts-based interventions as both a clinician and as a researcher. We felt that working with an art therapist would support the development of the *No Barriers Here* approach and make sure that it evolved into a tool that could be used by a wide range of health and social care workers. Our intention was not to develop an art therapy intervention but to develop an arts-based intervention and research method. The role of the art therapist was important in navigating the boundaries between art therapy and arts-based methods and approaches.

Working in Co-Production

Box 4   What Is Co-Production?

Co-production is not just a word, it is not just a concept, it is a meeting of minds coming together to find shared solutions. In practice, co-production involves people who use services being consulted, included, and working together from the start to the end of any project that affects them. When co-production works best, people who use services and carers are valued by organisations as equal partners, can share power and have influence over decisions made.

(Think Local Act Personal National
Co-production Advisory Group, 2022)

How Did We Do It?

At the very beginning of the journey to develop *No Barriers Here*, co-production was a key foundation (see Table 5.1). Earlier work by the hospice in partnership

Table 5.1 Embedded co-production across the five phases of model development

1. Preparatory Stage	2. Planning and Developing Stage	3. Delivery Stage	4. Evaluating and Disseminating Stage	5. Next Steps
• Development of relationship with advocacy organisation	• Developing, testing and evaluating the tasks and activities	• Experiencing the intervention	• Making a film	• Supporting development of model for use with other underserved populations
• Service visits, improvement to hospice, peer reviews, etc.	• Revising and influencing change	• Co-delivering workshops	• Creating and co-delivering education sessions	
• Invitation to participate, co-production group formed (varying abilities and skills inc. people with lived experience, researchers, healthcare staff, advocacy staff	• Developing resources	• Data Analysis	• Conference papers and writing journal articles and book chapters	

with a local learning disability advocacy service (Allen, 2021) had led to people with learning disabilities and/or autism contributing to reviews of accessibility of hospice services and the original idea for the project came from listening to people with learning disabilities and/or autism who were taking part in a bereavement workshop.

Foundations

Building on the existing partnership between the hospice and the advocacy organisation, local discussions about death and dying for people with learning disabilities and/or autism had been shared during local partnership meetings and focus groups and an easy-read advance care plan had been developed.

Planning and Development

The co-production group developed the workshop content, tested out art materials, use of language and accessibility of the planned sessions. The project was also named by a co-production group member with lived experience who stated:

if it's about removing barriers, let's call it No Barriers Here?

(Co-author and co-production group member)

Delivery

Over several months three cohorts of participants took part. Participants were predominantly people with learning disabilities and/or autism, but, importantly, also included support staff. One cohort included other professionals involved in research concerning people with learning disabilities and/or autism.

Three workshops were delivered over three weeks, each lasting two hours. The themes for each workshop were (see Figure 5.3):

- week one – All about me? Introducing myself and what makes me who I am. Explored through creating an image together
- week two – What matters to me at the end-of-life? Four questions explored through textiles:

  - who are my important people?
  - where would I like to be cared for?
  - what are my funeral and other wishes when I die?
  - what are the three most important things to me at the very end of my life?

- week three – What is my legacy? How would I like to be remembered? Explored through weaving

The workshops were delivered online and facilitated by the art therapist researcher and co-facilitated by a co-production group member including people with lived experience. The presence of a person with learning disabilities in the workshops

Figure 5.3 Photograph showing the three creative activities in the three sessions of *No Barriers Here*.

helped participants feel safe. The presence of support staff allowed those staff to hear the stories and priorities of the people they looked after very differently and led to each person's personal plans being updated following the workshops.

Evaluation and Dissemination

The content of the workshops was analysed using thematic analysis (Braun and Clarke, 2022), and themes developed which supported the delivery of education sessions for health and social care staff involved in ACP. People with learning disabilities and/or autism co-delivered these education sessions. The impact of the arts-based approach and the co-delivery by people with lived experience led to greater impact of the training and led to participants being able to hear the stories and experiences more effectively.

Next Steps

The co-production group has continued to be involved in the dissemination of the *No Barriers Here* approach and the development of it with other underserved groups. The approach is included in several good practice guides and toolkits and further research has been carried out with other groups (Jerwood and Allen, 2023; NHS England, 2022; Derbyshire Community Health Services NHS Foundation Trust, 2023).

Challenges of Working in Co-Production

Bringing the voices of people with learning disabilities and/or autism into clinical practice, research and service development can often be misguided, tokenistic and lack authenticity (Russell, 2023). Co-production is often confused or misrepresented by engagement and consultation whereby people with lived experience are invited to be involved in work that has either been completed or key decisions have already been made. This results in restricting how people with lived experience can change, challenge or offer a different perspective.

There is always good intention when organisations want to work in co-production with people with lived experience, yet often the timeframe for doing so is insufficient. This can create tension, particularly when working to deadlines set by others or within the restrictions of inflexible funding programmes. Allocating sufficient time ensures people have the time to review and feedback information alongside any additional support a person may require such as a co-worker, family member or support worker to help them to prove new information.

Ensuring funding is available to recompense co-production partners for their time is a challenge. Time and contribution of people with lived experience is often not properly costed into funding bids or included within funding guidelines.

Opportunities for Working in Co-Production

Working authentically in co-production offers an opportunity to see from another person's perspective with a greater emphasis on finding solutions together, instead of making presumptions or doing something in a way that has little impact on the people the work is aimed at. It provides alternative views and will often create other further opportunities and greater impact if people feeling empowered to share their experiences and know that these are valued.

Working in co-production disrupts traditional power imbalances and enables everyone to be able to contribute in a way that will build on people's existing abilities, strengths and skills. Engaging meaningfully with people prior to co-production work is important and will build a foundation for trusted reciprocal relationships. It is important to use the skills, knowledge and experience of everyone within a co-production team, identifying the individual strengths of each member and allowing both the time and space for existing skills to be shared and new skills to be developed. Here, two of the co-authors explain how working in co-production made them feel and the personal benefits of being involved.

> *I felt relaxed and comfortable working together with the researchers and staff on No Barriers Here because they didn't apply pressure on us. They let us be ourselves. When we all got together and did the work it brought out a different side to us all and as a group, we all became personally involved and felt able to share our feelings and make our own decisions.*
>
> (Co-production group member and co-author)

> *It made feel confident and happy.*
>
> (Co-production group member and co-author)

Considerations when Working in Co-Production

When working in co-production with people with learning disabilities and/or autism reasonable adjustments must be considered to ensure equitable participation. These may include the way and format that information is shared and at a pace that is comfortable for the individual.

> *The main difference when working with people with learning disabilities and/or autism in a co-produced way is time. Everything must be done at an individual's pace. There is always intention to work inclusively, it just never gets the time allocated to make sure this does happen in the most meaningful way.*
>
> (Co-author and co-production group member)

Thoughts from the Co-Production Group

The members of the co-production group with lived experience identified the important elements of working in co-production:

- co-production is about including our own ideas, thoughts and designs
- everyone's voice counts. Listen to us
- working in co-production is good because you will hear everyone's views, and these may be different to yours
- to work in co-production, you need to trust and respect one another to work as a team

Impact of the *No Barriers Here* Approach

The impact of *No Barriers Here* has been far-reaching and multi-faceted. We often talk about the need to 'amplify voices' when talking about underserved or marginalised people and communities. One of the most significant impacts of the *No Barriers Here* project was gaining insight into the need for clinicians, researchers and other professionals in the healthcare workforce to listen, to hear more effectively, not to amplify voices. People should be heard and listened to no matter how loud their voices are. The combination of the use of arts-based methods and the co-production of the project with people with learning disabilities and/or autism at the forefront of its development and delivery seemed to enable others to really hear what was being said in a far more effective way than previously.

The objects and artefacts that were made, the impact of allowing space for exploration as well as expression of views and experiences and the direct voices of people with learning disabilities and/or autism as facilitators, participants and co-trainers have led to changes in policy, practice and processes for the delivery of ACP within and beyond the learning disability field.

Working in co-production had an impact on us all. The people with learning disabilities and/or autism gained new skills and confidence with one person gaining employment following the project. Members of the group were interviewed on BBC News advocating for prioritisation of the first COVID-19 vaccines for people with learning disabilities. The fear of talking about death and dying has reduced for all of us and we have become advocates for ACP within our communities. We have spoken at national conferences, made a film which has been seen across the world and we are now co-authoring a book chapter together.

For the people in the co-production group without learning disabilities, those involved due to their roles as art therapist, researcher, advocacy worker or hospice staff we have all gained insight into the power of working in co-production. We have learnt the value of working alongside people with lived experience and learnt to share the power and privilege which come with our respective roles. We have learnt how to come into, create and challenge spaces of equity together with those who experience inequity and to reflect on our own identities throughout our work.

The use of arts-based methods within *No Barriers Here* has led to a change in perception of the value of less verbal approaches within palliative care. Often viewed as vocational, less robust or not relevant, arts-based approaches to both clinical working and to research are key when delivering equitable care and opportunities. Many people need a different approach to process information, and *No Barriers Here* demonstrated the result of adopting a less verbal approach throughout its development and delivery. Using arts-based approaches allowed wider access to participate, reduced fear and stigma, allowed space for exploration as well as expression of views and delivered powerful messages which could be more easily heard by the workforce who can improve care for people with learning disabilities and/or autism.

No Barriers Here is not an art therapy intervention. It was designed to be delivered by a wider workforce, as an art therapy-informed intervention and research method. *No Barriers Here* has become an equity-oriented intervention for ACP and a research method for exploring themes of inequity. The role of the art therapist researcher in supporting the development, design and delivery of the *No Barriers Here* approach was essential in creating a safe and supportive model, highlighting the place of art therapy-informed research methods in healthcare research.

Conclusion

This chapter has presented the evolution of an art-therapy-informed ACP intervention and research method. Co-production with people with learning disabilities and/or autism was the foundation of the project and continues to be as the approach has grown into a larger movement addressing inequity in ACP and palliative care more widely.

The final words belong to the people with learning disabilities and/or autism in the co-production group and co-authors of this chapter.

> *We all have different stories to share and working this way as a team, with trust and respect, we were able to be ourselves. We used art-making to show other people with learning disabilities and/or autism that when we can't find the words to speak we can still think about and share the way we want to be cared for in the future*
> (Co-author and co-production group member)

An easy-read version of the this chapter is available via this QR code:

References

Allen, G. Exploring loss and Grief with People with Intellectual Disabilities. *BMJ Support Palliat Care* 11 (2021) (Suppl 2) A1–A96: A21. https://spcare.bmj.com/content/bmjsp-care/11/Suppl_2/A21.3.full.pdf.

Braun, V., and Clarke, V. *Thematic Analysis: A Practical Guide*. London: Sage Publications Ltd, 2022. https://uk.sagepub.com/en-gb/eur/thematic-analysis/book248481# description (2022, Accessed 28 December 2022).

Derbyshire Community Health Services NHS Foundation Trust. *The Dementia Palliative Care Service: Service Improvement & Delivery Toolkit 'How to Guide' – Flipbook*. Derby: NHS England Midlands, 2023. https://dchs.nhs.uk/our-services-and-locations/ az-list-of-services/living-well-dementia/dementia-palliative-care-service-toolkit/ dementia-palliative-care-service-toolkit-flipbook.

Elbrecht, C. *Healing Trauma with Guided Drawing: A Sensorimotor Art Therapy Approach to Bilateral Body Mapping*. Berkeley, CA: North Atlantic Books, 2019.

Ferguson, M., Jarrett, D., and Terras, M. Inclusion and Healthcare Choices: The Experiences of Adults with Learning Disabilities. *British Journal of Learning Disabilities* 39 (2011): 73–83. https://doi.org/10.1111/j.1468-3156.2010.00620.x.

Fraser, K.D., and Al Sayah, F. Arts-Based Methods in Health Research: A Systematic Review of the Literature. *Arts Health* 3 (2011): 110–145.

Gruber, H., and Oepen, R. Emotion Regulation Strategies and Effects in Art-Making: A Narrative Synthesis. *Arts Psychotherapy* 59 (2018): 65–74.

Heslop, P., Blair, P., Fleming, P., et al. *Confidential Inquiry into Premature Deaths of People with Learning Disabilities (CIPOLD) Final Report*. Bristol: Norah Fry Research Centre, 2013. https://www.bristol.ac.uk/media-library/sites/cipold/migrated/documents/fullfinalreport.pdf.

Jerwood, J., and Allen, G. *No Barriers Here: For People Excluded by Identity, Culture, Ethnicity and Race*, 2023. https://www.nobarriershere.org/wp-content/uploads/2023/04/No-Barriers-Here-ICER-Research-Report-March-2023.pdf (accessed 30 September 2023).

Kara, H. *Creative Research Methods in the Social Sciences: A Practical Guide*. Bristol: Policy Press, 2015.

Kuper, H., and Scherer, N. Why Are People with Intellectual Disabilities Clinically Vulnerable to COVID-19? *Lancet Public Health* 8 (2023): e325–e326.

Malchiodi, C. Art Therapy and the Brain. In *Handbook of Art Therapy*. New York and London: The Guildford Press, 2003, pp. 16–24.

Mannay, D. *Visual, Narrative and Creative Research Methods: Application, Reflection and Ethics*. London: Routledge, 2015.

NHS England. *Personalised Advance Care Planning through Art-Based Methods for People with Learning Disabilities*, 2022. https://www.nobarriershere.org/wp-content/uploads/2023/01/NHSE-Case-study-Dudley-No-Barriers-Here-FINAL-2.pdf (accessed 30 September 2023).

Public Health England. *Deaths of People Identified as Having Learning Disabilities with COVID-19 in England in the Spring of 2020*. London: Public Health England, 2020. https://assets.publishing.service.gov.uk/media/5fa91fcc8fa8f578988a866c/COVID-19__learning_disabilities_mortality_report.pdf (accessed 30 September 2023).

Read, S. A Year in the Life of a Bereavement Counselling and Support Service for People with Learning Disabilities. *British Journal of Learning Disabilities* 5 (2001): 19–33.

Russell, C. The Helper's Crossroads. *Nurture Development Blog*, 2023. https://www.nurturedevelopment.org/blog/the-helpers-crossroads/ (accessed 29 September 2023).

Ryan, S. *Love, Learning Disabilities and Pockets of Brilliance*. London: Jessica Kingsley Publishers, 2021.

Sudore, R.L., Lum, H.D., You, J.J., et al. Defining Advance Care Planning for Adults: A Consensus Definition from a Multidisciplinary Delphi Panel. *Journal of Pain Symptom Management* 53 (2017): 821–832.

Think Local Act Personal National Co-production Advisory Group. *What Is Co-Production?*, 2022. https://www.thinklocalactpersonal.org.uk/co-production-in-commissioning-tool/co-production/In-more-detail/what-is-co-production/ (accessed 25 August 2023).

White, A., Sheehan, R., Ding, J., et al. *Learning from Lives and Deaths – People with a Learning Disability and Autistic People (LeDeR) Report for 2021 (LeDeR 2021)*. London: Autism and Learning Disability Partnership, King's College, 2022. https://www.kcl.ac.uk/ioppn/assets/fans-dept/leder-2022-v2.0.pdf..

Chapter 6

Self-Doubt and the Art of Listening

A Story about Geoffrey

Claudia Rossi

Positionality Statement

I, Claudia Rossi, have written this chapter as a white female Italian/Australian with lived experience of family with disability and working as an Art Psychotherapist in Melbourne, Australia. The character of Geoffrey is a composite narrative (McElhinney & Kennedy, 2022). Following guidance (Duffy, 2010) I constructed a case, a character, by taking details and impressions of several other clients where my experiences had paralleled my work with the core client. This approach protects the identity of single individuals. And so, Geoffrey is a character created to share my experiences culminated over many years of my work as an art psychotherapist in the disability sector. This chapter seeks to describe the teachings I've gained while working with these clients and how I have grown as a result, as therapist and person, with thanks to the generosity and wisdom of my clients.

Introduction

Sometimes a client arrives and brings with them teachings that are ripe for learning. For me, it was Geoffrey (not his real name). Geoffrey was a man with learning disabilities that created a barrier to his being heard and understood. His learning disability acted like a moat that effectively isolated Geoffrey, leaving his many colourful stories of a well-lived life, unheard. Art therapy became a bridge to Geoffrey; Life Story Work, a receptacle offered to Geoffrey to hold the stories that suddenly tumbled out and onto the pages of his journals. Geoffrey changed me as an art therapist and as a person. He taught me to listen and to be brave in the face of the unknown. In short, Geoffrey helped me to grow. Geoffrey introduced me to his internal landscape held fast, precious and mostly unshared, unvalued in his world. He opened my eyes to the lives unheard and unnoticed that many people with learning disability are sadly ascribed without choice, often unable to request otherwise, rendering them a benign participant in an unhearing world.

We form a tapestry for the people we love that tells a story

—Claudia Rossi

DOI: 10.4324/9781003350736-9

My Mother Died

My mother died three years ago today, the day after my birthday. She was a loved woman; she loved her family and had lived a full and rich life. She died alone in hospital, during a long and heartless Covid lockdown that prevented her family from being by her side or saying goodbye.

I was assured that nurses were with her when she passed and they expressed their care and fondness for her, which I believed to be true. In the end, it was the carers that attended to my mother, and I can only reconcile that that is ok, because it came at the end of a lifetime of love and belonging.

My mother came to know the staff on the hospital ward during her many stays. They became a kind of second family that heard and understood my mother in her last years. And although I thought I heard and understood her, I wonder now, did I? Did I really listen, give time to understanding what was being said behind the words? She had many people in her life, and I think that as a community, we listened and, I hope, heard. Perhaps that is all we can hope for, that together with our collective listening, we form a tapestry for the people we love, that tells the story of their life.

How must it be to live a life where nobody hears you or really listens?
—Claudia Rossi

An Unwitnessed Life

But what happens when the tapestry is never woven? No weavers, no subject, no story told.

How must it be to live a life where nobody hears you or really listens or even notices that you have something to say? Where a lifetime goes by unwitnessed, invalidated and unvalued. When, because it can't be voiced, can't be heard, it therefore doesn't exist. How does someone hold onto memories when they can't be shared, when a photo is a sole reminder without context, without story and without witness? What does it do to a person when nobody is interested in their life? Are remaining memories co-opted into the service of photos, reduced to the confines of the frame? What about memories without evidence? Do they evaporate, or vanish forever? Does one's story, one's lived life, slowly evaporate with them? What does that do to a person?

These questions highlight the power of listening. As Alan Alda wisely said: "Listening is being able to be changed by the other person" (Kotelnikov, n.d.). This principle of being truly heard is at the heart of our work in the art therapy room.

Being Changed by Listening

A long time ago I had the experience of being changed by listening to another person. Although I've learnt many more things since then, I have tended the memory to keep it alive. It is a buoy that I return to when I'm adrift at sea; when, as a therapist, I have lost my way.

In the art therapy room as I sit with my client, I adopt a calm and patient presence. It is like the feeling of being held by still water as you float, steadied on its surface. It is a receptive space of trust and gentleness. There I wait, as the words of the person sitting opposite break the calm surface and set the ripples in motion. The course for the session is charted by their words and in my responses. We are suddenly in the flow of a current created in the space between us and between our words, journeying somewhere together. But sometimes the process isn't so smooth, and I'm taken by surprise. The ripples change to sudden waves, the sea grows rough and I'm swept away, dragged off course, far away from that peaceful, steady place to somewhere unknown, unfamiliar and alone. I don't understand the words, I have no response, I feel a panic rise up and I have nothing to hold onto.

I am adrift.

I have no life raft to save me; the theories escape me. I have no buoy to hold onto; my therapeutic interventions are useless. This isn't the still space I was in before. I am treading water just to stay afloat, as self-doubts rise up in the bubbles caused by my flailing. Together, my client and I struggle there for what seems an age but is just a moment. I have lost connection with my client and with myself and the therapy stops. It's in that moment that I try to recall what I learnt from working with Geoffrey. Through the whirlpool stirred up by my flailing, comes the image of Geoffrey and I'm reminded to observe the person sitting opposite me, to hear them, to listen carefully to the spoken words and for those unsaid, and in that place I always find something to hold onto, and I am returned from the stormy sea to the present, to the person sitting opposite me in the art therapy room. I am reminded that my client directs the course of the therapy, but I must be attentive for the signs. When I allow myself to trust this process, the direction becomes clear and together, we are once again travelling.

A Story about Geoffrey

It was 2015 and I began working as an art therapist within the recreational programme of a busy disability day-centre in Melbourne, Australia. The day-centre was a hectic hive of activity that had started its life as a pre-school, which meant that some clients had attended since they were children, some for 40 years. The buildings were old and dilapidated, the stained and damaged walls painted in dreary, depressing, long faded colours and it looked more like an abandoned institution than the "school" that most of the clients referred to it as. But what the centre lacked in aesthetic it made up for in heart, and the devoted clients revelled in the camaraderie of their peers and the love and support received from the staff. From Monday to Friday, at least 100 adults with disabilities participated in the various daily programmes on offer and went out on excursions.

I had been working as the only art therapist at the day-centre, earning my stripes co-facilitating day programme art groups when after six months I was given the chance to start a weekly four-hour art therapy group for six clients. I worked on contract as an art therapist, filling a gap in services offered at the centre. It was not uncommon to see clients spend entire days colouring in. Management, alarmed by this wanted more meaningful engagement in artmaking. Although intern psychologists serviced day-centre clients, many clients were unable to engage meaningfully in verbal therapy. It was hoped that art therapy could provide for these clients.

I was given the "old art room" to use, which had once been a staff room and a client lunchroom. The room was sandwiched between the corridor and the outdoor breezeway. On one side were big windows onto the busy corridor and the windows on the other side looked onto the breezeway. Both supported the high foot-traffic of almost all clients, who rushed down the corridors rowdily to get to their group rooms. The art room was also a shortcut between the corridor and breezeway, so clients frequently bustled through the room on their way to somewhere else.

The large room was set up with a long central table. Brown vinyl-laminate desks with computers ran along two walls. On the third wall, a long bench ran almost the length of the room with a small sink set into the bench, which was often filled with the dirty cups and dishes of the previous day. The remaining bench was covered in boxes, outdated notices, scraps of paper, old lunch boxes, lost clothing and other discards. The noticeboard running above the bench had pinned photos of clients in their younger years, outdated timetables, Fire Safety Signs and cardiopulmonary resuscitation posters. On the fourth wall was a door to a storeroom where oddments of art materials, accumulated over the years, lurked unused in filing cabinets.

Management determined the art therapy group members based solely on "an interest in art" and I was given the group list of six clients. The cohort consisted of clients with vastly varying disabilities and support needs. On the first day, the clients trickled in curiously, wondering what they had been signed up to, and took a seat at the long table. Each week the same six clients attended, plonked down their bags and lunchboxes and waited patiently for the surrounding hubbub of morning activity to subside, so that the group could start.

I began seeing some of the day-centre clients individually for one-on-one art psychotherapy sessions. These were held in a room down the same busy corridor with two glass sliding doors, each at opposite ends of the room. The doors were often suddenly opened, then slammed shut, by clients who mistook them for the adjacent bathrooms. Strategic placing of art on windows created a somewhat private art therapy room.

Each morning at the day-centre buses and taxis would arrive from the suburbs of Melbourne. The room reverberated loudly with the excited greetings of clients, heightened behaviours, yelling, screaming and laughing. Friends and enemies gathered rowdily for brief acquaintance before heading to their activities. Geoffrey came to my attention partly for his dapper presentation, an older gentleman in his sixties, dressed with consideration and style, but mostly for the loud and angry invective, threats and abuse that he directed at some of the clients, his unfortunate targets. He repeated this on a regular basis and it was instigated by the mere sight of those he'd earmarked as the enemy. The morning gathering in the hall gave Geoffrey a steady staple of victims. So, I was less than enthusiastic to find that he was one of the six clients directed towards my art therapy group. Little was known about Geoffrey's medical diagnosis, other than that he had learning disabilities and had attended the day-centre since childhood. Fortunately, Geoffrey appeared to get along with the other art therapy group members. He was the most independent member of the art therapy group and didn't need any physical assistance, unlike the others.

"Tell me! What Are You Trying to Say?"

At the start of each group, an art therapy directive was given and the art materials were set out. I helped Geoffrey to start the activity and would then work my way around the room, supporting the other participants. Geoffrey would sit at the table, continually muttering to himself quietly as he worked. It soon became apparent that the only mark Geoffrey could make on paper was the letter "g" in lower case. Asking Geoffrey to scribble on the page resulted in a page of "g"s. "Draw a face" was a "g" centred on the page. "Fill the page with colours and shapes", a page full of colourful "g"s. Geoffrey signed each artwork with a row of "g"s. We made clay beads and painted them. Geoffrey painted each one with the letter "g".

What Geoffrey was unable to communicate through art materials, he made up for with talking.

Each week for the duration of the four-hour group, Geoffrey would follow me around the room talking continuously in a way that was unintelligible to me. He did this no matter what I was doing, who I was helping or talking to. I found it exhausting. I would try to stop and listen but by then Geoffrey would be onto another unintelligible topic. I just didn't have the time to devote to him, so I accepted that Geoffrey would follow me around and talk at me as I went about my work. One particularly exhausting day, Geoffrey had been shadowing me all morning. The other group members were busily engaged in artmaking. I finally flopped into a seat while Geoffrey invariably followed, sitting down next to me, talking all the while. In exasperation I turned to Geoffrey, faced him squarely and said, "What Geoffrey? Tell me! What are you trying to say?" Geoffrey looked into my eyes, took a breath and said, "I miss my Pop".

"Storytelling"

I gave Geoffrey magazines to cut pictures from and invited him to show me what he was trying to tell me. I helped him cut out a picture of a rugged-looking old man, a truck, dried landscapes in golden colours and a glass of beer. Geoffrey glued the pictures face down. Together we re-glued them face up. We worked like this for about half an hour, the images torn and crinkled aggressively and haphazardly slapped onto the paper, and images and paper covered in a sticky mess of glue. We looked at the artwork together.

He turned to me. "I miss my Pop".

As I sat facing Geoffrey, I listened intently with strained focus, to decipher his words, to try to understand his verbal style, almost a foreign language that I hadn't yet developed an ear for. I heard Geoffrey tell me about "Pop", his grandfather, about how Pop had liked a beer and how Geoffrey was given the occasional illicit sip, how Pop could fix things like cars and how Geoffrey so loved him and how terribly he missed him, now that Pop had died. Geoffrey spoke softly, calmly and clearly, with sadness and reverence. My listening had enabled Geoffrey's storytelling. And that's how Geoffrey and I started two years of individual art therapy sessions and how together we made two journals of Geoffrey's life story.

Geoffrey lived in supported independent living for people with disabilities and appeared to have no surviving family. His day-to-day needs were well met and by all accounts, he lived in a very good house, where fun events took place, good meals were cooked and residents left the house each morning clean, groomed and well-dressed. Geoffrey had lived there for innumerable years, "a long time", and was happy there. Geoffrey was fortunate in this regard. Geoffrey had his social needs attended to, not only by the staff at his home but by the day-centre programme as well.

On any given day Geoffrey was there, at the day-centre, laughing, yelling, accosting, riling staff, wandering the halls and going on excursions. Geoffrey's care and social needs were catered to in these busy shared environments, personalised attention, which was highly sought from staff, was time limited.

This is where the shortfall appears in the lives of many with learning disabilities, where those fortunate enough have their physical and social needs met but not their emotional needs, so much. And subsequently, many people with learning disabilities have to hold inside, stories that remain untold or that fall on the deaf ears of busy people. In the worst case scenario, there is a presumption that people with learning disabilities have nothing to say, other than the niceties they might have been schooled in or scripted conversational phrases they have become adept at delivering.

A Makeshift Art Therapy Room

A makeshift art therapy room was provided for me to see day-centre participants individually. As one wall of the room was lined with head-height windows looking onto a very busy hallway, all those who walked down could look into the room, knock on the windows, say hello and maybe intrude. Needless to say, working in the therapy room was challenging. Geoffrey was not much help, jumping out of his seat to bang on the windows and yell at the passers-by he objected to, frequently shattering the quiet focus of the session and, very nearly, the glass. A few strategically placed artworks on the windows helped reduce the distractions somewhat. The noisy location, the easily distracted Geoffrey, the frequent disturbances and Geoffrey's rapid, breathy speaking style challenged my hearing and focus but ultimately trained them to find the stories in his words. The process was slow. Weekly art therapy sessions with Geoffrey tested my patience frequently. He brought conflict, anger and window-banging into the room. He was in equal measures of the charming gentleman and the nasty aggressor who targeted sweet and harmless participants at the day-centre.

"Stories Tumbled Out"

Geoffrey's stories tumbled out, had to be extracted, were fractured and broken, fluid and articulate, came in fits and starts, were repeated over and over, were denied, changed, were unreliable, consistent and explored. Stories were transcribed onto the page only to be contradicted, redacted, inflated or minimised. Pictures were glued down, torn off. Words were crossed-out only to be re-written. Stories of trauma and abuse were told and later denied, were changed and then told again. It was confusing, sometimes deeply meaningful and at times apparently meaningless.

As the sessions progressed with regularity, Geoffrey very seldom missing a session, the story of his life was slowly revealed onto the page. Geoffrey's medium of choice was collage, and he would fly through magazines in seconds, tens of pages at a time, not finding anything useful. Slowly, patiently, together we would work our way back through the magazines, to find the right fit of image to word. Geoffrey's stories began to stick, not just in the pages of a journal, he appeared to remember them more deeply. He moved from the collage table to the sand tray and played out his memories, walked through them again, to tell them, perhaps for the first time. Over the two years of art therapy, the stories became familiar to Geoffrey. He wore them proudly like a badge, showing his artwork to the important people in his life, receiving the validation he had always sought but never found and finally being heard and seen. The rich life of Geoffrey began to be known by those around him. Geoffrey's stories were unlocked and voiced in a way that could be heard by others.

After two years of working with Geoffrey, he moved on. Geoffrey had completed two journals packed with the stories of his life, the golden years of his youth, his mum and dad, his loving and loved Pop who let Geoffrey drive his car, the escapades; sneaking out of home and sleeping rough, the time he willingly got into a car full of "bad people", getting drunk, eating foods he wasn't allowed to, loving girls, fighting enemies, the heartache he caused others and that others caused him. He kept the journals under his bed, along with his "private things" and only showed them to a select few, but the stories were alive again in Geoffrey, having been witnessed, heard and documented. They now accompanied him, as stories do, and informed others, because Geoffrey could now show a page of his journal and tell one of his stories of joy and sadness in a life well lived.

To truly listen means surrendering into unchartered waters

Claudia Rossi

Adrift

We therapists are taught a lot about listening, but to truly listen means surrendering into unchartered waters without a life raft. Really listening can leave you adrift, exposed, vulnerable and inadequate. It can leave you without a game plan, your toolkit left ashore. It leaves you alone with the client, exposed to the elements, in a foreign landscape. And then stranded and lost, you struggle together in the wilderness, work together to build a path out. With each new session both client and therapist venture together into the unknown. In other words, I have to let go of my deliberate approach and my conscious intentions in order to remain present with the client and to fully experience the moment. Otherwise, I miss the subtle cues, which are the signposts directing the course of therapy.

I spent too many years working in this way. I built what I thought was an adequate professional persona. But it felt like a puffy coat, bloated with air and not a lot beneath the thin fabric. It felt superficial. I had the skills, the education, but the link to the client was missing and I held deep doubts about my effectiveness as a therapist. I was focused on myself and less so on my client. We know that the therapist develops with practice and the practice of working with difficult clients is where the greatest development lies.

Geoffrey provided that development for me because nothing worked on Geoffrey. I threw everything at him. All my art materials. All my therapeutic approaches. All my methodologies. I cajoled, supported, encouraged, enthused and directed; nothing worked. My prescribed, deliberate approach was inadequate.

I had to listen hard to Geoffrey, with conscious effort and determination to understand his words. It was difficult to stay tuned to his unique language and to avoid falling to shortcuts to understanding, which were always tempting.

"Listening is being able to be changed by the other person".

Listening to Geoffrey changed me.

Anchored

"'I want to change but not if it means changing,' a patient once said to me in complete innocence", wrote Stephen Grosz (2014). The therapy work with Geoffrey was never in my comfort zone and the path that was offered instead was wobbly, unstable and without destination. Accompanying Geoffrey on his therapy journey meant I had to stay in the present to keep pace, be receptive, keep my wits about me and try to maintain my bearings. We were at once in the throes of sadness and grief and the next, rollicking along in the back of a car of drunken men. One moment yelling at the football, the next crying over a grave. Geoffrey, weeping silently in his chair, next banging his fists on the window. I'd catch my breath, find my bearings and begin my way back to Geoffrey, who was left alone in his story, waiting for me.

I had to trade a professional position for one of receptive humility in order to stay present. Eventually what arose in me was an attitude of reverence, gratitude and privilege for the honour of being escorted through Geoffrey's life. I changed in the two years that I worked with Geoffrey. I learnt patience, respect, acceptance, humility and hopefully grace, and to this day the memory of Geoffrey is like an anchor that makes me stop and reminds me to be courageous.

Historically, people with learning disability were considered unable to benefit from psychotherapy and were considered lacking:

> ... the cognitive capacity for reflection and being unable to conceptualise the importance of narratives and relate these back to their everyday lives.
>
> (Cottis, 2009, p.40)

However, Cottis considered that

... people with intellectual disabilities, like all human beings, have the same desire for self-expression and the need to process or make sense of their life experiences. Because they may struggle with language, and their cognitive capacities for conceptualisation and reflection may be limited, this does not mean that they cannot find meaningful ways to express themselves... creative expression can play a vital role in facilitating both self-expression and a working through of emotional issues.

(Cottis, 2009, p.43)

Geoffrey's therapy was slow. As the therapeutic relationship built, the dialogue deepened and Geoffrey addressed bigger, difficult and painful topics. Incrementally, Geoffrey began to change in small ways, assuring me that the therapy was worthwhile. The small internal changes began to manifest externally. The calm and centred state Geoffrey acquired in sessions began to accompany him out the therapy door.

The Internal Family Systems model, developed by Richard C. Schwartz, emphasises the Eight C's as central to the work and crucial to successful therapy. He categorises the Eight C's: Calmness, Curiosity, Clarity, Compassion, Connectedness, Confidence, Creativity and Courage (Schwartz 2023b, p. 149).

Geoffrey made progress at a glacial pace over a very long period of time. There were times when, stubbornly, Geoffrey refused to progress and would slip back into his old self. His behaviour would decline. He was more aggressive and picked on the vulnerable people around him. It was hard to like Geoffrey at these times. All our work felt pointless. All the effort, a folly of time wasted, for want of something better to do. But the anchor would bring me back to the task at hand, and I'd return to my place of patient waiting. "Being a compassionate witness" (Schwartz, 2023a) on the journey through Geoffrey's life helped me to tolerate setbacks in the therapy. It enabled me to maintain the earth so that something might grow, retain a non-judgemental attitude and a welcoming space that Geoffrey could return to when ready.

At the end of therapy Geoffrey did not appear, on the outside, too different to how he was before. But he had been heard. Someone had stopped and listened and found his stories interesting enough to write down, value and keep. And Geoffrey found those stories valuable enough to keep and to share with those he trusted. Geoffrey might not have owned a photo album but he captured a lifetime of memories in the stories of his journals.

Reflections

People living with learning disabilities have stories too but aren't always able to share them so easily or frequently. They may need more time to tell them than we have to hear. They may not have the words to form into a story. They may need help to remember them. They may never be asked. But the stories are there. Given dedicated, regular time, patience and the means, the stories will emerge. Provide materials, magazines, a sand tray, pen and paper, movement and music, and the stories can be shared. Genuine interest, compassion and mindful presence is a powerful tool of connection that many people with learning disabilities, like Geoffrey, are seldom afforded in a busy world.

Geoffrey changed during the course of art therapy. I observed that he became happier, more content. His anger reduced and his aggressive compulsions deflated. His perpetual need to be noticed seemed to subside and, instead, his communication became intentional and purposeful. Where he once stood alone in the hall, vying for attention, harried and on edge, he was now self-contained, confident and no longer alone.

And he was proud of his forebears and of their stories, cradled within the pages of his journals, and of the person that they made him today.

Acknowledgement

I acknowledge the Traditional Custodians of the land on which this chapter was written, the Dja Dja Wurrung and Taungurung peoples and also the Bunurong peoples of the Kulin Nation and pay my respects to Elders past, present and emerging. I acknowledge their continued practise of custom, cultural, physical, social, historical and economic relationship with the land and waters that make up their Country.

References

Cottis, T. (ed.). (2009). *Intellectual Disability, Trauma and Psychotherapy*. Routledge. ISBN: 9780415421676.

Duffy, M. (2010). Writing about Clients: Developing Composite Case Material and Its Rationale. *Counseling and Values* 54: 136–153. https://doi.org/10.1002/j.2161-007X.2010.tb00011.x.

Grosz, S. (2014). *The Examined Life: How We Lose and Find Ourselves*. Vintage. ISBN: 9780099549031.

Kotelnikov, D. (n.d.). *Learning from Great Masters; My Teachers – Alan Alda*. Available at: https://denkot.ru/en/teachers_quotes_alda.html.

McElhinney, Z., & Kennedy, C. (2022). Enhancing the Collective, Protecting the Personal: The Valuable Role of Composite Narratives in Medical Education Research. *Perspectives on Medical Education* 11(4): 220–227. https://doi.org/10.1007/S40037-022-00723-X

Schwartz, R. C. (2023a). IFS Therapy: What Have We Learned and Where Are We Going with Richard Schwartz. *The Master Series Oxford Conference*. Oxford, September 2nd.

Schwartz, R. C. (2023b). *Introduction to Internal Family Systems*. 2nd edition. Vermillion. ISBN: 9781683643616.

Chapter 7

Finding Connection through Group Art Therapy and *"Being in a Book"*

Elizabeth King

Positionality Statement

I (Elizabeth King) have written this chapter as a white woman without learning disabilities working as an Art Psychotherapist. Where I include the words of the group participants with learning disabilities I use their direct quotes. Those individuals and their parents who I have written about gave their permission for me to use their words and were pleased and proud to be a part of this piece of work.

There were two other professionals who supported me in running the group. They are Lauren Fletcher and Elaine Ford. Lauren was a trainee co-art therapist in the group at the time of writing this chapter. She identifies as a white woman without learning disabilities who was in her final year of an Art Therapy Master's Degree whilst co-running the group with me. Elaine was also a co-therapist at the time of writing. She identifies as a white woman without learning disabilities who has worked at the school as a teaching assistant for 19 years.

Introduction

This chapter focuses on group art therapy sessions for five children with severe learning difficulties, aged nine- and ten-years-old, and demonstrates how the sessions helped them to unblock channels of communication through art-making, practicing taking turns, finding their voices and words for their felt experiences, to be listened to and feel heard and to interact with each other and be part of a cohesive group. At the time of writing, the group had been running for two school years, so its culture was well established.

I aim to demonstrate how children with severe communication issues can take ownership of an art therapy group by setting their own boundaries and rules, and how this enabled them to feel equal, worthy, safe and able to communicate.

Reported below are the significant moments and breakthroughs of the group art therapy sessions illustrated through accounts of the first-hand experiences of the children involved.

DOI: 10.4324/9781003350736-10

Being in a Book

In late April 2023, I told the group, "we have a really exciting opportunity for you to talk and for people to listen", "people from all over the world".

I had already spoken to all the parents regarding consent for the children to be included in this chapter (all had agreed) and now hoped to gain assent from the children. It was clear that it may take some time for the children to be informed as to what they were consenting to.

We all looked at an art therapy textbook and saw that some pictures would be included. Jordan commented that the pictures in the book were better than theirs, and we looked further through the book to seek some comparison. The children understood that if they agreed to "being in the book" they would be able to look back at it in years to come as it would be permanent.

I asked the children how they felt about being in a book and if they felt they could talk about being in the group. Children in the group chose their own pseudonyms for the purposes of "being in the book".

The Setting

The specialist support primary school where this work took place is based in an area of the North West England, which is ranked among the top ten most deprived local authorities in England, out of 326 (UK Government, 2019).

The school caters for children with profound multiple learning disabilities, severe learning disabilities and autism. At the time of writing, there were 150 pupils and every child in attendance had an Education, Health and Care Plan (EHCP). Children with an EHCP require additional or different support to children in mainstream school, the children on the plan will require extra support to access the curriculum.

Both the UK Government Departments of Education and of Health respectively state that educators of children with special educational needs (SEN) must provide a culture of high expectations including and offering children with SEN the opportunities available to other children so they can achieve the best possible outcomes (UK Government, 2024; UK Government, 2015).

In addition to art therapy, the school employs the services of various professionals to support the children's holistic education: physiotherapy, orthoptist, occupational therapy, child and adolescent mental health workers, speech and language therapists, music teachers and visual and hearing impairment teams. The school ethos has an emphasis on personal, social and health education which is embedded in a broad and balanced curriculum, including core subjects.

The school year runs from September to July divided into three terms: autumn (early September to mid-December), spring (early January to Easter) and summer (Easter to July). The terms are around 13 weeks long with a week-long half-term break. The full year amounts to 39 weeks and 39 therapy groups.

It is a refurbished building that was part of a mainstream school that it is still joined to. Sections of the school and corridors have magnetically locked doors for the safety of the children, to prevent unaccompanied access to places such as the hydrotherapy pool and external doors. School closures during the Covid-19 pandemic had a negative impact upon many pupils.

The indirect impact of Covid-19 through school closures and social isolation measures may have profound short- and long-term effects on children's well-being. Findings from global studies completed between 2020-2021 show that more than 1.5 billion children and young people have been affected worldwide by school closures in 188 countries (United Nations, 2020).

A review investigating the impact of school closures found that 27 studies from 20 countries identified negative impact on children's emotional, behavioural, restlessness and attention problems. In these studies, 18–60% of all participants scored above risk thresholds for anxiety and depression (Viner, Russell, Saulle et al., 2022).

The Art Therapy Group Structure

I have run the art therapy group for over ten years, and when a member leaves the school, the group takes on a new member. However, due to the COVID-19 pandemic (2020–2021), the current group of individuals all began at the same time. All children had demonstrated heightened anxiety post-pandemic.

A new member of the group was introduced after 18 months and another for the final summer term. The group members have grown their own culture and supported new members joining.

The rationale for the group was to encourage social skills and working with others. Taking place in a dedicated therapy space, separate to their usual classrooms, the expectation is that the children will express difficult feelings and form and share their own thoughts through their art-making. This is aimed at enabling the children to tolerate frustration and to build self-esteem, confidence in their expression, to introduce and support self-regulation and to also feel a part of something.

The group has a clear structure of check in, spontaneous art-making, sharing and check out. Research has indicated that "art therapy enhanced the ability of children with ASD [Autistic Spectrum Disorder] to engage and assert themselves in their social interactions, while reducing hyperactivity and inattention" (D'Amico & Lalonde, 2017).

All the children had a diagnosis of severe learning disabilities, of either autism or global development delay. In addition, all had either experienced illness in the family or fear of death and dying. The topics explored in the group were spontaneously brought in by the group members and supported by the therapist. The range of topic areas covered in the sessions include loss, gender, sexuality, illness, death, everyday fears and magic potions to cure cancer, syndromes, everyday blues and the realisation that these issues cannot easily be resolved.

The first session I cover here was in early December 2022. The themes in the group have centred around death and dying since it began, but when Queen Elizabeth II died on 8 September 2022 the group had rarely left this theme.

Checking In

Nico, age ten years, joined the group this year. He checked in using the word "hate" and then changed his mind. He said he felt "helpless and confused". He has a diagnosis of global development delay and quickly demonstrated his sense of humour and joy in making others laugh when he settled into the group. He was referred due to anxiety around death and illness, often put his own needs behind others, and put himself in the firing line. Nico chose his name because he liked it.

Jordan checked in, "disappointed [because of] the mess in the session last week". Jordan, age ten years, had a diagnosis of autism and was referred due to anxiety at night focused on death and dying of himself and his loved ones. Jordan has an incredible ability to retain knowledge from his research. He understands complex theories but at times struggles to understand the impact of this knowledge. Jordan chose his name for inclusion in this book based on a famous YouTuber he admired.

Taylor, age ten years, checked in, "frustrated… disappointed and fear". He was diagnosed with global development delay and was in mainstream school until he was eight. Taylor had a busy social life outside of school and experienced complex communications from his peers. He has a language for relationships, he talks about kissing girls and having a girlfriend, his understanding of this is not always clear. His grandmother died during his time in the group and he spoke about to this often. Taylor was referred to the art therapy group support him to, understand his communications, and to aid self-regulation.

Claire checked in "happy". Claire, age ten years, had a diagnosis of global development delay and autism and was referred to enable her to manage transitions, understand her sense of self in a group, and help her to express her anxiety. She started in mainstream school and, during her time there, Claire would "turn a classroom upside down". She had a dark sense of humour that enabled her to enjoy calamitous situations, especially when she can observe them. She had difficulty in verbal expression of feelings and sometimes used her actions rather than her words when distressed. Change was very difficult for Claire she formed close bonds with adults to help her to cope.

Lily checked in, "happy" too, age ten years, she had a diagnosis of autism, she was referred for her anxiety, to offer a safe space to begin to communicate with her peers and to offer her the opportunity her to experience altruism. Lily was often very quiet and, very focused on her own tasks, she often reminded others of the rules especially when it becomes noisy and disruptive (see Figure 7.1).

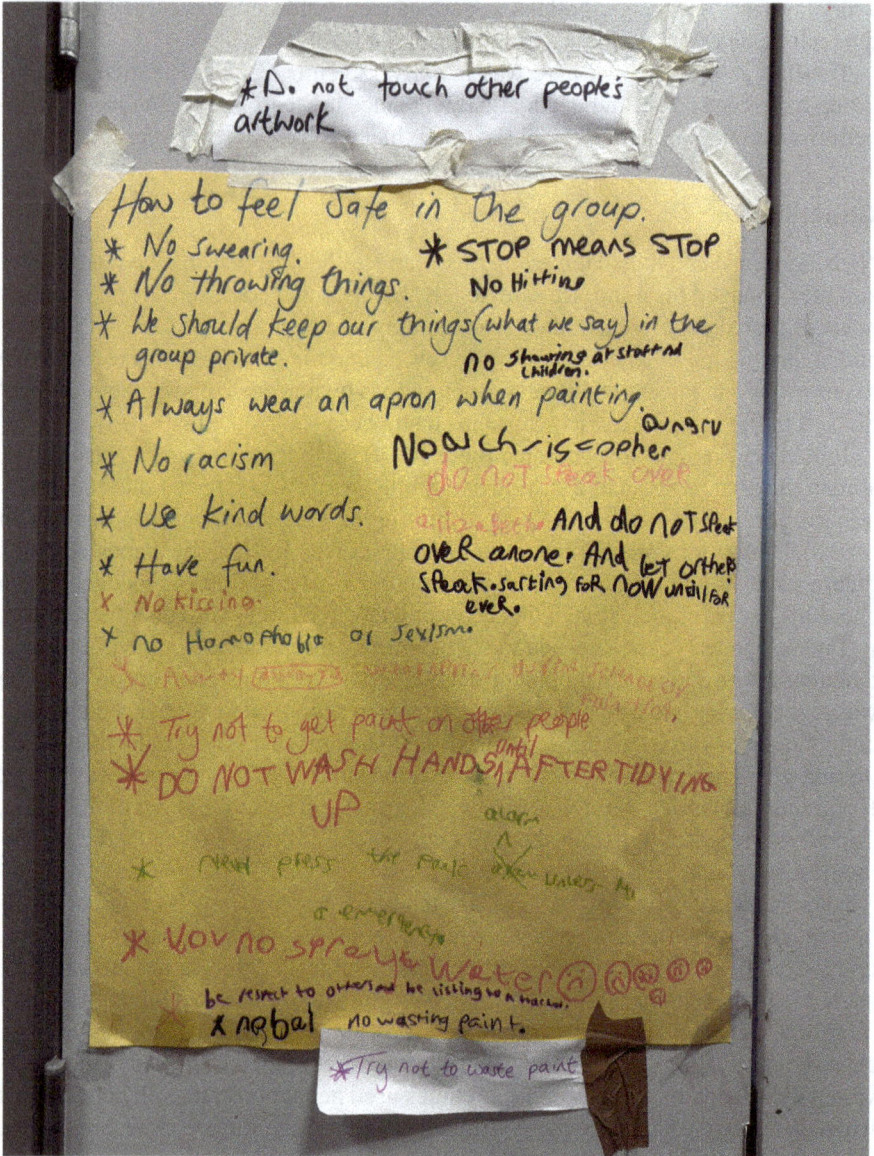

Figure 7.1 Photograph of co-created group rules.

Peter, joined the group in June nearly nine months after the others, aged nine, he was the youngest in the group. He, had a diagnosis of autism and was referred to the art therapy group as he was anxious about illness and death like many of the others. His referral was urgent as he was acutely distressed at night.

Art-Making

The children moved quickly to creating, each with their own idea. Mess soon became the focus, with all three boys excitedly chatting and playing around the sink. The "science project", as named by Taylor, mainly centred around paint and water, until paper and sponges were added to the "potion". There was an excitement about its potency. "This is a really strong potion", commented both Nico and Taylor. "It's going to do so much good", replied Jordan.

Lily had been ill and had missed two sessions in a row. I had a sense that for these children with fears of death, dying and illness, that the potion-mixing was an attempt to address their fears and, through play, experience overpowering and defeating the enemy, in this case illness. Taylor had previously made a science project that had helped him process being bitten badly by a child from another class. He had named it "prison food" and he said he felt less angry as a result.

During this process, the girls happily coloured foam shapes they had found in the junk modelling drawers. Claire talked about feeling better about respite (time away from home) and how she likes it now.

Sharing

In the final part of the session, everyone sits around the table and is invited to present their art. This enables the whole group to see what their peers have been working on in the session and to respond to it. It can feel exposing for individuals, but positive responses and genuine interest soon help the children to enjoy and look forward to the experience. It also enabled them to notice similarities in themes and ways of working, and show others how challenges of using certain materials may have been overcome, helped strengthen skills, or conquer fears. Sharing gives a reflective quality to the discussion which can enable members to refer back to a previous session and their feelings around that.

Members often request to "go first" and today that was Lily. Lily named her reindeer Daisy, made out of a 2D foam and coloured in with felt pend. She interacted playfully with Daisy, introducing her to the group members, and later helping her to check out "happy". Lily stated, "I am very proud of Daisy".

Claire showed her snowman, a 2D foam shape coloured in with felt tip pens, she commented, "I enjoyed the colours".

Taylor shared several images, a pot of potion and a potion cake for people to eat. He hoped it would help cure all illness (Lily had been ill and missed two sessions in a row). Taylor talked about his wish to save the world and global warming.

Nico and Jordan worked together on creating a "cure all potion". Jordan wished his potion could cure cancer, all illness and all syndromes, and expressed sadness as he realised this was not possible. He continued to think about it and explained that if it were possible things would be different. He could not say more. Nico remained excited at the prospect of the potion he had created, "to make old people young again".

Jordan had talked about the Queen dying and said that as "she was old, this seems ok". He then talked about how this isn't always possible, "people don't always get old" [before they die].

Checking Out

The session ends with all members checking out verbally. Marking the end of the session and assessing people's feelings. Nico checked out "happy" that he had his new youth potion, Jordan checked out "unhappy", and he said he had "…struggled with the mess". Lily checked out "happy" as did Claire. Taylor remained "unsure" of his feelings.

"Being in the Book"

The session began and Jordan checked in with: "Help me I'm the biggest hater of art therapy, too long, missing forest school". Nico checked in "happy to be in the group" and drew Taylor and someone else (himself), commenting, "Taylor is my friend". Nico proceeded to draw a clear boundary around his image meaning "nobody to touch".

As the group began to make their own art on the joint image, Taylor settled down to using magic clay, squeezing it, seemingly to help manage his feelings. I was concerned for Taylor as he was distressed, and it was important to acknowledge that in this session. I reminded Taylor that I had noticed he was sad. Taylor was clearly uncomfortable with the idea of being in a book and was struggling to understand it. Taylor often moved around the room at check in, making his ability to take in the information tricky.

Jordan stated, "Taylor isn't my friend". Taylor responded, "That's ok, I have loads of friends", although his body language suggested differently as he withdrew from the check in, refusing to join in with the group image. Taylor was invited to try to say what he was feeling, but he struggled. I suggested he was sad because Jordan had said something hurtful. He nodded and started to "make science". Lily checked in "happy", and Claire checked in "happy and excited about [an upcoming] trip to Alton Towers".

All members were engaged in some form of art-making and Nico, potentially sensing the same tension as myself, pressed the room's emergency alarm button, prompting people to rush in and assist. Taylor became very distressed by this. He left the room and sat on the floor whilst saying, "Nico did that on purpose he knew I would hate that", an amusement park.

With encouragement, Taylor returned to the room once the alarm had been switched off and said that he had "…felt like kicking doors". It was suggested to him that he could put the feeling into some art-making, so he used magic clay to help. Taylor became very attached to the clay and asked for it to be bagged up and kept safe with his name on, he wanted to take it home with him. Perhaps in an attempt at reconciliation, Nico joined in with the "science project" with Taylor for a while before settling with the clay and creating an alien.

Lily was silent during the alarm, but clearly struggled with the noise and movement in the room. Lily settled back into image making, but perhaps expressed her feelings about the session with finger painting instead of using her usual drier materials – something she rarely manages to do.

Claire appeared to be excited by the commotion and remained in her seat, while pointing out repeatedly that "Nico pressed the red button". Claire often expresses her distress by throwing large objects, and as a group we gained an understanding that at times this meant its "too much, I need to return to class". On this occasion she remained in the room.

During check out we discussed group members' feelings again. Claire was "happy" and we discussed afterwards how she seemed more available to the group and the members. It was possible that the chaos, anger and distress were expressed so well by Taylor, that it gave her space to sit back and create. Claire tended to engage more with staff but today she had been very chatty with all members. Lily checked out as "proud of being able to be messy" and said that she was "happy".

Nico checked out understanding what the alarm did, saying, "I know what the red button does". I suggested that, "It is a very tempting button, you have been wanting to press it since you started", and he agreed. "I have, but I won't do it again", he said he also commented, "I can't help it".

Taylor checked out not wanting to stop making, non-verbally, and made an image of a face looking worried. He found leaving the clay in the room, in a safe space, difficult but agreed to let it remain. He was calmer and was able to be in the room. Jordan checked out feeling "so much better for bashing the clay". All the children had engaged with the group image except Taylor. Taylor remained unsure about taking part in being in the book and appeared to be the most distressed by it.

The Following Session

In the following session, Jordan had added a new rule "do not press the alarm button unless there is an emergency". When I asked if anyone had remembered the exciting news from previous weeks, Taylor had asked "are old members coming back? New members coming in?" Taylor expressed that he felt "like smashing the room up", so he was encouraged to bash some clay.

Nico expressed excitement "I'm going to be famous" while Lily commented, "I am being an artist". Discussion around each other and their images appeared to grow, and it was difficult to know if the impact of 'being in the book' on the group was felt negatively.

Taylor expressed in a check out, "I don't want people reading the book about me". We discussed the meaning of confidentiality again and how he would change his name, which when he settled and said, "I will be called Taylor". He also commented how "nobody will know it is me". We all discussed how important the group is and how it would be helpful for other art therapists to know so more people could go to a group. The boys appeared to accept they would be anonymous and as a result would compete to be the centre of the art-making and discussion.

The Final Term

A new group member, Peter, was introduced, during the final term with just six sessions to go (Figure 7.2). Peter joined after a meeting with me and having a discussion about being in the book and how he was perfectly able to say no. Peter immediately knew he wanted to be a part of it, and he chose to be named after his favourite superhero, Peter Parker, Spiderman.

Nico picked up a pen, threw it and hit Lily, who began to cry. Nico then went over to her to comfort her and said, "I'm sorry it was an accident like the ball in my face at break". Lily gathered herself and said, "I want to stay". After this, the group settled to art-making although the atmosphere still felt difficult. During the art making part of the session Peter discovered that his clay figure is broken.

It was time to clean away the art materials to talk about what was happening in the group I acknowledged that he might be feeling upset and he replied, "I am, but its OK". During clean up Claire accidently got paint on Taylor's arm, who declared, "I'm going to smash everyone". I spoke about other incidents in the group and he said, "yes but I'm still upset" I agreed that's ok, but it's not ok to be hurtful to each other. "Ok", he responded.

We gathered around the table to try and help everyone talk about how they felt about this session. There was discussion about how the breakage of Peter's art work happened. Taylor confessed and commented, "it was an accident".

Everybody began talking at once and it was difficult to manage to understand for a while until there was a lull in the chatter. Peter said, "Let me tell you what happened, Jordan said something mean to Taylor then Taylor said some unkind things, then Taylor and Jordan were arguing then Taylor broke my clay, then Taylor and Nico were arguing".

It felt like when we brought up the idea of "the book" the children had become rivalrous again, feeling the need to be heard and centre stage. Peter felt able to speak up, despite this potentially making him unpopular.

In our final session of the year, a discussion around their chosen names began, with all of the children checking I had remembered what name they wanted. There was a true sense that the children had now fully understood the meaning of 'being in the book' and that their words were important. Jordan asked again, "is it going to be translated?".

A group sculpture was made at the end of term, collectively named "The Group Tower" (see Figure 7.2). The conflict that regularly rumbles through the group was notably absent, as all members discussed their need and appreciation for the group. Cohesion returned.

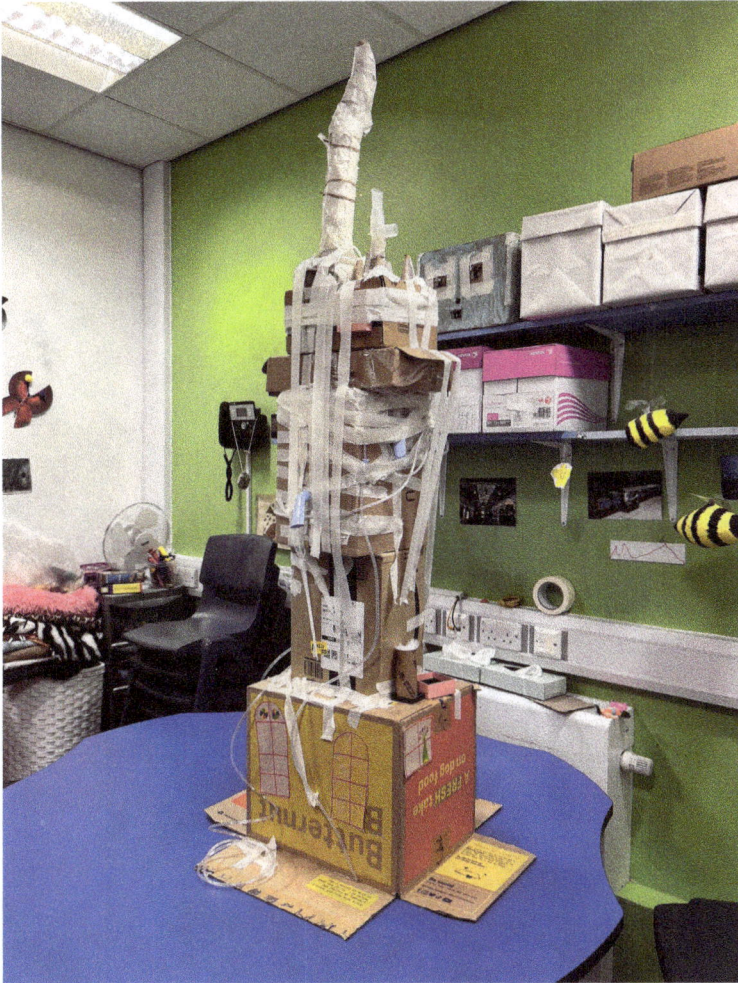

Figure 7.2 Photograph of "The Group Tower" a group sculpture made at the end of term.

After the Summer Holiday

In the first session after the summer holiday, the children were excited about the prospect of the group and 'being in the book'. Taylor asked, "what's happening with the book?" and Jorden asked, "what's needed for the book? Do you need anything else?". I asked if they felt they wanted to add anything else. They unanimously said they found the rules for the group the most important as when they forget to share or use kind words, they can refer to them on the wall all the time. Following this Nico and Jordan both commented that they felt that the rules needed writing again neatly.

Nico added that he felt that the time machine he had built needed to be added to the book. Nico continued, explaining that it was his favourite project as he enjoyed the sharing when everyone "had a go at time travel". Nico was clear he had made the machine for Taylor to visit his Grandma who had died, but that the fun they had together playing with the machine was an unexpected (Figure 7.3).

Figure 7.3 Photograph of the "Time Machine" *in action.*

Conclusion

The individuals within the group needed careful and thoughtful support during times of conflict ensuring all members were able to communicate their feelings, as such to be able to gain a greater understanding of themselves through the material and other members of the group. Foulkes regarded group therapy to be the main focus for change, stating that the individual would recreate typical conflicts using "…other members of the group, including the conductor" (Foulkes, 2018: 157). This was clearly indicated with the members of the group gaining an understanding of each other and themselves.

The group as a different space outside of the classroom offered freedom to create and express feelings. Support was sometimes demonstrated through a non-verbal dialogue between therapist and children, such as the 'interactive square', an approach devised to enable children on the autistic spectrum to access art therapy (Bragge & Fenner, 2009).

The group setting accelerated the learning of social skills and enabled positive social interactions, through making humour and play. The children may have needed time during the session to withdraw but they learned through the support of the group that they could state how they were feeling and remain in the room. Group interactions can also enable a reduction in hypersensitivity and inattention (D'Amico & Lalonde, 2017). This was true of the group when they were able to share their joy and play together with the creations they had made. Humour and the spontaneity of the art materials may have also been beneficial (Wright, 2023).

The children's art-making became increasingly collaborative to the point that they would make things to enjoy together during sharing. As Case and Dalley state (2002), the therapist must "work with the group and with the images of the individuals within the group and those of the group as a whole, and how the transference relationships that develop within this are understood" (2002: 215). The children had a sense of belonging and of each other. This was key to the success of the group.

For a group of children who struggled with communication, the dynamic communication and understanding that they achieved through their art-making was remarkable. They became able to hold conflict and cohesion within the group scenario, something they were unable to do at the start (Yalom, 1995). Tolerating the chaos offered a place for self-growth, expression, self-regulation, and connection that has enabled them all to share their experiences through "being in the book".

References

Bragge, A., & Fenner, P. (2009). The Emergence of the 'Interactive Square' as an Approach to Art Therapy with Children on the Autistic Spectrum. *International Journal of Art Therapy*, *14*(1), 17–28. https://doi.org/10.1080/17454830903006323

Case, C., & Dalley, T. (2002). *The Handbook of Art Therapy*. Routledge.

D'Amico, M., & Lalonde, C. (2017). The Effectiveness of Art Therapy for Teaching Social Skills to Children with Autism Spectrum Disorder. *Art Therapy*, *34*(4), 176–182. https://doi.org/10.1080/07421656.2017.1384678

Foulkes, S. H. (2018). *Group Analytic Psychotherapy: Method and Principles.* 4th Edition. Taylor & Francis.

UK Government (2015) *Special Educational Needs and Disability Code of Practice: 0 to 25 Years. Statutory Guidance for Organisations which Work with and Support Children and Young People who Have Special Educational Needs or Disabilities.* Department of Health & Department of Education. (January 2015). Online resource. Available at: https://assets.publishing.service.gov.uk/government/uploads/system/uploads/attachment_data/file/398815/SEND_Code_of_Practice_January_2015.pdf.

UK Government (2019). *The English Indices of Deprivation 2019: Statistical Release* (IoD2019). Ministry of Housing, Communities and Local Government. (26 September 2019). Online resource. Available at: https://assets.publishing.service.gov.uk/government/uploads/system/uploads/attachment_data/file/835115/IoD2019_Statistical_Release.pdf.

UK Government (2024). *Academic Year 2023/24: Schools, Pupils and their Characteristics.* Department of Education (6 June 2024). Online resource. Available at: https://explore-education-statistics.service.gov.uk/find-statistics/school-pupils-and-their-characteristics.

United Nations Sustainable Development Group (2020). *Policy Brief: Education during COVID 19 and Beyond.* August 2020. Online resource. Available at: https://unsdg.un.org/resources/policy-brief-education-during-covid-19-and-beyond.

Viner, R., Russell, S., Saulle, R., et al. (2022). School Closures during Social Lockdown and Mental Health, Health Behaviors, and Well-Being among Children and Adolescents During the First COVID-19 Wave: A Systematic Review. *JAMA Pediatrics*, *176*(4), 400–409. https://doi.org/10.1001/jamapediatrics.2021.5840

Wright, A. C. (2023). Art Therapy with an Autistic Person with Learning Disabilities: Communication and Emotional Regulation. *International Journal of Art Therapy*, *28*(4), 154–166. https://doi.org/10.1080/17454832.2023.2172439

Yalom, I. D. (1995). *The Theory and Practice of Group Psychotherapy.* Basic Books.

Chapter 8

"Art saved my life; it saved my life"

How Art-making Creates Connection and Builds Resilience

Emma Gentle and Tomas Calhoun

Positionality Statement

I, Emma Gentle, am a neurotypical female working as a researcher and Art Psycho-Therapist. I used a participatory action research frame so that all quotes and information were approved by the research participants for the original research and for the follow up. Participants told me they wanted to be involved and were pleased with what I had written. While I wrote much of this chapter, Tomas, a neurodiverse male and my co-author, has shared his experiences, his artwork, and his words in this chapter.

My co-author Tomas Calhoun is a prolific artist, practising for as long as he can remember. Tomas agreed to co-author this chapter because he likes being involved in artistic pursuits and enjoys the recognition he receives for his artistic talents. Tomas attends social events in the regional town he lives and enjoys creating and dancing. He has a Down syndrome diagnosis and works with other neurodivergent artists in art studios or on his own at home.

Introduction

I have been enriched personally and professionally by my interactions with neuro-divergent people, some of whom are people with learning disabilities. The isolation and social disconnection experienced by so many people with atypical neurological functioning is inequitable and avoidable. This disparity negatively impacts neuro-divergent people, their families, friends, and communities. When I attended the International Association for the Scientific Study of Intellectual and Developmental Disability (IASSIDD) World Conference in Melbourne in 2016, the *Welcome to Country* (an aboriginal welcome ceremony) from a Wurundjeri Elder, from the Kulin Nation, said her people would never have needed a conference like this because all people born on Country are part of the Mob, they have always been included. Disability was not a concept. That stuck with me because it mirrored my own view that society is not improved by excluding people because of difference to a perceived "norm." If cultures that have continued for tens of thousands of years are inclusive, then we have a guide. Most family members of neurodivergent people I have met feel the same. A lack of inclusion and therefore understanding

DOI: 10.4324/9781003350736-11

around human diversity seems to be the core problem. Getting to know people through their art provides a nuanced window into the artist's experience.

My involvement in the arts and "disability" sector, alongside my practice and research in art therapy, has shown me that it is our society as a whole that suffers most when diversity is not appreciated. I conducted research with neurodivergent artists to better understand the nuances of inclusive art workshops in regional Australia, which grew from my experience in facilitating art-making groups with diverse populations. This chapter is drawn from my PhD thesis on art-making with neurodivergent adults (Gentle, 2018). That research established how a range of therapeutic aspects of group art-making can create and/or enhance connection. Such connections improve quality of life (QoL) and build resilience. It is clear to me that for any of us to survive and have a life worth living we need human connection. It seems that our existence and journey through life can be enhanced when we have acceptance for who we are.

Exclusion from society can have detrimental impacts on mental and physical health and increase mortality rates (Cacioppo & Cacioppo, 2014). Neurodivergent people have repeatedly faced structural and social discrimination and exclusion. Everyday ostracism seriously depletes coping mechanisms, so strengthening people's ability to buffer such negative effects is imperative to maintaining good mental health (Williams, 2009). A recent literature review by Williams and Nida (2022) on ostracism and isolation illuminated how the long-term impacts of social disconnection can manifest in feelings of helplessness, unworthiness, alienation, and depression. The authors recommended countering these effects by focusing on real-world, longer-term interventions. Though there are various ways to counter social disconnection, research, and practice in the field show art-making groups to be an excellent conduit (Gentle, 2018, 2020; Gentle, Linsley, & Hurley, 2020; Gentle & O'Brien, 2021; Gentle, O'Brien, & Parmenter, 2022).

This chapter explains how neurodivergent people in Australia can use the National Disability Insurance Scheme (NDIS), a user-led funding scheme to access art groups. It elaborates on how using an art therapy frame in group art-making supports connection to the artwork and the self. This chapter shows how that process can become a conscious reflective practice, where the artist shows their work to other artists within the group who then acknowledge the artwork and thereby the artist. This art ritual supports the continued formation of the artist's identity which is scaffolded further through artistic and social exchanges that create authentic connection (Gentle, 2018). Such social opportunity can reach beyond the studio to create richer connection to the community, where the artist displays their work by creating in a public space or by exhibiting their work with their peers. Such exhibitions add to the connection to self and to peers, as the artist community formed during the group work interacts with the wider community. Thus, each connection enhances other connections. I use the neurodiversity model where a humanistic view of our individual capabilities and differences are a natural part of society. Obejas (2015), a neurodivergent person, explained the neurodiversity model like this

Every type of mind is equal, that they are all valuable, they are all normal, healthy. That there is not one type of mind that is superior to another, this contrasts with […] there being one type of mind that is healthy to exist and everyone else's are somehow flawed or broken.

(Obejas, 2015, 02:02-02:27)

The medicalised and normative term "disability" is particularly redundant in an art space, as the strength of an artist lies in their artistry. An artist's creative perspectives have the potential to open viewers' minds to a plethora of interpretations and responses, thereby enriching them. I was lucky that one of the art group participants from the research agreed to be reinterviewed and to show me some of his recent artworks.

I visited Tomas to talk about how he felt about the project we created together all those years ago, this book chapter, and his current art practice. His mother was there to support him if he wanted help understanding, explaining, or showing me his artworks. She is his main advocate and ensures Tomas's voice is heard. As a neurotypical person, I am privileged to have been given such a great wealth of perspectives from a range of neurodivergent artists and their advocates, which my visit to Tomas reconfirmed to me.

An Australian Context: The NDIS and Art Groups

The detrimental impacts of marginalisation of neurodivergent people are now well understood (Williams & Nida, 2022). Australia finally took on the relegation that most neurodivergent people experienced by developing the NDIS. The NDIS roll out was completed in 2020. The scheme provides individualised funding to eligible people to gain more time with family and friends, greater independence, access to new skills, jobs, or volunteering in their community, and an improved QoL (NDIS, 2022).

I have worked with neurodivergent artists in different countries in a range of settings as a community arts worker and art therapist. On my return to regional Australia, I asked one of the groups I had previously worked with if they would be interested in being part of an art-making research project. I explained it would be like their usual art group but I would facilitate, record, and then take notes afterwards and then check with them I had written the notes accurately. I asked if they would be comfortable including a few other artists from another art studio who they were familiar with. They agreed to having a larger group and being part of the research. All were enthusiastic to be involved and signed the necessary consent forms. This art group became the focus of my PhD research in 2017/2018. I made sure the newly formed group ran during the same time the participants would have usually been attending their art studio so I didn't interrupt their routine. The art space was provided by non-governmental, grassroots disability services that survived from a variety of funding streams before the NDIS roll out. In the late 1970s, some of the participant's families had seen a need for services with art studios that were inclusive and vibrant.

Since the research project finished, Australia has fully rolled out the NDIS. As illuminated by Hadley and Goggin (2019), the adjustment to the NDIS was not without problems, which played out in many grassroots arts organisations. An example of some of the issues was the many grassroots community-based services, like the ones the research participants utilised, were superseded by for-profit service "providers." However, clients can now choose whether they want to employ a provider or to choose their own services, or both. The participants I researched within 2017/2018 now have individualised NDIS packages so they can join any art group they choose. Most of them find themselves together again as nearly all use the same NDIS provider.

They informed me that the art groups they attend are not usually led by artists or art therapists but by different workers who may or may not have particular creative skills to share. These art sessions do not take place in an art studio designed specifically for art-making. Thus, in this instance, regional artists' access to an art studio changed considerably when the NDIS came in. Ironically, in some instances, the spaces have been described as a return to the "sheltered workshop" that grassroots services had worked to change before the implementation of the NDIS.

Opportunely, there has been some movement very recently from regional arts organisations to provide more inclusive creative studios. Now, rather ironically, most of the original research group are returning to the artist-led art studios they used to attend.

Art as Therapy or Art Therapy?

The NDIS includes art therapy as a means to build capacity by increasing skills, independence, and community participation, so it can be included in an NDIS package. However, the term "therapy" can feel loaded. Understandably, the term does not always sit comfortably with neurodivergent people who have historically been treated as people who needed "fixing" (Lige, 2011). There are arguments that art-making as a form of therapy for neurodivergent artists is medicalising the experience (Lige, 2011), and conversely, that neurodivergent people who have been born into a world that has oppressed their diversity will have felt the effects of marginalisation (Gentle, 2018). With 60% of disabled adults in Australia experiencing high or exceedingly high psychological distress, compared to 8% of their non-disabled peers (Australian Government, 2022), the impacts are still being felt. It would help if therapeutic art-making spaces were readily available without having to be labelled as therapy.

Most of the art groups that are accessible to neurodivergent people in regional Australia could be considered "art as therapy" as described by Edith Kramer. That is, the act of making art is in and of itself therapeutic (Kramer & Gerity, 2000)

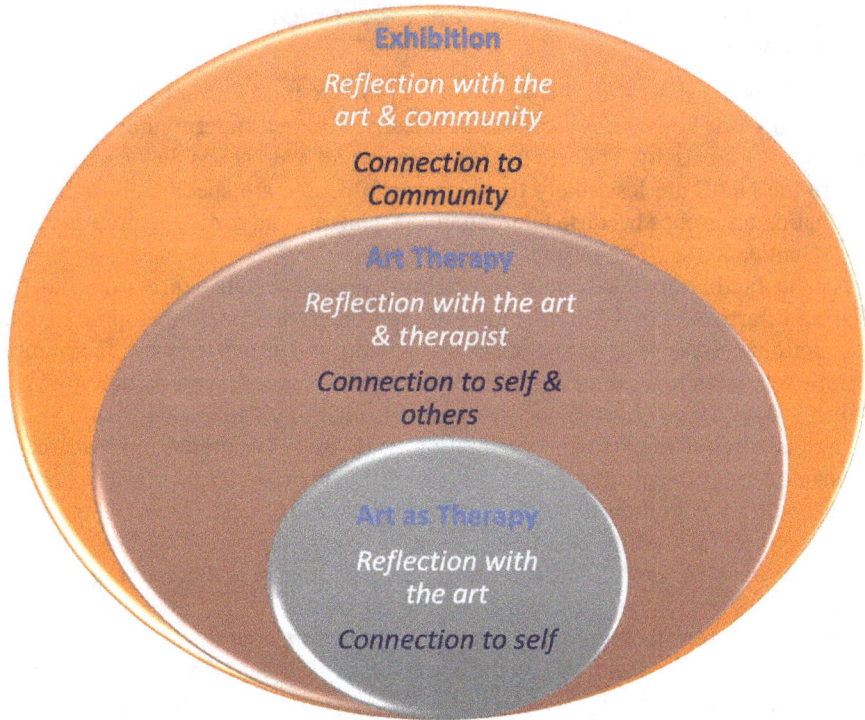

Figure 8.1 Map of therapeutic arts practices showing three levels of art connections with reflective frames.

and does not rely on the therapist for reflection as in "art therapy." Art groups operated by NDIS providers can be facilitated by people with little experience in art facilitation or group work and may not take place in an art studio. Thus, the remedial aspects of art groups are highly variable. The therapeutic potential remains but could be further enhanced with an understanding of the significance of reflective processes and cultivating connection. These components create a dynamic therapeutic space without a "therapy" label. Figure 8.1 shows three main types of therapeutic arts practice: art as therapy, art therapy, and exhibiting the artworks. The practices are aligned with three main connections through different reflective processes.

Connection and Creativity

This section explores the central role of the facilitator in supporting connection to the self through art-making to others in the group and to the wider community beyond the group. Examples of each type of connection are shared.

Making Connections Possible: The Importance of Facilitation

Connections are pivotal to the success of an art group. As an art therapist, I am trained to work holistically and therapeutically, without undermining the artist's autonomy or creativity. The less dynamic "sheltered" workshops that were in place before the NDIS are less likely to re-emerge if people are specifically trained in facilitating art groups because facilitation can generate and fortify genuine connection (Gentle, 2018, 2020; Gentle & O'Brien, 2021).

As the facilitator, I was sure to celebrate authentic self-expression and the sharing of artworks at different stages of their creative process to support group connection. I have found that including person and group-centred facilitation techniques helps to achieve this. The therapeutic aspect of "art as therapy" has often been with them throughout their lives, but ensuring a group is enriching to all participants requires particular facilitation skills. As a facilitator and researcher, I became part of the group whilst maintaining a safe holding space where participants could fly with their ideas and interact in ways that were respectful and supportive. Such facilitation techniques have the capacity to enhance participant's resilience because they encourage a deep sense of agency and belonging (Gentle, 2018).

These art group facilitation techniques can support connection to the created artworks, to self, to others, and to the community, building identity and resilience (Gentle & O'Brien, 2021; Gentle et al., 2022). Art therapists are well placed to facilitate art groups; however, artists also have the capacity to utilise a therapeutic frame. They can model how to reflect, explore, and create authentically and then co-organise local exhibitions to celebrate the group's artistry. Using person-centred, inclusive practice is therapeutic, whether a group is advertised as therapy or not.

Models for Facilitators to Enhance Connection

The data collected during the research contributed to the creation of a six-stage model that shows how connection can be developed during the life of an art group (Figure 8.2). Each stage of the model is discussed further in Gentle (2018, 2020). Throughout my practice and research, connection usually formed in direct relation to the artmaking process. I had begun to understand that this was where the "magic" of the art group happened. I now gauge the potency of art therapy groups or for that matter any art group, by the connections formed within the space. Figure 8.2 also shows how facilitation can enhance connection throughout the term of the art group.

Connecting to Self through Art-making

Creating artworks can produce a state of flow through mindfulness, providing connection to self, which helps to strengthen identity. Physiologically, artmaking has

Stage 1	Stage 2	Stage 3	Stage 4	Stage 5	Stage 6
Setting Up	Making Art	Showing & Discussing	Enrichment	Taking the Lead	Transition
FACILITATION					
SELF					
Self-esteem					
Agency					
	Identity as an Artist				
	Focus				
	Positive Feeling				
	Expression				
		Pride			
			Flow		
	SOCIAL				
		Forming relationships			
		Community of Practice			
				COMMUNITY	
				Making Art Outside	
					Exhibiting

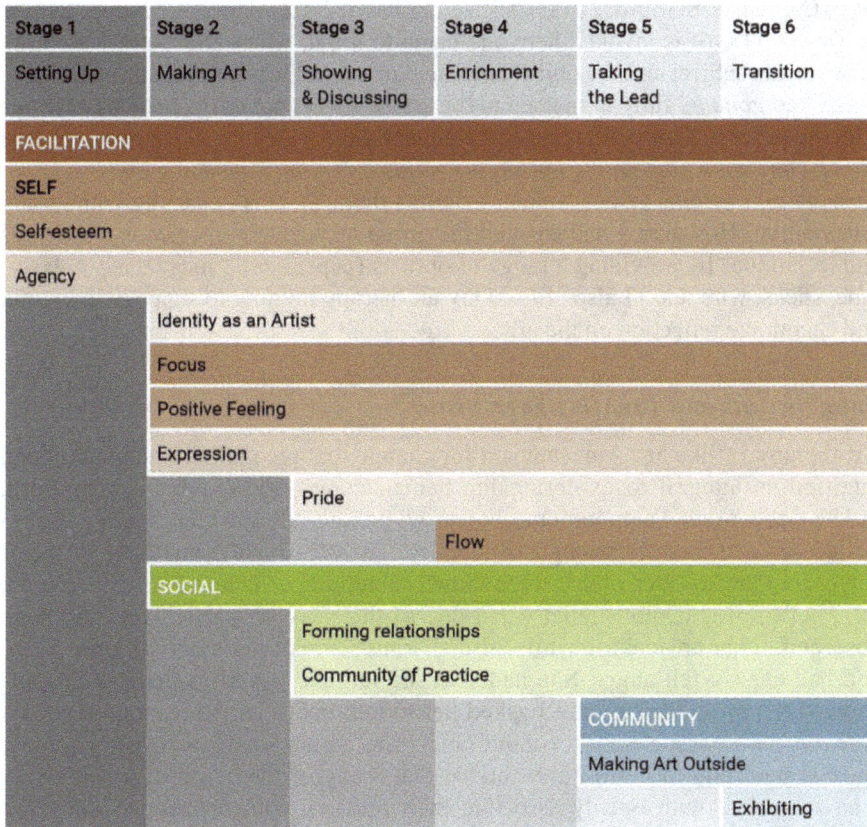

Figure 8.2 Diagram of the six-stage group art-making model, originally published in Gentle, 2018.

been shown to lower cortisol levels (Kaimal, Ray, & Muniz, 2016). It is the space where "art as therapy" (Kramer & Gerity, 2000) is evoked, the place we can escape our lives, a place of refuge and safety where the art and the artist connect.

From the beginning of the research project in 2017, the participants engaged in their art-making as artists. They were deeply absorbed in their process. When I asked each participant how they felt when they were engrossed in creating art, they gave responses like *"relaxed," "it feels good actually,"* and *"feels brilliant!"* along with other calm and positive descriptions. Even though the temperatures over the year the study took place ranged from six to 38 degrees Celsius in a shed with no heating or air conditioning, I regularly observed a *Zen-like* atmosphere within the art space. During these times, I would gently check in with how the participants of the group were feeling. They would reply that they were *"relaxed, concentrating," "happy,"* and *"good"* as they made art together. I reflected that they were connecting with their respective artworks, it was like they were in a state of flow (Carolan & Stafford, 2018; Csikszentmihalyi, 2002). The reflexive arc termed by Dewey (1896) is invoked here and came to mind, where the Cartesian clarity between the subject and the object became blurred and was no longer distinct. The artists had *gone in,* fully immersed in the art they were creating. They were at one with the process. One participant had eloquently described it as: *"Nothing to think about. Only what I am doing. I get in the mind set of what I am doing and can't concentrate on anything else."* Kramer's "art as therapy" was occurring without my intervention. However, I had ensured the group had agency in selecting materials and techniques by providing a range of options (paper, paint, magazines, polystyrene, sticks, wire, etc.) I also utilised my art therapy training to support discussion and encourage reflection on the art.

Imagination and Identity Formation

Art therapy is, like art, a mechanism for change that recognises imagination and intuition as integral to exploring the human experience (Carolan & Stafford, 2018). I encouraged autonomous choices with materials and techniques and suggested loose themes to strengthen identity. The artists put something of themselves into the art, then others were shown something of themselves (Malchiodo, 2012). This was demonstrated when one of the research participants had been absorbed in her art-making whilst also sharing some of her story with the group and had clearly felt angry. She had said she felt she would explode. When she showed the group her art and I asked her to talk about it, she responded *"It's a volcano."* She associated her mood and ideas immediately with her painting. It came naturally to her. I have noticed that many of the neurodivergent artists I have worked with openly associate their artwork with themselves and their experiences. My research and experience have shown that a supportive, less directive art group is helpful to this process.

Connection to Others: The Group Experience

Social disconnection has been shown to negatively impact mental health (Wang et al., 2017). Art groups have been championed as a way to counter this by providing a range of opportunities to connect. Group connections form organically in an art studio where the same people gather regularly. However, art offers something particularly enriching because, as I referred to earlier, it has a symbolic reference to the artist within the art. The nuance of the art comes from the artist, so sharing the artwork with the group communicates something distinctive. The richness of such a sharing adds depth to the interactions of the art group. One participant said of another's work as they showed the group: *"It's good Paul, I like it!"* Paul and his artwork were acknowledged; this produced a smile and contented look from Paul.

Art therapy groups will often explore their creations at the culmination of the artmaking session. Throughout the research, the participants had shown each other their artworks at the end (and often during) the session. I recorded a moment that illustrates how a group can support each other through showing their art and reflecting:

> *One participant held up her work to the group, then another suddenly held their work up and was very happy with it. He...was very strong in how he showed the group. Another quieter member then said: "Look what I did!" and proudly held up her work with new brush strokes on it. She was noticeably proud of it.*
>
> (Gentle, 2018)

This pride in showing and influencing each other supported the group's authentic connection to one another and to their artwork. The art object was subject, thus the connection extended again to themselves through the interactions with the group. Our sense of self supports our identity formation which in turn strengthens confidence and builds resilience. Tomas referred to the social aspect when I asked about going to an art group he said, *"I like drawing with my friends and my friends make art, and we talk."*

The influence artists have on each other and how art studios can become places of extraordinary creativity is well documented. However, for neurodivergent artists using the NDIS, they need to know where the studios are and how to access them. Organic collaboration opportunities arise from shared art spaces. The co-creation of art forms exciting connections between artists, thus has a range of benefits.

Connection to Community: Outside the Group

Many neurodivergent people in Australia have experienced segregation, meaning most have experienced exclusion, othering, and bullying. As I have touched on, having an art therapist or an artist who uses person-centred practice when facilitating art groups can support the agency and belonging many have missed out on. When the research group decided to show their artwork publicly, it further supported the development of their artist identity, agency, and sense of belonging (Gentle, 2018; Gentle et al., 2020; Gentle & O'Brien, 2021; Hall, 2010, 2013). However, for this to occur, it was imperative we collaboratively planned this event, and further exhibitions with the group. Tomas and his peers came up with ideas throughout the planning process during the research and then saw their ideas implemented. Each had agency in how their work was displayed, if they wanted to sell it and when they wanted the opening. This collaborative planning increased the depth of connection that was already growing in the art studio. Additionally, the exhibition gave the artists an opportunity to richly communicate their stories to their communities and beyond, and again, this increased their sense of identity, their agency, and sense of belonging.

During the exhibition, the community learnt more about the artists as well as placing their own meaning onto the artworks. This form of affiliation to the art goes beyond people and beyond the artwork, as it is the liminal and somewhat existential wonder of art that is so often felt by the viewer. This experience has no bounds, and these elements are not confined to specific artworks. The artist is the artist; the viewer is the viewer; neurodivergent or not. The exhibition demonstrated that the power of an artwork is not enhanced or reduced in its capacity to communicate by the neurological functioning of the artist or viewer. The artists beamed as they talked about their work or watched as people became immersed in their displayed artworks.

Thus, finding a space where neurodivergent artists can confidently express themselves and show some of their authentic self through their art is a useful way of reconnecting communities. The exhibition offered a space for real inclusion, for artists to deeply express themselves and then to see themselves celebrated on the walls, floors, and ceilings of galleries. These aspects contribute to the hope and self-esteem that form cohesion (Yalom & Crouch, 1990). Communities are less likely to stigmatise when they are invited into people's worlds in a way that gives them a better understating of the richness in diversity. The connections formed at an art event go beyond the artwork, the artist, and the group. They extend to all who attend an exhibition or art event where the artists are front and centre. The sense of pride expressed by the artists during their exhibition was palpable. Art exhibitions hold a distinctive position as they have the capacity to support societal changes in unconscious perceptions of people with diverse ways of being. Art is an undervalued technique for connecting and thus enriching society on a community level.

Re-Engaging with Local Artist, Tomas

To finish, we return to Tomas and how we collaborated during the writing of this chapter. Since the facilitation model was developed, I have continued working around the area I researched but rarely see the artists. I was curious to see how they were doing and what their art practice looked like, as I had heard they were not attending specific art groups. Most of the artists were either working or very difficult to contact after the changes in their support services since the NDIS. I knew how to contact one participant, Tomas Calhoun through his cousin, who was able to reconnect me with him. Tomas had made it clear before and during the research project that he liked to be seen and heard as an artist and welcomed this attention. He was prolific with his work both at home and in the studio. Tomas said he was keen to meet up again, as I had hoped. His cousin informed me that he was no longer attending a dedicated art group, but he continued his arts practice at home.

When I visited Tomas, he didn't want to talk too much, he chose to sing and show me his artworks. When Tomas did use his words to describe his art-making and attending an art group, they were poignant. He said, *"It saved my life; art saved my life."* A man of very few words that day, but the ones he chose he repeated each time I asked him, with an obvious deeply felt passion. He backed up his claim by showing me images that showed parts of his story, and his Mum chimed in to give me anecdotes that revealed just how important his artmaking practice was to him then and now.

During my visits, he had shown me his art on the wall in his room. He then asked me to record and said pointing to a picture *"This is Tomas Calhoun."* He said,

"I am an artist and [I] paint and draw." He then pointed to himself and smiled broadly saying, *"I made it!"* I asked whether he sold his art or gave it away to others, to which he responded, *"Yes- they are presents. I made it, I painted it."* He then showed me his art book. His Mum described it as his journal. He has used journals throughout his life. Tomas was vocal about wanting to become a star, actually, that he already was a star *"a super star!"* which obviously made him overjoyed as he smiled broadly with his head held higher than it already had been. He smiled and grinned and continued to hold the artwork up to ensure I got the photo. He had created artworks of himself as a super star, a king, and created pieces called *"the pretty girls."* He said they were his girlfriends in his imagination. When he spoke about these artworks he showed excited delight, as though these ideas were real to him. He was reconnecting with himself through his art. The image below shows Tomas presenting his self-portrait and a picture from his sketch book to me. His unfettered self-expression has provided all who see his art with an enhanced understanding of Tomas's authentic self and also possibly provided a window to themselves (Figure 8.3).

Our imaginations have the capacity to make us feel better, to take us to other self-created realities. Yet Tomas, who has a Down's Syndrome diagnosis, inhabits his imagination seemingly more often than the perceived world neurotypical people ordinarily inhabit. His advocate and mother said he has always been like this.

Figure 8.3 A photograph of Tomas with some of his artworks.

When taking part in a church ceremony Tomas had looked at his mother and back at the bread they were being given and said, *"That's the universe, all the universe is there."* Like so many artists, his inner world is awash with ideas and possibilities.

Conclusion

There is a depth and authenticity in artmaking that allows people to fully express themselves without having to rely on verbal communication. Relating is the crux of human endeavour, therefore valuing people for their authentic selves enriches us personally and societally. Utilising therapeutic facilitation frames has been shown to provide a rich source of connection. Creating together and exhibiting support agency and belonging thus quality of life is enhanced and resilience nurtured. Moreover, art holds a wonderfully unique position to communicate the rich inner worlds of artists. Tomas's mother and advocate gave me an anecdote whilst Tomas was showing me his sketch-book before I left. With Tomas's permission, she told a story about how Tomas helped her see the everyday from a unique angle.

> *One day ducks were flying in front of us and he said: 'Ahhhhhhh! Love with wings!' when I asked, he said it was because the ducks' bottoms looked like hearts. Then when we got home Tomas drew a picture of love hearts with wings.*

She was enriched at the time, again whilst telling me the story, and fortunately I now have the image of the ducks' bottoms as hearts with wings that always makes me smile when I see ducks flying by. Art has the capacity to connect us. It is a communication tool, a reflective experience, an embodiment of self, a salve, a distraction, and, possibly above all, a key to valuing a diverse range of human perspectives.

Acknowledgments

I acknowledge the place where this research took place, Gumbaynggirr country. I pay my respects to the Gumbaynggirr people, to their Elders past, present and emerging. Creativity is central to their culture, as it is for most First Nations peoples in Australia and throughout the world. I am exceedingly grateful for the knowledge the Gumbaynggirr people and Aboriginal Australians continue to generously share.

I would also like to express my gratitude to Tomas Calhoun, Jenny Arkle, Edward Barns, Marnie Russell, Paul, Tim Pearson, Stuart Relf, Olivia Dean, and Kylie for their enthusiasm and understanding of art processes that formed my PhD research. The research was supervised by Professor Emerita Patricia O Brien, Professor Colin Rhodes, and Professor Emeritus Trevor Parmenter. Their professional support, expertise, and regular supervision ensured I could carefully reflect on my work with the participants and the project as a whole.

References

Australian Government. (2022). People with Disability in Australia. *Disability.* Retrieved from https://www.aihw.gov.au/reports/disability/people-with-disability-in-australia/contents/health/health-status.

Cacioppo, J. T., & Cacioppo, S. (2014). Social Relationships and Health: The Toxic Effects of Perceived Social Isolation. *Social and Personality Psychology Compass, 8*(2), 58–72. https://doi.org/10.1111/spc3.12087.

Carolan, R., & Stafford, K. (2018). Theory and Art Therapy. In R. Carolan, & A. Backos (Eds), *Emerging Perspectives in Art Therapy: Trends, Movements, and Developments* (pp. 17–32): Routledge.

Csikszentmihalyi, M. (2002). *Flow: The Classic Work on how to Achieve Happiness.* Rider.

Dewey, J. (1896). The reflex arc Concept in Psychology. *Psychological Review, 3*(4), 357– 370. https://doi.org/10.1037/h0070405

Gentle, E. (2018). *Autonomous Expression and Creative Connection: An Exploration of Art-Making with Neurodivergent People in Regional Australia.* https://ses.library.usyd.edu.au/bitstream/handle/2123/20416/ex_final_thesis_gentle.pdf?sequence=1

Gentle, E. (2020). Facilitating Art Groups: How Art Therapy and Community arts Paradigms can Intersect to Support Connection with Marginalised Groups. *Journal of Creative Arts Therapies, 15*(1), 82–93. https://www.jocat-online.org/a-20-gentle

Gentle, E., Linsley, P., & Hurley, J. (2020). "Their Story is a Hard Road to hoe": How Art-Making Tackles Stigma and Builds Well-being in Young People Living Regionally. *Journal of Public Mental Health.* https://doi.org/10.1108/JPMH-10-2019-0087.

Gentle, E., & O'Brien, P. (2021). Forming Relationships through Group Art-making: An Exploration with Neurodivergent People Living in Regional Australia. *Health Promotion Journal of Australia, 32*, 308–319.

Gentle, E., O'Brien, P., & Parmenter, T. (2022). "Me an Artist!" Building Relational Communities with Neurodivergent Artists in Regional Australia. *Journal of Rural and Community Development, 17*(3), 105–122. https://journals.brandonu.ca/jrcd/article/view/2085

Hadley, B., & Goggin, G. (2019). The NDIS and Disability Arts in Australia: Opportunities and Challenges. *Australasian Drama Studies 74*, 9–38.

Hall, E. (2010). Spaces of Social Inclusion and Belonging for People with Intellectual Disabilities. *Journal of Intellectual Disability Research, 54*, 48–57. https://doi.org/10.1111/j.1365-2788.2009.01237.x

Hall, E. (2013). Making and Gifting Belonging: Creative Arts and People with Learning Disabilities. *Environment and Planning A, 45*(2), 244–262. https://doi.org/10.1068/a44629

Kaimal, G., Ray, K., & Muniz, J. (2016). Reduction of Cortisol Levels and Participants' Responses Following Art Making. *Art Therapy, 33*(2), 74–80.

Kramer, E., & Gerity, L. A. (2000). *Art as Therapy: Collected Papers.* Jessica Kingsley Publishers.

Lige, S. (2011). *Adults with Intellectual Disabilities and the Visual Arts: "It's NOT Art Therapy!".* (Master of Arts). The University Of British Columbia (Okanagan).

Malchiodo, C. A. (2012). Psychoanalytic, Analytic and Object Relations Approaches. In C. A. Malchiodo (Ed.), *Handbook of Art Therapy* (pp. 57–74). The Guilford Press.

NDIS. (2022). *What Is the NDIS?* National Disability Insurance Agency. www.ndis.gov.au/understanding/what-ndis

Obejas, D. (2015, May 22). Neurodivergent Daniel Obejas speaks at USC Health Sciences Campus. [Video] YouTube. Available at: https://www.youtube.com/watch?v=i-vDqlCvY58

Wang, J., Lloyd-Evans, B., Giacco, D., Forsyth, R., Nebo, C., Mann, F., & Johnson, S. (2017). Social Isolation in Mental Health: A Conceptual and Methodological Review. *Social Psychiatry and Psychiatric Epidemiology, 52*(12), 1451–1461. https://doi.org/10.1007/s00127-017-1446-1

Williams, K. D. (2009). Ostracism: A Temporal Need-threat Model In M. P. Zanna (Ed.), *Advances in Experimental Social Psychology* (Vol. 41, pp. 275–314). Elsevier Academic Press. https://doi.org/10.1016/S0065-2601(08)00406-1

Williams, K. D., & Nida, S. A. (2022). Ostracism and Social Exclusion: Implications for Separation, Social Isolation, and Loss. *Current Opinion in Psychology, 47*, 101353. https://doi.org/10.1016/j.copsyc.2022.101353

Yalom, I. D., & Crouch, E. (1990). The Theory and Practice of Group Psychotherapy. *The British Journal of Psychiatry, 157*(2), 304–306.

Section 3

Advocacy

Chapter 9

Advocacy and Art Therapy

"It helped me piece together what happened"

Toni Leigh Harrison and Lizzy

Positionality Statement

I (Toni Leigh Harrison) have written this chapter as a white British woman without learning disabilities. I have worked within Learning Disability Services for ten years, practising as a qualified Art Psychotherapist for five years. I follow a person-centred approach to therapy where possible, and in writing this chapter I have given careful consideration to how I could present information to my co-author and welcome her contributions. Lizzy (the client) has co-authored this chapter. She has given permission for her words and images to be used and for her story to be shared with others.

Introduction

I found art therapy extremely helpful as I was able to express myself through art about what I needed and my memories. By drawing its less traumatic but extremely effective how it was done. Its really helped me massively.

—Lizzy

This chapter demonstrates how art therapy can be used to actively advocate for clients with learning disabilities in a range of areas, beyond the art room. I will outline how the relationship built in art therapy was used to promote one client's voice, in settings where they found it difficult to overcome communication barriers and to have their views heard by others. I will discuss a long-term piece of individual work with Lizzy (the client) which began during the COVID-19 pandemic in 2020 and continued over a period of 27 months. I will discuss a range of areas in which I was able to support Lizzy, advocating on her behalf in relation to her health and social care needs, communication with others, accessing information and navigating a complicated complaints process with the help of an independent advocacy agency. The art therapy work was provided in the UK National Health Service (NHS) in North East England.

Lizzy's art therapy journey is one which is difficult to describe chronologically, due to the nature and complexity of her situation. To try to describe Lizzy's

DOI: 10.4324/9781003350736-13

journey, I will first describe our work together relating to Lizzy's main reason for accessing art therapy. Primarily, this was related to her coming to terms with an accident which left her with life-long physical changes. I will then discuss how Lizzy was able to use art therapy to support her communication with others and describe some of the resources co-created during art therapy which she has been able to use in other settings. These pieces of work often occurred simultaneously in sessions or during times when we were waiting for information from external sources before we could continue to think together about Lizzy's accident. This chapter will describe how the art therapy sessions were used to introduce and work alongside an independent complaint advocate in order to explore Lizzy's past experiences, which had left her with many unanswered questions. Lizzy hoped that art therapy could help to bring her some closure around a traumatic past experience with previous caregivers, which had taken place some years earlier.

Before starting this chapter, I approached Lizzy to ask if she would like to contribute her experiences of the work we did together and I was pleased that she expressed how important our collaboration had been for her. Lizzy's words, as written by her, are included throughout this chapter in *italics*. Lizzy's involvement in telling this story is an essential part of the writing process, just as our collaborative working was an essential part of the therapy. Lizzy read and added to the first draft of this chapter and was happy for me to share details of her story and our work together in art therapy.

Let's Meet Lizzy

Hi, I am Lizzy I have a learning disability and a brain injury I have been through mental health services for many years and struggled with communication barriers as I would get agitated. When this opportunity [art therapy] came forward it felt right to me. I didn't know what to expect at first. It was a difficult journey for us all involved. But it was made easier by art therapy as I was able to draw the trauma that was showing in my head.

- Lizzy

Lizzy's Referral to Art Therapy

I wanted to try something I have not tried before. And as I felt that it would help me explain everything regarding my accident. Art give[s] my brain a rest as I don't need to verbally say anything and express myself in the most confident way possible.

—Lizzy

Lizzy was referred to the art therapy team in April 2020 from a Community Learning Disability Team after expressing an interest in art therapy due to difficulties with communication. At the time of her referral, Lizzy was 32 years old. Lizzy has a diagnosis of mild learning disability and was struggling to understand and come to terms with life and health changes since an accident which occurred in 2017.

Lizzy was experiencing flashbacks and anxiety and had difficulty in expressing how she was feeling. During the time we worked together, Lizzy also received a diagnosis of a brain injury, sustained due to her accident.

When I accepted Lizzy's referral, I was working in a secure inpatient setting with a reduced caseload due to COVID-19 restrictions on the secure wards. I was able to take on Lizzy's case with an aim to have weekly telephone or video call contact until we were able to meet face-to-face when COVID-19 restrictions were eased. Online meetings were not part of my usual practice, but the pandemic restrictions necessitated new ways of working for art therapists, and a move to online practice was experienced by many practitioners worldwide (Zubala & Hackett, 2020). Over the course of therapy, Lizzy attended a total of 12 telephone appointments, 6 online appointments and 73 face-to-face appointments which took place between April 2020 and July 2022. Lizzy's face-to-face sessions took place in a Community Learning Disability Team setting on a weekly basis for 60 minutes.

Starting Face-to-face Sessions

I was anxious, nervous, not knowing what to expect with the covid 19 restrictions.

—Lizzy

In June 2020, we met in person for the first time. We had already completed her art therapy assessment and had begun to form a positive therapeutic relationship through weekly telephone contact over the previous two and a half months. During our telephone calls, we had discussed Lizzy's preferences for art materials and her current coping strategies, which had involved colouring and baking, which prompted me to create a set of mindful colouring worksheets which I was able to send to Lizzy for her use at home. Based on Lizzy's preferences, I provided a range of felt-tip pens, pencils, paints, paper and craft items for use within sessions, as well as some sensory items for relaxation.

We were now able to meet for the first time in person, following social distancing guidance and wearing appropriate personal protective equipment (PPE). During our first face-to-face session, after completing the formal paperwork (therapy contract, consent forms, adapted mood assessments) Lizzy and I created a resource for use as a mood "check-in" at the beginning of each session. Lizzy was familiar with, and comfortable using, a "Red-Yellow-Green" traffic light system in order to rate her mood, and as this had been discussed during previous telephone contact, I brought a template traffic light worksheet with me to use within the session. Lizzy was keen to discuss this and was able to explain to me what each colour meant for her:

- Green: *"Good, no issues"*
- Yellow: *"Something is wrong/happening, but not sure how to explain or find the right words"*
- Red: *"Complete danger, something has happened, or I may do something to myself"* (Figure 9.1)

RED

Complete Danger

Something has happened or I may do something to myself

YELLOW

Something is wrong/has happened

Not sure how to explain or find the right words

Could mean some negative behaviours (self harm, withdrawal from services, not going to appointments)

GREEN

Good

No issues

Figure 9.1 An image of Lizzy's traffic light mood rating system.

This resource gave us an opportunity to think about how Lizzy might feel and how she might present if things were not going well for her. Lizzy identified that when she was "Yellow", she may display some negative behaviours such as wanting to withdraw from services or missing appointments or that it could lead to self-harming behaviours (although she reported that she had not self-harmed since before her accident three years ago). Further exploration in this session allowed

Lizzy to think about what would help when she was feeling "Yellow" or "Red", and we created a list of ways in which others could help her during these times. This included not having too many people talking to her (one-to-one contact was preferable) and that tone of voice was very important as she found that loud, deep or aggressive tones could heighten her distress. We agreed to use the traffic light system to check-in on how Lizzy was feeling each week, and it was used to good effect for the duration of her art therapy, proving to be especially helpful when Lizzy was unable to verbalise her emotional state at the beginning of some sessions.

This was the first of many worksheets and resources co-created in order to help Lizzy to explore her feelings and to help her communicate them to other professionals involved in her care.

I absolutely love these work sheets it's so helpful. I still use them now.

—Lizzy

This session also highlighted some of Lizzy's sensory issues relating to loud or unexpected noises, as during the session a police siren could be heard outside. Lizzy became extremely distressed; her hands rapidly covered her ears to block out the noise, she closed her eyes tightly and her breathing became fast and panicked. The sirens quickly passed, and Lizzy took a few moments to recover from the noise, I spoke softly, telling her she was safe. Seeing how distressed she had become, I asked Lizzy how we could manage future unexpected noises and suggested that we could introduce some relaxation music into our sessions in order to dull down any noises external to the room. This was provided in our second session when a personal alarm was activated in another room nearby. Lizzy used an iPad to select some nature sounds that she found relaxing (birds, rainstorm, waves), which proved to be useful to help Lizzy to relax and mask the sounds of the alarm. For the rest of our time working together, I would have the relaxation sounds playing before Lizzy entered the room and for the duration of the therapy sessions.

This also led to further consideration of our environment at the time and the importance of ensuring that the setting felt safe to Lizzy. UK art therapy practice-based guidelines (Hackett et al., 2017) highlight "providing a safe experience for the service user" (p 89) and suggest adaptations should be made where possible to meet the needs of the client surrounding environment or timing of sessions. I was acutely aware of how Lizzy's environment could impact her ability to engage with therapy and, where possible, made changes to ensure that she felt protected and comfortable within the art therapy room. This necessitated changes in the timing of our therapy sessions in order to avoid weekly fire alarm tests in the building. Another significant challenge to some of our early sessions was building work occurring outside of the venue, and with help from other professionals within the service, we were able to reach an agreement with the building workers that they would not carry out any loud work during the time of Lizzy's weekly appointments.

Figure 9.2 Photograph of a section of Lizzy's artwork showing a timeline of events surrounding her accident.

Lizzy's Story

With the groundwork now in place to create a safe environment for Lizzy's sessions, we were able to begin to explore her reasons for coming to art therapy, and create some therapy goals. They included *"understanding my accident"*, *"accepting all of the changes since my accident"* and *"feeling let down by professionals in the past"* and they became the main focus throughout therapy.

To understand the importance of these goals, there is a need to know a little about Lizzy's accident and how we worked together in art therapy to think about this. Lizzy was able to use artmaking to piece together her memories of the accident which had occurred three years earlier. Whilst Lizzy was detained under Section 5(2) of the Mental Health Act (UK legislation which covers the assessment and treatment of people with mental health disorders, Department of Health, 1983), she had experienced a traumatic fall which resulted in serious physical injuries, brain injury and significant mental distress.

Lizzy wanted to understand her accident but felt she had a lot of gaps in her memory and questions around what had happened. To explore this, Lizzy used several pieces of A3 paper, taped together to draw out her memories in a time-line, using felt-tip pens. The image below shows Lizzy's drawings relating to her memory of being airlifted to hospital after the accident (Figure 9.2).

Lizzy's injuries led to her having a stoma bag fitted (colostomy bag which collects bodily waste), and problems with her mobility meant that she became a full-time wheelchair user and needed to live in adapted accommodation to maintain independence. Lizzy was initially mobilising to sessions by walking and using the bus. When Lizzy became dependent on using a wheelchair (due to reduced sensation in her legs and feet), this necessitated a further change in therapy space within the building, to accommodate her wheelchair and allow easy access to a table and art materials.

To try and answer some of the questions she had around her accident, Lizzy had previously tried to request her medical notes from prior care providers through the community learning disability team. Some information had been received by the team and I reviewed this information to see if there were any answers to Lizzy's questions. Unfortunately, the information received related to Lizzy's care had not included any information from mental health teams during the time-period of her accident. Lizzy was understandably disappointed by this and requested that I try to find the right information for her to piece together the story. This proved to be a difficult and time-consuming process, taking six months in total, but I was able to submit a subject access request (a request which can be made in order to access personal information that an organisation holds) on Lizzy's behalf and received information from her previous care teams along with a police report from the date of the accident.

The information was vast and difficult to process, not easily accessible to read for Lizzy and certainly would have been hard for her to understand. I gave careful consideration to how I would feed back this information to Lizzy and asked her how she would like to explore it, being careful to explain that some of it would be difficult to hear. Lizzy was determined that she needed to know, and we made a plan to address each of her questions that had arisen in the timeline of events that she had drawn out in therapy.

Reviewing the information took time and it was necessary to be mindful of how much of it was relevant to what Lizzy wanted to know. I had received hundreds of pages of clinical notes and medical reports. Holding and digesting the information was a powerful and moving process, and for a time, it seemed to me that I was the only person who understood the importance of this information and the impact it would have for Lizzy. Being able to organise and locate the relevant pieces of information to address Lizzy's questions was a difficult, but privileged task, and one which I am grateful to have been able to carry out for Lizzy.

I was able to prioritise this, and within a week or so, I had created an easy-read timeline document containing information about the time leading up to Lizzy's accident and what happened afterwards. We went through this information together in a session, looking at which questions had been answered and which remained a mystery. Listening to the information was difficult for Lizzy to process, and after this session we met again the next day on a video call, so that Lizzy had time to think about any new questions she might have about it.

It didn't process straight away. It took time. Overwhelmed by feeling and emotions.

—Lizzy

After Lizzy had taken some time to consider the information we had about her accident, she decided that she wanted to raise a formal complaint about the care she had received. Lizzy explained that she had made a complaint previously but felt that it had been dismissed by the organisation involved. Lizzy now wanted to get more answers from the people who were involved in her care at the time and asked me to help her to make a complaint, which she hoped would help her gain some closure about her accident.

> *I [k]new when I was in the ward I was not treated right. After my accident things didn't feel right when I was looking for answers it felt like people were covering up or making accuses [excuses].*
>
> —Lizzy

My work with Lizzy up until this point had been complex, and the things we had worked on had been achievable within my job role; however, a request to raise a formal complaint was something I felt was beyond my capabilities. As an alternative, I suggested to Lizzy that I could, with her permission, pass some of her information on to an advocacy service that specialised in supporting people to raise complaints about their care. In the UK, individuals have the right to complain to an organisation which has provided care, if they feel it has been unsatisfactory; Local Authority, Social Services and National Health Service Complaint Regulations 2009. Lizzy agreed to this, and in early 2021 I made a referral on Lizzy's behalf to an advocacy group who could help her with this request.

The advocacy group agreed to take on Lizzy's request and we decided it would be helpful if the advocate could meet with Lizzy and myself during our usual art therapy session in order to make a first introduction.

Before this meeting, Lizzy asked that I share some information about her communication difficulties and preferred ways of communication with the advocate. I encouraged Lizzy to draw some images related to the difficulties she'd had since her brain injury, to help her visualise and think about the issues. Lizzy drew images relating to her struggle with decision making, noise sensitivity, conversational difficulties, having no verbal *"filter"* and feeling she may upset people unintentionally. Lizzy expressed feeling frustrated and overwhelmed at times due to her communication difficulties. This led to the creation of another resource for Lizzy, which she was able to use many times with many other professionals during her time in therapy in order to let other people know the best way to communicate with her. It turned out to be quite a comprehensive document, outlining 12 things that others could do or consider when meeting with Lizzy or whilst sharing information with her. Lizzy has been able to use this document with housing professionals, other members of the multidisciplinary team (MDT) and new professionals who began working with her during her time in art therapy.

> *It has been extremely helpful as people are aware In advance[,] I have communication difficulties and need things adapted. It elim[in]ates any breakdown in communication.*
>
> —Lizzy

After sending this document to the advocate, we met via video call during our usual session for Lizzy to be introduced and to start to find out the process of making a complaint. This first meeting is where the independent advocate became part of our work, and we would continue to work with them (via video call in our sessions) for a period of 18 months from January 2021 to June 2022.

Having an independent advocate take on the responsibility of progressing Lizzy's complaint meant that I was able to focus on supporting Lizzy to process and reflect on the information we would receive and to manage her anxieties between meetings with the advocate.

Working through Lizzy's Complaint

The process of helping Lizzy to work through her complaint was a lengthy piece of joint work between Lizzy, the advocate and myself. The advocate's hard work liaising between the complaints team at the previous healthcare setting and feeding back information to us was absolutely instrumental in Lizzy obtaining more answers.

Navigating the complaints process was complex, and despite outlining Lizzy's communication needs to the complaints team, their replies and information were often complicated to read and did not contain easy-read summaries as requested. Lizzy began to use our art therapy sessions to create images which told a story about who she was and how the accident had changed her life. These documents were sent to the complaints team in order to highlight Lizzy's feelings around her physical and mental health difficulties throughout the complaint process. One document created within the sessions contained drawings of the events leading up to Lizzy's accident, an account of Lizzy's story as written by herself, and a powerful final line stating, *"I am a human being, with feelings and emotions, not just a number"*. Throughout the process, Lizzy continually stated that she just wanted to make sure that what she had experienced did not happen to anyone else; she wanted her story to be told and for others to learn from it.

> *I am using my story to make awareness to help other including professionals so mistakes do not happen again. Which could lead to someone either commit[t]ing suicide or life changing injuries. My aim is to prevent this.*
>
> —Lizzy

The complaint process ended with an official meeting with representatives of Lizzy's former care team. This was a face-to-face meeting with Lizzy (and her partner), myself and the advocate, with the former care team representatives on video call. Preparing for this meeting was extremely anxiety provoking for Lizzy, and we spent the weeks running up to the meeting thinking about how we could best support her through it. Lizzy brought along an item from home for comfort (her favourite teddy) and I brought along some calming sensory items (a sensory liquid timer, fidget items and soft therapy putty), which she had used in our sessions, as well as paper and art materials.

The atmosphere in the meeting was tense; the previous organisation had a lot to say, much of which was not easy to understand. The advocate took the leading role, pressing for answers to Lizzy's questions and letting Lizzy ask questions herself. My role in this meeting was to offer support to Lizzy and to act as a silent observer, taking notes so that Lizzy and I could go back over the information at a slower pace once the meeting was concluded. The outcome of the meeting was generally positive with some verbal acknowledgement of failings in communication and care; however, some things remained unanswered and unacknowledged for Lizzy.

After this meeting we had a break in therapy (at Lizzy's request) in order to give her time to consolidate and process the information, and when Lizzy returned to therapy, she felt ready to put the complaint behind her and think about her future.

Advocating for Lizzy Outside of the Complaint Process

Coming to terms with her accident was a key reason for Lizzy accessing art therapy. Lizzy described wanting to *"work it all out in her head"* and learn how to be the *"New Lizzy"* since her fall and process the feelings of grief for the *"Old Lizzy"*. In our sessions, she was able to draw pictures which explained her physical health and life changes since her accident, and a resource was created to illustrate her difficulties. Lizzy was able to show this to new professionals that she worked with, as a way to inform them about her physical health difficulties and, in turn, avoid having to tell her story over and over to new people. Lizzy also created a health folder during our sessions, which included sections for each of her health issues (with images painted as separators for each section) and spaces to keep her appointment letters and correspondence for each health issue.

Lizzy described finding it very difficult to explain her pain levels or sensations during appointments with health professionals, which led us to the creation of another resource relating to her pain levels. Lizzy found this to be very helpful during health assessments and appointments where she often struggled with the 0 to 10 pain scales which doctors often work with. The numbers for Lizzy had no meaning in relation to her pain. The process of creating this pain chart took place over a number of weeks. Lizzy created images relating to her physical pain, and we both spent time thinking about what words could be used to describe them (Figure 9.3).

Been able to have a[n] easier way to communication how my pain is so much better. Rather than me feeling frustrated that I can't understand what there on about.

—Lizzy

Working with Other Professionals

During our time together in art therapy, Lizzy had a lot of involvement with an Multi Disciplinary Team (MDT) looking at her physical health, her housing situation and her mental health. Lizzy voiced that she struggled to build trust with professionals due to her past experiences and that she found it difficult to *"keep telling*

Number	Pain Faces	Different Pains	Feels Like...	Words to describe the Pain
10			Worst Pain Imaginable, like when I fell from the bridge. Spasms and something else at the same time might be a 10.	• Heavy • Intense • Can't think • Crying
9			Elephants Stamping on my head/brain	• Big • Banging • Rattling • Throbbing / Pulsating • Can be sickening • Tiring • Exhausting • Pressure • Tight pain • Powerful: takes over • Demanding: can't concentrate • Upsetting: crying • Heavy
8			Elastic band being twanged across my pelvis	• Constant pain • Twanging • Popping • Throbbing
7		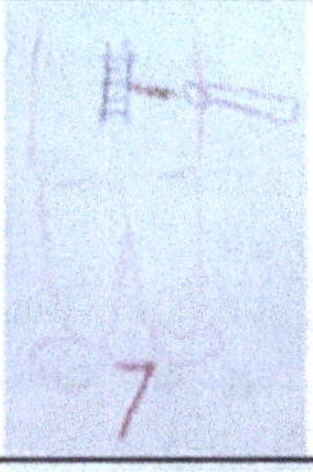	Someone using a screwdriver in my metal spine-work	• Tight • Twisting • Sharp • Annoying • Prolonged • Constant • Hot/warm pain • Tender to touch • Unbearable • Debilitating

Figure 9.3 An image of part of Lizzy's pain chart.

my story". Lizzy struggled to work with male professionals and with professionals who had certain job titles. Throughout her time in therapy, Lizzy often voiced feelings of *"not being listened to"* or understood by other professionals in her care team. Lizzy used our sessions to create plans and questions for other professionals and often requested that I share her wishes with the rest of the MDT. Lizzy could, at times, be quite demanding of services and would often ask the same questions to a multitude of different professionals and external services, making it difficult for the MDT to know what information had been shared with Lizzy. After some discussion around this with Lizzy, she decided that having a *"single point of contact"* would be beneficial in order to give her information and that it would be me who took on this role. Lizzy's thoughts about professionals could often be very *"black and white"*, identifying professionals as good or bad, and this opinion could often change quickly, leading Lizzy to disengage or demand new professionals to work with, which meant that her contact with services could end abruptly and that it was not always easy or timely to get referred back into a service. In order to contain Lizzy's anxiety and tendency to send multiple e-mails asking questions between sessions, I gave Lizzy a notebook and discussed that it would be helpful for future work if she could write things down and bring the notebook to our sessions. This was useful for Lizzy, and she often came to sessions with a list of questions and information to pass on to me, as well as requests for other professionals.

> *I find [the notebook] extremely helpful. I still do it now.*
>
> —Lizzy

At times, advocating for Lizzy with other professionals meant that I was involved in making a lot of telephone calls, chasing updates and getting answers for Lizzy, as well as facilitating meetings with other professionals during our art therapy sessions. I was able to support Lizzy to explain her thoughts and wishes to others in a concise manner and to help her to process information and think about how to answer questions from others. Miller et al. (2020) highlight how art therapists can promote autonomy and self-advocacy in clients with learning disabilities, by "reducing barriers to participation" on both a local and national level. Supporting Lizzy's self-advocacy became central to our work together, and by helping her to have her voice heard by others, she was able to start to work with other professionals and groups more confidently.

Taking on this role of advocating for Lizzy was not one which I envisioned when I accepted Lizzy's referral, but over the 27 months that we worked together, it became a natural part of the art therapy, and one which Lizzy expressed gratitude for during many of our sessions. Had my regular caseload not been reduced due to COVID-19 restrictions and had I not received the continued encouragement from my line manager in supporting Lizzy's complaint, I do not think it would have been possible to provide the depth of support that I was able to give Lizzy, both within and outside of the therapy room. The long-term nature of the work was also a new experience for both of us, as my work was usually time-limited within an inpatient service and Lizzy's previous experiences of therapy had not been long-term. In a recent systematic review of art therapy with people with learning disabilities, data suggests that the median length of treatment is 14 sessions of one-to-one art therapy (Power et al., 2023). Having an opportunity to attend sessions long-term with a professional who had time to work at her own pace and to give her the time she needed to process information has gone a long way towards repairing Lizzy's past negative experiences with professionals and, in turn, has given her a positive experience which might help her in future engagement with services and professionals.

I feel that because I was able to have a long time with you. Set days, times, location really helped. The fact you were really patient, kind, understanding, compassionate with. It has given me hope for the future.

—Lizzy

Preparing to End Therapy

During the later stages of Lizzy's complaint process, there were a lot of sessions where we did not yet have the replies we were waiting for and Lizzy did not have any other particular issues that she wanted to work on. Things were relatively calm for Lizzy in her life outside of therapy, and we decided to work on a positive piece of artwork as a way of bringing therapy to an end and to think about what would come next for Lizzy when the complaint was resolved. During some of our early sessions, we had worked together to paint a mandala canvas, as a calming activity when she was feeling overwhelmed and did not want to focus on anything too difficult during the session. We revisited this idea, and Lizzy and I worked over a number of weeks to co-create a canvas painting of Sunflowers, which Lizzy said made her feel *"hopeful"*. Lizzy was extremely proud of the Sunflower canvas once it was completed and asked that we try to get it displayed somewhere others could see it. This canvas has been put onto the wall in the Community Learning Disabilities Team reception area at Lizzy's request along with a short piece of writing explaining the meaning of her picture.

Upon the completion of her complaint, it seemed that the therapy was coming to a natural end, as Lizzy had found out all she could about her accident. I had spent time in supervision reflecting on how to approach the ending of therapy with Lizzy, given that we had worked together for such a long time, and I envisioned that this might be a difficult process for her. Dunn et al. (2024) discuss the potential for therapeutic endings to be experienced by people with learning disabilities as a loss and suggest that in order to alleviate the feeling of loss, endings should be well planned, include reflection on emotions and highlight a continuity of care from a wider MDT or the individuals' support system. With this in mind, I had planned a phased ending process for Lizzy that would allow time for her to process the ending of our work and to consider how others would support her after therapy.

However, to my surprise, when Lizzy arrived for her session the next week, she came with her notebook at the ready and had decided her own ending date, which would be 3 weeks later. We spent some time thinking about how to spend our last session and how to review her artwork (of which there was a very large amount). Lizzy spoke about some of the more difficult images she had made in our sessions, saying that she did not want to keep those, and joked that perhaps she could use a shredder to destroy them. I told Lizzy that if she wanted to shred her unwanted pieces of work, I could facilitate this, and it became part of the plan for our final session.

Something felt right to ask for that date. And I felt like I had the choice of be able to destroy or keep my drawing and choose to destroy as it was the end of the chapter And new beginning.

—Lizzy

When our final session arrived, Lizzy found reviewing her artwork to be difficult at times but was able to choose the pieces she wanted to keep. Lizzy chose to shred artworks relating to her accident, past relationship and anything which she felt was negative. The process of shredding her unwanted artwork was very satisfying for Lizzy and she was visibly pleased that she was able to do this in our final session. It seemed an appropriate and symbolic final act to help Lizzy to move on from this

Figure 9.4 Photograph of Lizzy's artwork called: "There is always hope in life".

difficult chapter in her life, and to move forward, taking with her a collection of personalised resources to use and share in the next part of her journey.

Conclusion

To end this chapter, I will share some words from Lizzy, submitted to an organisational bulletin to describe her experiences of art therapy, and her reflections on our Sunflower canvas (Figure 8.4):

Me and my art therapist have tackled a challenging piece of work together. My art therapist made sessions easier through art, drawing, painting and glitter... Since having this opportunity of expressing myself through art and having the right worker who has been patient and calm and understands my needs... Giving me hope for the future. And opening my eyes to how good art therapy can work for me.

—Lizzy

There is always Hope in Life
Sunflowers to me represent growth, strength, hope and accomplishment.

—Lizzy

References

Department of Health (DH), (1983, Amended 2007, c. 12). *Mental Health Act (England).* Available at: Mental Health Act 2007 (legislation.gov.uk) (Accessed 12 February 2024).

Dunn, Y., Summers, S. J., & Dagnan, D. (2024). Facilitating transformative endings: Therapists' experience of ending therapy with people with intellectual disabilities—An interpretative phenomenological analysis. *Journal of Applied Research in Intellectual Disabilities*, 37(2), e13162. https://doi.org/10.1111/jar.13162

Hackett, S. S., Ashby, L., Parker, K., Goody, S., & Power, N. (2017). UK art therapy practice-based guidelines for children and adults with learning disabilities. *International Journal of Art Therapy*, 22(2), 84–94. https://doi.org/10.1080/17454832.2017.1319870

Local Authority Social Services and National Health Service Complaints (England) Regulations 2009. Available at: The Local Authority Social Services and National Health Service Complaints (England) Regulations 2009 (legislation.gov.uk) (Accessed 20 February 2023).

Miller, S. M., Ludwick, J., & Colucy Krcmar, C. (2020). Professional considerations for art therapists supporting the work of people with intellectual disabilities. *Art Therapy*, 37(2), 83–87. https://doi.org/10.1080/07421656.2020.1757376

Power, N., Harrison, T. L., Hackett, S., & Carr, C. (2023). Art therapy as a treatment for adults with learning disabilities who are experiencing mental distress: A configurative systematic review with narrative synthesis. *The Arts in Psychotherapy*, 88, 102088. https://doi.org/10.1016/j.aip.2023.102088.

Zubala, A., & Hackett, S. (2020). Online art therapy practice and client safety: A UK-wide survey in times of COVID-19. *International Journal of Art Therapy*, 25(4), 161–171. https://doi.org/10.1080/17454832.2020.1845221

Chapter 10

Finding Connection Using Attachment-Based Art Psychotherapy in Secure Care

My Experience of Working with a Young Man with Limited Verbal Communication in Long-Term Segregation

Mizuho Koizumi

Positionality Statement

I (Mizuho Koizumi) am a Japanese woman without learning disabilities who speaks English as a second language, working as an Art Psychotherapist in the United Kingdom (UK). The man (Jayden) whose story I share in this case vignette has limited verbal communication skills. His voice is shown in images of his artwork and through my description of the creative process in art psychotherapy. Sometime the experience of being with Jayden, I have understood, as being unconsciously projected material located in the artmaking, which may relate to his experiences of complex trauma which could not be verbalised.

Jayden gave me permission to show his artwork and to write about his life. He signed an easy-read consent form, which I created to be accessible for him. His family also gave me verbal and email consent to write this chapter. The multidisciplinary team in the organisation where I work also agreed to this chapter being written. I will use the term 'patient' to refer to Jayden, as he was an inpatient in a forensic setting, receiving treatment for his mental health.

Introduction

When I started working as a trainee forensic art psychotherapist, my first lesson was: *never assume anything,* which became my mantra. Everyone has a different background, life experiences, and communication ability. This shapes how they see the world and the people in it. I learned too, how trauma could further compound someone's ability to connect. A rigid mind would not help me to empathise with individuals with complex histories. I am particularly drawn to working with people with communication difficulties because of my experience as an immigrant. When I arrived in the UK, I was a young adult with limited English skills and no social status. It was a challenging experience not having my voice; I felt I was regressing – a child's communication ability in an adult's body. I experienced embarrassment, humiliation, and anger with how some people undermined

DOI: 10.4324/9781003350736-14

me because I was unable to express myself. I know I had these feelings in common with my patients whose communication challenges impacted their experiences. It was not only the language issues but cultural differences in communication style that were also a barrier for me. For instance, in my cultural background, people often have a pause before responding. I was used to thinking first before answering, but many people I met in the UK saw this as a lack of understanding English.

My supervisor, when I was still a trainee, wrote: "Working with intellectual disabilities in a locked setting is like working in the dark" (Rothwell, 2015, p. 18). Her words have stayed with me. My work is to look for a light in the dark and search for hidden gold that has yet to be discovered within the individual. The unspoken voice may be heard, seen, and felt using all senses when working with people with communication differences. For me, it is a touching and fascinating experience. This is how I have tried to find connections with the patients I work with.

Context

Currently, I work with people with learning disabilities and autism (LDA) in a Forensic Psychiatric Inpatient Unit in London. It was on one of these wards, a Medium Secure Unit, where I worked with Jayden (pseudonym). An entire multidisciplinary team supported Jayden, and the treatment included psychiatry, speech and language therapy, and occupational therapy, alongside art psychotherapy.

All patients we work with are sectioned under the Mental Health Act 1983, and the majority have either been diverted from the criminal justice system straight to our hospital or transferred from prison. Some patients have no criminal record, but their diagnosed mental disorder(s) are deemed to require treatment in the hospital.

Before being Sectioned by a court, most of this patient group depended on their family or an institutional facility. I often wonder if there was better support earlier; for families from a range of education, health, and social care services, if some of these patients may never have arrived in this locked environment. Patients with learning disabilities and/or autism are likely to stay with us, in forensic services, longer than patients without. This is because they are more likely to need a greater level of support, including future housing arrangements, before they can return to live safely in the community.

Supporting Patients; Supporting the Team

In my clinical experience, caring for vulnerable adults often generates conflict between members of the care team. The patients' dependent lives can lead to infantilisation, where the staff become the decision-makers. This could reduce the sense of self-control and advocacy for patients, which is particularly relevant in a forensic setting, in which risk is strictly managed. For all staff in forensic settings, our professional training, unique life experiences, and socio-cultural beliefs will influence aspects of our professional attitude. In addition, the patient's life experiences and family background, particularly when trauma has been experienced, may be re-lived within the forensic setting. Past relationships and ways of interacting may be projected onto the staff, which can divide the patient's care team. These challenging dynamics manifest distinctly within the restrictive forensic psychiatric setting, and especially in the LDA Service, where communication can be limited. The splitting of opinions generates extended meetings and disagreements between the team. Staff may become burnt-out emotionally and physically from working in such a challenging environment (Chung et al., 2009). Therefore, teams must have a confidential, safe space to speak about their feelings without judgment (O'Driscoll, 2014). Our daily safety huddle and monthly reflective practice are regular spaces for us to share our feelings.

Jayden

Jayden is a young man of mixed heritage in his twenties with co-morbid diagnoses of mild learning disability, autism, and challenging behaviour. He also has speech, language, and communication difficulties, including echolalia. He came to us following an incident of 'arson with intent to harm' and a significant violent assault on a female staff member. He is the sole patient placed onto a fully staffed forensic ward, as his risk of violence was deemed too severe for him to be on a populated ward.

During childhood, Jayden's parents were not together. His mother suffered from a mental health condition and struggled to look after him. At age six, he was taken into the care of Social Services. He was placed into various foster care families, but none of them could keep him long, and before arriving to us, he was in a children's home. Pictures in his photo album showed him smiling, surrounded by many peers and staff celebrating a birthday. He told me each name while looking at the pictures. It seemed a happy place, but he had to leave when he reached 18 years old.

Day-to-day he used very few words to communicate, but he spoke sentences fluently when acutely agitated. Jayden was easily triggered and responded with aggression, and as a result, staff were often injured. The front-line nursing team were becoming burnt-out, and the ward, at times, needed additional staff resource to rota enough staff each shift. It felt like we were driving a vehicle in the dark, without directions.

We observed him and shared our experiences of what we knew about Jayden. Once, the team heard Jayden shouting: *"Don't bring a belt!"*. We wondered whether he experienced a flashback, but there was no way to find out for certain.

Jayden could not tell many of his stories; not all of his history was available to me. It was apparent that he was a young man who had experienced prominent childhood trauma, and he could not regulate his anxiety.

Clinical Approach: Attachment-Based & Trauma-Informed Art Psychotherapy

Disability psychotherapy highlights the potential links between adverse events in childhood and emotional development (Cooke & Sinason, 1998; Buchanan, 1991) which may be experienced as early developmental trauma and impact a person across their life. My clinical practice uses a growth-based reparatory approach that takes place over several years. This is informed by Frankish's (2016) approach to trauma treatment in psychotherapy, which requires "an attachment figure (the therapist) and working through of past trauma" (Frankish, 2016, p. 110). In attachment-based psychotherapy (Brisch, 2012), developing the therapeutic relationship involves building a "therapeutic bond" (Brisch, 2012, p. 100) through reciprocal interaction, which references the early bond relationship between mother and infant, building on the foundational work of Stern (1985).

Art psychotherapists have the advantage of using art as an aid to help people address complex emotional problems and process traumatic memories. I spent much time thinking and preparing for sessions. I was influenced by Corbett (2018) who advised using creativity, playfulness, and judgment of boundaries surrounding the work depending on the patient's level of disability. I also anticipated the long-term nature of our work, as leaving Jayden prematurely could be another rejection, which would be more hurtful than helpful.

The Beginning of Our Therapeutic Relationship

On the ward, Jayden's multi-disciplinary team supported him with many areas of life, including producing visual resources to communicate with him and provide necessary information related to his care. Meanwhile, my aim in art psychotherapy was to support him to find his voice and explore how he could safely express his inner world.

I met Jayden as a newly qualified Art Psychotherapist. Then, at the start of my career, our relationship became a significant learning experience for me. Jayden always had an interest in Japanese culture. In the first session, he pointed at me and said: *"Japanese"*. I said: *"Yes, I am Japanese. Is that good or bad?"* I made a hand gesture of thumbs up and then thumbs down. He paused, then said, *"Good"*, with his thumbs up. This was enough to confirm we would start working together.

We began meeting twice weekly; at least three staff were present for safety in every session. He did not maintain eye contact in the first meetings, sniffed staff's hands, and made grunting sounds. I laid out some basic art materials (paper, colourful pens, crayons, and pastels) on the table. He wrote 'SMTV' on paper, and I asked what this referred to. It was 'Saturday Morning Television', a children's programme he knew and liked. I printed several pictures from SMTV in advance of the next session. This enabled us to make our next connection. He chose what he wanted, and we stuck them down to create a collage. The SMTV images enabled Jayden to see that I had understood something he shared about his history. The programme also included Pokémon and Power Rangers, which are Japanese. Jayden indicated that he liked them and acknowledged that I was Japanese too, which was a safe and happy connection.

In these early weeks, Jayden would come to the art table and wait for my instruction. Frequently, he would say *"finish"* and leave the session abruptly. At first, I didn't know why. I wondered if Jayden felt a need to take control by disengaging (Rothwell, 2015). I knew I needed to adapt to meet Jayden's needs.

Jayden's verbal communication was limited, and I would rely on his facial expression, body movement, and tone of voice to try to understand him. I also had my bodily responses as communication. Now I understood that I could feel his anxiety as though it was my own, like tuning in to the same radio channel. I felt frustrated when Jayden repeated the same words, and I could not understand what he meant. Seeing his irritation grow was like watching boiling water in a saucepan. I felt rushed, I had to do something to stop it from boiling over; my reaction could make him go either way. I sensed Jayden's annoyance in our inability to understand each other. I experienced powerful feelings of *countertransference*, a useful tool for therapists to understand the patient's feelings through our own responses (Sinason, 2010). Trying to hide my nervousness, I spoke calmly, although my hands shook.

Also at this time, I noticed that our sessions were often terminated by the observing staff. It appeared that everyone felt intolerant of our powerful non-verbal communication, afraid perhaps. I felt incompetent as a clinician when the sessions were abruptly ended. It was hard to contain not only Jayden's and my anxiety but also the staff team's perception.

We persisted, session after session. Jayden began to get used to seeing me regularly at a consistent time. It was predictability and perseverance to communicate which seemed to contain his anxiety gradually. I also learned to tell the team that I needed to be in control of ending the session, and like Jayden, the staff started to accept me more.

Finding his Voice Using Clay: Trauma and 'Projective Identification'

A significant moment when trust deepened in the therapeutic relationship involved sensory work with flat clay. Jayden used match sticks to poke into the clay (Figure 10.1). Jayden became engrossed in this and made slow, decisive movements. As he worked, I could see the many old scars from cigarette burns on his hands from childhood. I noticed his facial expression had changed, he seemed distraught. He could not explain what had happened but appeared to remember something. I experienced powerful emotions watching him with the clay and said: *"It looks painful"*, and Jayden responded: *"Painful"*. Rather than just repeating my words, he appeared to embody this traumatic memory using the art materials. I was able to mirror it through my words, which he acknowledged verbally. Jayden knew I saw an aspect of his abusive history that he could not verbalise.

After the session, I had my supervision and burst into tears, which had never happened before. I realised it was projective identification (Klein, 1946), a defence mechanism in which the patient splits part of the self that they find intolerable and projects it onto the psychotherapist unconsciously, so they feel these feelings. Jayden needed to protect himself from the pain. The supervision was a safe space to understand where the overpowering emotions came from and differentiate what was mine from his. Supervision with an experienced supervisor who specialised

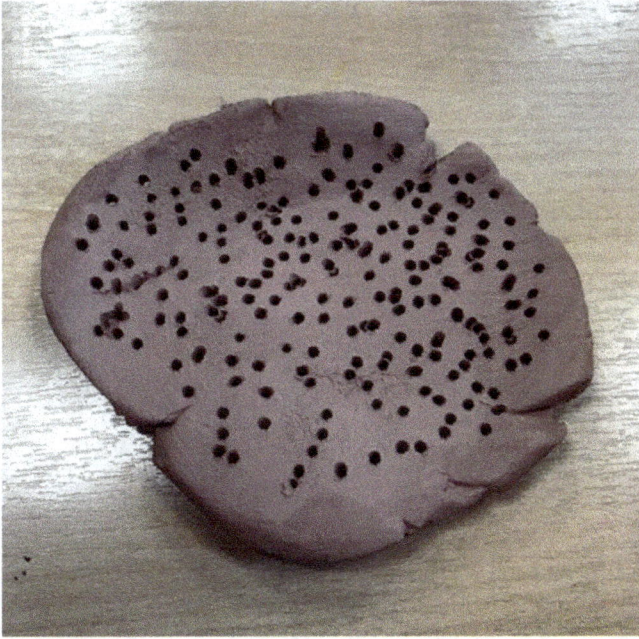

Figure 10.1 Photograph of clay object made by Jayden.

in non-verbal communication was vital in my early therapeutic relationship with Jayden.

I also undertook long-term personal art psychotherapy, which helped me to identify particular art materials that may precipitate memories. For example, I found that clay is a primitive and raw material that feels like skin.

Sharing his History: Identity and Collaboration

Jayden often repeated the words *"British Airways, Jamaican Airlines"* as a metaphor for his dual heritage identity. He would also say: *"Pack a suitcase"*, which made staff concerned that he was agitated and may ask to leave the locked ward environment. Then, the team discovered from his grandmother that he had travelled to Jamaica on holiday when he was younger. I wondered what these words meant to Jayden.

In one session, I asked him if he would make an aeroplane with me. He nodded enthusiastically, which I had never seen him do before. We began making model aeroplanes from plastic water bottles wrapped in Modroc (Figure 10.2), with each of us pointing out what needed doing next. Working side-by-side enabled us to share responsibility in co-creating our models. We also made a suitcase and through imaginative play discussed what he would like to pack for his travels. I entered

Figure 10.2 'British Airways, Jamaican Airlines' photograph of aeroplane sculptures by Jayden and Mizuho.

these aeroplanes into the *Koestler Arts Awards*. Jayden received a 'Commended Award', and we displayed the certificate on his ward. We also held an in-house art exhibition with his consent; he was proud for other patients to see his work. This was particularly important to foster a sense of community for him.

Communication through the Body and Insecure Attachment

After working intensively for two and a half years, Jayden's attachment issues began to emerge. He verbally 'pushed me away' when I told him I would be away for ten days. For the first time, he did not want me to join a walk with other staff saying: *"Bye, Mizuho"*. Moreover, Jayden stopped engaging in art psychotherapy after the Christmas break. He said: *"No art therapy"*, and sometimes: *"No Mizuho"*. Staff were concerned about the risk to me, but I still went to his ward and spent an hour there to ensure he knew I was around if he changed his mind. This continued for three months, until Easter came.

Jayden gradually re-engaged with me and agreed to return to the off-ward therapy room. On session 167, I arrived on the ward to collect him. One of the escort staff asked me if we should take Jayden's iPad with us, and I said: *"No, we don't need it"*. I knew Jayden's iPad was precious to him, but I did not think to ask him about it. A few seconds later, Jayden ran behind me and shoved me forcefully in my back and shoulder. There was no warning. We all felt shocked. I turned to him and asked: *"What's wrong?"* as calmly as possible. I cannot recall clearly what he said. He was angry and shouted the F-word. Staff responded swiftly and moved Jayden to his bedroom.

Afterwards, it felt surreal; his impulsive reaction overwhelmed me. Although my body ached, my brain focused on analysing the incident. Something triggered him, and I wanted to understand it as soon as possible, because talking to Jayden about past incidents had been problematic. With the nursing team's help, I returned to speak to him later that day. Jayden looked very remorseful. He sat with his back to me, curled up, and was staring at the floor. Occasionally he looked towards me while I talked to the nursing staff in the nursing station. The team reported that he did not believe what he did to me. Jayden said: *"Sorry Mizuho"*. I also apologised to him for hurting his feelings. I guessed that it was some misunderstanding about his iPad. I told Jayden I would never take his precious iPad away. His body became tense for a second, but he listened to my words carefully.

There were many physical assaults on nursing staff members, each time we reflected on the incident and adjusted his care plan as a team. I continued to work with him but was always aware of the risk. Another incident happened the following year, again in the Easter period. After spending one hour together in the art therapy room, on the way back to the ward, he suddenly pushed me in my back, and I was injured again. The escort staff appeared horrified. I hid my shock and said: *"What's wrong?"* He shouted: *"Because you are naughty!"* I was unable to find out what this meant to Jayden. It was a painful discovery for me, but we had learned that the Easter bank holiday season destabilised his mood. As a team, we suspected a traumatic event had happened during the bank holiday period. Although we could not know for certain, we learnt from these incidents and proactively planned some fun activities for him to redirect his focus before the next bank holiday season at Easter.

Attachment theory helped me to understand the motivation behind Jayden's behaviour. Brisch (2012) suggests that if a psychotherapist offers more closeness than a patient can handle, they may feel threatened and this "may trigger a premature desire for separation and/or more distance in the therapeutic relationship" (p. 103). I also considered again the impact of past trauma on Jayden's relationships in the present. Here, disorganised attachment (Main & Solomon, 1986), which may be more common in this population (Hamadi et al., 2019) and can lead to a lack of trust and hyper-vigilance as an adult, supported me to make sense of the assaults.

I suffered from the shoulder injury for two years after these incidents. Whenever I felt pain in my shoulder, it reminded me of Jayden, and I wondered if he also had experienced a lasting pain but could not let other people know. It felt like he unconsciously expressed his pain to me by injuring my body. How could I ensure we could feel safe again in each other's presence? Jayden liked to hug male staff members, particularly those with a large build. I could not give him physical containment through a hug, but I wanted to try something so that he could relax with me. I found that body massage could reduce autistic children's symptoms, such as anxiety, and help them bond with carers (Walaszek et al., 2017). With his agreement, I experientially gave Jayden a back massage using a hand massage tool, which he liked. Then I started to ask if he would like this in the closing of our sessions; he never refused. It became a ritual to end the session. The ward staff also adopted the idea and occasionally gave Jayden a massage.

Life after Secure Care?

Jayden's lifestyle has changed over the years. Nowadays, with staff members escorting him, he goes swimming, cycling, shopping, watches football games, visits museums, and experiences activities in the community. The commissioner of his care acknowledged his risk reduction and commented that as a team we have transformed his quality of life. These changes in his quality of life align with the most recent UK recommendations for this population detained in hospitals (Department of Health & Social Care, 2023).

Together, we have used various materials and sensory art-based activities in the last six years. In art psychotherapy, we explored his senses, for instance, using scented pens, painting with spray bottles, and making slime and utilising sand trays. We have also made pancakes and gingerbread houses, grown plants from seeds, carved a pumpkin head, jet-washed a car, and shopped for his new trainers, to name just a few of the non-art activities we have engaged in to strengthen our relationship. I also accompanied him on his first bus ride as an adult, which was an intense experience for both of us and for the wider team, as we had no idea how he would react on public transport. It went well and became the turning point in his care. His psychiatrist at the time was excited and commented: *"I'm over the moon"*.

He has a discharge plan, which we've been working towards for the last few years. We have voiced strongly that his subsequent placement must be his permanent home. Jayden calls the Medium Secure Unit his *"home"*, and it is the place where he has stayed the longest. We have invested time to understand his needs and adjusted our communication strategies to provide the best care possible for him. It works, but the problems could re-occur when staff or the environment change. He will always need people who understand him and can create safe relationships with him in the long term.

Conclusion

Jayden has experienced many ruptures and repairs (Bowlby, 1988) in relationships with numerous staff members. His adverse early childhood attachments were reshaped through healthier interactions on the ward, and he became more resilient and tolerant. To prepare for healthy separation, we have gradually reduced our session frequency. Jayden and I have recently been creating photo albums, which include many photographs of him visiting places with staff members. I print these pictures and we place them in his album together, so he knows, I know what he has been doing. We have started the second album and will continue until he moves to the community. He will take the albums to remember the many smiles he came across.

I feel privileged to have witnessed Jayden grow and become *"a man, no boy"*, as he often said. I also grew as an art psychotherapist, with thanks to him, I continue as a specialist in this area. Art psychotherapy with Jayden was complex, challenging, and painful, but he taught me it was possible to change his life for the better if his needs were met. I learned to listen to the person's voice, using all my senses, and together we built shared experiences.

References

Bowlby, J. (1988). *A Secure Base: Parent-Child Attachment and Healthy Human Development.* 1st Edition. New York: Basic Books.

Brisch, K. H., (2012). *Treating Attachment Disorders: From Theory to Therapy.* 2nd Edition. New York: Guilford Publications, Inc.

Buchanan, A., and Wilkins, R. (1991). Sexual Abuse of the Mentally Handicapped: Difficulties in Establishing Prevalence. *Psychiatric Bulletin,* [online] 15(10), pp. 601–605. https://doi.org/10.1192/pb.15.10.601.

Chung, M.C., and Harding, C. (2009). Investigating Burnout and Psychological Well-Being of Staff Working with People with Intellectual Disabilities and Challenging Behaviour: The Role of Personality. *Journal of Applied Research in Intellectual Disabilities,* 22(6), pp. 549–560. https://doi.org/10.1111/j.1468-3148.2009.00507.x

Cooke, L. B., and Sinason, V. (1998). Abuse of People with Learning Disabilities and other Vulnerable Adults. *Advances in Psychiatric Treatment,* 4(2), pp. 119–125. https://doi.org/10.1192/apt.4.2.119

Corbett, A. (2018). *Intellectual Disability and Psychotherapy.* London: Routledge.

Department of Health (1983). *Mental Health Act* [online]. Available at: https://www.legislation.gov.uk/ukpga/1983/20/contents

Department of Health and Social Care (2023). *Baroness Hollins 'final Report': My Heart Breaks-Solitary Confinement in Hospital Has No Therapeutic Benefit for People with a LearningDisability and Autistic People.* [online]. Available at https://www.gov.uk/government/publications/independent-care-education-and-treatment-reviews-final-report-2023/baroness-hollins-final-report-my-heart-breaks-solitary-confinement-in-hospital-has-no-therapeutic-benefit-for-people-with-a-learning-disability-an

Frankish, P. (2016). *Disability Psychotherapy: An Innovative Approach to Trauma-Informed Care.* London: Routledge.

Hamadi, L Hamadi, H. K. (2019). Are People with an Intellectual Disability at Increased Risk of Attachment Difficulties? A Critical Review. *Journal of Intellectual Disabilities,* 2(1), pp. 114–130. https://doi.org/10.1177/1744629519864772

Klein, M. (1946). Notes on Some Schizoid Mechanisms. *The International Journal of Psychoanalysis,* 27, 99–110.

Main, M., and Solomon, J. (1986). Discovery of an Insecure-Disorganized/Disoriented Attachment Pattern. In T. B. Brazelton, and M. W. Yogman (Eds.), *Affective Development in Infancy.* pp. 95–124. Westport, CT: Ablex Publishing.

O'Driscoll, D. (2014). The Case for Dr Freud. *Learning Disability Practice,* 17(3), p. 11. https://doi.org/10.7748/ldp2014.03.17.3.11.s11

Rothwell, K. (2015). 'Disobedient Objects: Group Art Therapy for Male Patients with Mild Learning Disabilities in a Locked Environment. *Group Analysis,* 48(1), pp. 16–37. https://doi.org/10.1177/0533316415569661e

Sinason, V. (2010). *Mental Handicap and the Human Condition: An Analytic Approach to Intellectual Disability.* 2nd Edition. London: Free Association Books.

Stern, D. (1985). *The Interpersonal World of the Infant: A View from Psychoanalysis and Developmental Psychology.* 1st Edition. New York: Basic Books.

Walaszek, R., Maśnik, N., Marszałek, A., Walaszek, K., and Burdacki, M. (2017). Massage Efficacy in the Treatment of Autistic Children – A Literature Review. *International Journal of Developmental Disabilities*, 64(4–5), pp. 225–229. https://doi.org/10.1080/20473869. 2017.1305139

Chapter 11

The Creative Corridor

A Transitional Space between Arts Therapy and Educational Creative Practice

Tania J. Rose

Positionality Statement

I (Tania J. Rose) have written this chapter as a neurodivergent white woman, working as a teaching artist, creative collaborator, educator, and Arts Psychotherapist. My writing includes the narrative account of a now-deceased artist with cognitive differ-ability (learning disabilities) who was unable to provide permission for the telling of their story. I have included the words of this artist in direct quotation marks. The ethical dilemma as to whether to share their story was significant for me and I considered a wide variety of factors, including the voicing of their ongoing challenges faced in their life in not being heard. It was for this very reason that I decided to push ahead and write about their experiences, with the sincere belief that this publication could serve not only as preserving their personal story but also by providing an example of different ways a voice may be heard.

Introduction

I invite you on a journey to visit a *Creative Corridor* between arts therapy and educational creative practice, where unique forms of expression emerge and evolve into novel modes of communication and genuine authenticity. I will introduce you to "Paul", a creative artist with cognitive differences, and share his journey towards empowerment through creative process. Join me to consider the ethics of sharing another's story and examine some of the challenges faced by people with cognitive differ-ability (learning disabilities), as we contemplate communication and accessibility. Let's explore a person's rights and the impact that historical and contemporary sociocultural systems may have on an individual's voice. Moreover, we will contemplate the significance of creativity and its perceived worth, envisioning a future where inclusivity and access define the landscape of artistic endeavours.

In our culture of meaning-making, I chose to draw from the word *difference* in place of disability. I come to this position via two paths; through my experiences working with others labelled as disabled and through my own experience of

DOI: 10.4324/9781003350736-15

recently becoming labelled. Differ-ability is a non-ableist term replacing disability (Makkawy, 2018; Smith, 2021), and I choose to use the term cognitive differ-ability for this reason.

The Rights of a Person to Share and Express

The United Nations Convention on the Rights of People with Disability or UNCRPD (United Nations, 2006) recognises that any person has the right to make their own choices and participate in decisions that concern themselves, including rights to enjoyment and belonging. It also raises concerns that persons living with disabilities continue to face discrimination and roadblocks in participating and engaging in empowering opportunities.

It has been suggested that society may need to provide solutions to problems that exist due to cultural norms and perspectives on assistance (Arstein-Kerslake, 2018). Whilst the limitations of the medical model hold the narrow view that the pathology itself is the reason for the inability to activate independence (Bunbury, 2019), some argue that a rigid society disables a person's autonomy and self-advocacy, not taking into account the person as a whole (Degener, 2016). One could also assert that even through Convention ratification, interpretation of the rights of decision-making may not adequately align with the spirit of the intention (Watson, 2016) and that people with impaired cognitive function are often regarded with a simplicity which does not reflect the complexity of their lives or their communication needs.

The ethics of advocacy are sometimes lost in real-world situations where those entrusted with the support of a person may remain ignorant of the rights of a person (Bruce & Aylward, 2021). Additionally, the limitations of accessible support may exacerbate assumptions of a person's capacity (Scior et al., 2020). Communication and empowerment can take many forms, and one could argue that as a society we can appear stuck on the expectation that an individual should conform to a standardised view of communication. Let us consider for a moment the creative modalities of self-expression as a way of connection, interchange, and articulation of one's experience in the world (Jones, 2022). Perhaps there is a space where we can acknowledge an intersection between the world as it is on the outside and the world as it is on the inside and develop a mode of transmission between those worlds.

An Ethical Dilemma

I had known Paul for over four years (his name and details have been changed to protect his identity). We met when I was contracted as a teaching artist by an arts organisation to teach a weekly accessible theatre class. He first introduced himself as 45 years old and living in a "group home" (a supported living home shared with others with cognitive differ-abilities). I came to know him as having a gentle nature, an infectious smile, and a routine of considerable handshaking. I learned that Paul passed away some years ago. Not knowing his personal details outside of his first name on a theatre-class attendance sheet, I was unable to ascertain his next of kin to discuss sharing his story and gaining permission.

During our time together, Paul had told me he had no other family members and that he understood that *"the government is my father"*. Without details, it would be impossible to search for leads to secure consent. In considering the ethical dilemma I found myself in, I spoke to academic peers and deliberated for months over whether to move forward with bringing Paul's story public. There is, perhaps, a cruel irony in that the journey of individuals such as Paul is often lost in our history amidst the glamour of other stories. One's experiences then may become a type of hidden knowledge, known only by those present at events as they unfold. I lean into the rationale that if we don't speak about these experiences and give them voice, it's likely no one will ever know and pose a question: how can we learn about something not visible? In my role as a creative facilitator, I often learn far more than I teach. I consider that if society learned from those who have differ-ability, perhaps we would see the world through broader brushstrokes.

One might argue that this is a philosophical debate, but one that I nonetheless feel is important to bring to the fore. In my consideration, I thought a publication might not be the most appropriate forum, though if not this forum, then where? Perhaps there are other places where we can explore a voice and how it might be differently represented. Perhaps current models and ableist assumptions might limit the depth of knowledge we could access. Perhaps these questions can be reflected on as we search for meaning and answers, as we move from understanding to a deeper experience of knowing.

I gave considerable thought to Paul and his expressions of being heard in my deliberation. The themes he raised centred around recognition, sharing his plight and his experiences, remaining unheard, and the pain of silence. Paul's story has led me to ask many questions, to consider how we might be informed, and how the recognition of an individual's contribution can be broader in honouring their experience. Thinking differently is the overarching concept I am reminded of through my work. In addition, I consider that the context of a person can be contained in the ripples of change that radiate out from them, to places they may never go, to people they may never meet, with the potential to instigate positive change. In collaboration with the editors of this book, I made the decision to go ahead and share his story to give his voice a greater reach.

Paul's Story

In my first few sessions of the theatre class, I noticed Paul didn't participate in many activities, spending considerable time watching others in the group and only occasionally joining in. I considered his witnessing to be his participation style. Paul wasn't much of a conversationalist, and it took time to get to know him. Challenged by well-meaning support staff, it took several months of persistence to provide Paul with space for uninterrupted communication between just the two of us.

One session the class broke into groups and Paul sat in his usual witnessing seat. I sat next to him, and we shared some observations and a few laughs. I enquired why he chose to watch the groups rather than participate, hearing that he didn't like people telling him what to do. He wanted to do his own things. I asked Paul if he would be interested in creating a scene on his own to which he replied he would, but not to show the other groups. We both agreed that this was acceptable and for some time, Paul worked on his own improvisations during groupwork.

One day Paul seemed particularly agitated in theatre class. His support worker had informed me that his medication had changed, affecting his mood. He explained Paul had "unspecified intellectual and learning disabilities" and recently had begun having seizures again after 20 years seizure-free. Over the next few weeks, I noticed I felt uncomfortable with the communication style of Paul's support workers, witnessing Paul becoming increasingly dysregulated. Curiously, Paul spent much of this time at the furthest end of the room, looking down.

One morning, Paul was shouting at a support worker as they arrived, and soon after he walked briskly out of the room. I found him sitting in the foyer, crying, and I sat with him in silence. Eventually, he spoke to me about his acting, before talking about being *"bullied"* at his residence, being *"treated like a child"*, and being *"told off all the time"*. He said: *"Nobody understands me"*. He wished he could come every day to theatre class, expressing what he enjoyed about being here. He described annoyance with his doctor having changed his pills. Paul was convinced he wasn't having new seizures but instead daydreaming about theatre class. He said staff had told the doctor he was having *"absent seizures"* and that he would get annoyed with them when they broke his *"imaginings"*, shouting for them to leave him alone and stop bothering him. He suggested his doctor *"doesn't listen to my side"*, and now his new pills were giving him headaches, but he couldn't take headache tablets because *"there wouldn't be any left for everyone else"*. Paul told me he had had enough of everyone interfering, asking *"Why won't people just leave me alone?"*.

As we walked towards the door to the rehearsal room, Paul suddenly stopped walking and asked me if he could perform for the group after the break, which he used to create a performance work. Paul's performance of movement, dialogue, and vocalisations was extraordinary. When asked by group members what parts of it meant, Paul told them of his pain, his daydreaming, and of his need to be heard and have his feelings validated. He spoke of his frustration and anger, of the people around him treating him like a child, and he exposed the pain of his suffering. He shared all of this in the context of his performance.

Paul's performance and the discussion which followed deeply moved his peers, some of whom wept, whilst others punched the air in solidarity with acclamations of support. It was a powerful experience, with themes that resonated throughout the rest of our class time. At the end of class, Paul walked out of the room with an air unlike I had seen before; confident, calm, and laughing and talking with other members of the group. Paul's interactions with peers from that day forward seemed different. Given the opportunity, he began to perform his ideas regularly in front of the class and eventually began working in small groups, sometimes as a performer and even as a director. As time went on, Paul became a self-appointed mentor for new group members, explaining they could share the good things and the bad things in the group because everyone cared and would look after them. Paul advocated for others and sometimes delivered impromptu speeches on topics raised by other group members around self-advocacy, creativity, and the experience of disability. Paul found a new voice and developed a new way to be heard, to share, to self-advocate, and to create change.

The Label of Disability

Paul had been labelled disabled throughout his life. Unable to attend school and home-schooled by his single mother, he experienced barriers. A special school far from home was untenable, and his mother became ill. Paul reminisced about riding his bike to the library to borrow books until the librarian told him he couldn't come back without an adult, even though he was 18 years old. His mother died and he was moved into a home *"for idiots, they said"*, and *"against my wishes, you know"*. By this time Paul had a part-time job, having been the sole carer of his sick mother.

Paul's way of communicating with me was unconventional. He would often introduce topics via a series of gestural and somatic expressions to be later discussed in a conversational framework that incorporated whole-body gesturing and vocalised sounds. Paul taught me his language and was very clear in expressing his standpoint when he felt safe and supported but admitted that living within the disability system had taught him that expressing his will and frustration verbally could *"make people harm me"*, adding *"I don't want to be harmed"*.

A Creative Corridor

Over three decades of encounters with generous creative individuals living with cognitive differ-ability (or learning disabilities), I have discovered a transitional space between creative skill-building and arts therapy, which I call a *Creative Corridor*. To best understand this corridor, it is helpful to first consider what arts training and arts therapy are. Arts training focuses on skill-building outcomes and improved performance in a specific creative domain (Barrett et al., 2013; Posner & Patoine, 2009). Examples of this might be teaching the art of acting and voice-work aimed towards creating a theatrical performance showcasing these skills. Although there has been some conjecture as to a definition of creative therapies, a subscription to mental health outcomes notably aligns with creative therapeutic interpretations (Ulman, 2001). Whilst therapy using creative modalities may provide the exploration of a person's inner world with a therapeutic intent (Malchiodi, 2005), the *Creative Corridor* work makes no assumptions that an artist needs help, fixing, or support but rather acknowledges the artist's potential for authentic experiences of autonomy within a creative context.

Training in an arts practice provides a functional framework for the *Creative Corridor*, a schema free from therapeutic intervention. In this space, there can emerge a happening where the process of learning discipline-specific creative techniques transports the individual into an empowered position of exploration within and of the self. The teaching artist or facilitator considers the autonomy of the artist, assisting only with the emergence of a framework to apply a creative endeavour. Utilising a person-centred approach (Rogers, 1995) and following the artist's experience, the teaching artist or facilitator then moves to becoming the witness to the event, in and of itself a powerful alliance of the creative process. The overall experience can lead to previously unknown expressions of personal authenticity and communication, unconfined to a therapeutic context.

Just as in therapeutic practice, each emanation of this corridor will be unique. We can examine Paul's experience to identify several stages of emergence:

1 **The theme**: The artist (Paul) is provided an opportunity by the facilitator to consider important aspects to their unique experience. This is done using a person-centred approach of following the lead of the artist and remaining uninfluential (Paul expressed his experiences whilst I listened).
2 **The consideration**: The artist is given the opportunity, time, and space to explore their conceptualisation and examine which aspects resonate with the notion of a potential creative expression (Paul eventually moved from explaining his experience towards an urge to physically explore).
3 **The expressive exploration**: The artist moves into their creative modality autonomously (in Paul's case movement and performance) creating meaning-making and representation.
4 **The witnessing**: The artist presents the creative outcomes of their exploration (Paul's performance).
5 **The reflection**: The artist is provided with an opportunity to reflect on their experience (Paul invited discussion and reflection through a group process) and integrates it into their lived experience.

Though one might argue that this framework provides potentially therapeutic outcomes, it is not contained within a therapeutic model or cloistered within a therapy context. Rather it is explored as a creative process, expressed outwardly, in this case shared with an audience, and discussed as a creative expression. The transitional space of the *Creative Corridor* can provide personal explorative opportunities that may lead to the unearthing of new methods of creativity and expressing different aspects of the self.

Working within this *Creative Corridor* can be significant when working with people who have differences in self-expression or authenticity within a social construct of difference. Working within the *Creative Corridor* is not about intentionally helping a person heal or cope as perhaps in arts therapy, but rather it is about creating enabling conditions through a creative process, providing an alliance for a person exploring their voice in a world in which they may find attempts to silence them.

Creative Corridor work takes place with an artist working one-on-one with a teaching artist or facilitator with whom they have developed trust and positive rapport through a creative skill-building experience. What takes place will be unique to the individual, the creative discipline used, the facilitator, and the relationship between the artist and facilitator. For those who use verbal communication, the facilitator might begin by posing broad factual statement as a starting point. For example, "Here we are, in the acting space". It is vital for the facilitator to manage the time and space required by the artist, holding silence and stillness and resisting the urge to prompt a happening. For those facilitating a non-verbal *Creative Corridor*, it might begin with a gesture, a sound, or a movement which the facilitator has extracted from the artist's moments leading up to that moment. For example, the facilitator might hear that the artist arrives next to them and makes a loud exhale. This may then be mirrored by the facilitator as an invitation to a shared experience. Sometimes a dialogue may ensue in the form of an artist-led expression. A facilitator might become part of the artist's expression, such as when a dancer brings the facilitator into the dance space and instructs their involvement.

In many ways the artist becomes the teacher in the *Creative Corridor*, the facilitator following the artist moment by moment, becoming immersed in the artists' experience, conscientiously restricting any influence on the artist. This is a witnessing role, perhaps being a participant of the artists' experience is instructed to be so but allowing their own experience to be authentically shaped by the artist.

The Creative Corridor as a Transitional Space

I consider *Creative Corridor* work not to be specific to people who have been given a label of learning disabilities. The notion of opening-up experience rather than adding-on skills is the way I perceive working within the corridor. I spend time learning about each individual outside of teaching creative techniques. Much of the corridor work is providing an invitation for the artist to show and teach the facilitator. Through this transitional space, a person can bridge their actual experiences and their authentic expression within the context of their learning. Thus, they can form, explore, and express themselves in a way which is held with psychological safety, providing a vehicle for them to share with others, or alternatively explore inwardly. A person may use the *Creative Corridor* in any way they choose due to its loose framework. Herein lies its potential.

The *Creative Corridor* is not an intervention or therapy focused on changing or fixing the individual. In Paul's experience there is the premise that society was the disabling factor, and it was the harm from society's standpoint that required mitigation. In this instance, the therapeutic skills of the facilitator came into play, where a person-centred approach of safety and security provided a vehicle for authentic expression. However, therapeutic skills are only part of the picture. A facilitator must face their own ableism, conscientiously focused on understanding the context of the individual, and avoiding pitfalls, such as rescuing the artist by suggesting ideas, moving not at the artists' pace, or making assumptions. This is where a facilitator might benefit from professional supervision and peer support.

Unlike in arts therapy, Paul invited an audience, expressed himself as a performer, and invited participants to interact with his story, which in turn created the opportunity for new stories to emerge. Arts therapy does not generally provide this vehicle for unfacilitated collegial or peer interaction with the artist being the expert, yet one could also argue that there is therapeutic value in such a process. Creative education also does not in itself create this authentic transitional space, as it generally focuses on methodology, technique, and execution of skills, possibly run by practitioners with limited awareness of psychological experiences or disabling factors. From an educational-only standpoint, a participant is likely expected to regurgitate techniques, stay within a narrow instructional framework, and meet criteria directed towards an assumed outcome. Within the context of differ-ability, this then becomes another conformity risking attempt failures.

Paul's use of the *Creative Corridor* provided an avenue between his worlds of creativity, fantasy, and reality, embodying personal narratives diving outwards as an invitation to others to interact. He found an authentic voice here, springboarding towards his real-world experiences. Paul turned a history of obstruction into empowerment to not only advocate for himself but also to support others, providing both Paul and his peers with a living sense of inclusion and purpose.

The Importance of Finding a Voice and Moving Forward

An interdisciplinary approach to future support for people like Paul could recognise that modalities in creative practice can be important avenues for self-expression, communication, and autonomy, rather than the binary views of creative experiences being activity-based or therapeutic intervention. The power and importance of creative practice to harness meaningful individual expression could be used to enable a person to communicate experiences which better reflect the complexities and needs in their lives. In the future, we could do away with the constrained pigeon-holing of people via binary systems of can/can't or abled/disabled and simply be open to authentic communication and the sharing of experience.

Support programmes providing choice to individuals to access services which broaden their scope of support and experience may lead to empowerment and a greater voice in decision-making (Lakhani, McDonald & Zeeman, 2018). Government legislation may also help support a future commitment to accessible and inclusive communities and control over choice (Disability Inclusion Act for People with Disability, 2014). It is my hope that commitments such as these will result in real changes which reflect the actual needs and rights of the individual and provide opportunities to explore new ways of communicating and expressing an authentic sense of self.

Society has the potential to head towards a more humanistic approach in the future, where support systems steer away from iatrogenic harm and moral injuries often inflicted upon people living with differ-abilities by infantilising them. Enlightened professional practices across support networks could help establish more robust ethical principles which create alliances and support a wider perspective on the nature of identity and voice. For me, as an autistic academic and practitioner, these factors seem logical and achievable, free from the hierarchy of dictating who or how another person is in the world or what their identity should look like from a single-sided neurotypical perspective.

I imagine a time in the future when a person might go to their doctor and bring a painting to the session to explain how they feel about their treatment, or they might act out a scene to express their feelings about a service. In my world, these methods of communication are as normal and authentic as having a verbal conversation. Perhaps this concept is both naïve and too extraordinary to be braved by society, still I hope we will grow and mature as a community. For now, I can see how these ideas might seem astonishing, strange, and possibly even too incredible to some, but new ideas often are.

In Conclusion

Every person has a right to be heard, to give voice to their story, and to feel free to contribute to their own lives. It is important to acknowledge that different people discover and communicate their voices differently and to remain open to the authenticity sometimes brought about through unconventional methods such as the use of creativity as a medium for expression and even a *Creative Corridor* that might bridge the gap between worlds.

Paul's story highlights many things for me, not least of which is a person's right to express themselves with dignity and respect. Whilst governments and societies are moving towards a more inclusive attitude, we are still currently constrained by the perception of a person with differ-ability as being a person without something as opposed to a person having possibly more…more experiences, more challenges, and maybe more to express. Perhaps we could broaden our view to include creativity as a natural communication medium and find ways to incorporate new ideas into interdisciplinary practice.

The world of creativity is vitally important outside of educational and therapeutic settings, and perhaps the authentic embrace of inclusivity and access might unearth a richer and broader scope in the future of both communication and creative practice. Whilst we might be a long way from a utopia of expression that embraces communication approaches that reflect a wide diversity of differences, perhaps we can make a conscious effort to broaden our view of what it is to be a person and to express the human condition.

Acknowledgement

I recognise that my work and awareness have emerged through the generosity of those who have gone before me and have shared their knowledge and experiences, including those marginalised through social constructions of difference.

I acknowledge that I live and work on a number of indigenous lands, including Darug, Gundungarra, and Gadigal country, and pay my respects to the traditional custodians of country throughout Australia and their connections to land, sea, and community, and acknowledge all indigenous peoples. Always was, always will be.

References

Arstein-kerslake, A. (2018). Preface to disability human rights law. In A. Arstein-kerslake, *Disability Human Rights Law* (pp. vii). MDPI AG. https://doi.org/10.3390/books978-3-03842-388-1

Barrett, K. C., Ashley, R., Strait, D. L., & Kraus, N. (2013). Art and science: How musical training shapes the brain. *Frontiers in Psychology*, 4. https://sjdr.se/articles/10.16993/sjdr.741.

Bruce, C., & Aylward, M. L. (2021). Disability and self-advocacy experiences in university learning contexts. *Scandinavian Journal of Disability Research*, 23(1), 14–26. https://sjdr.se/articles/10.16993/sjdr.741

Bunbury, S. (2019). Unconscious bias and the medical model: How the social model may hold the key to transformative thinking about disability discrimination. *International Journal of Discrimination and the Law*, 19(1), 26–47. https://doi.org/10.1177/1358229118820742.

Degener, T. (2016). Disability in a human rights context. *Laws*, 5(3), 35. https://doi.org/10.3390/laws5030035.

Disability Inclusion Act for People with Disability, 2014 (New South Wales Government). Available at: https://legislation.nsw.gov.au/view/whole/html/inforce/current/act-2014-041

Jones, D. R. (2022). Reclaiming disabled creativity: How cultural models make legible the creativity of people with disabilities. *Culture & Psychology*, 28(4), 491–505. https://doi.org/10.1177/1354067X211066816

Lakhani, A., McDonald, D., & Zeeman, H. (2018). Perspectives of the national disability insurance scheme: Participants' knowledge and expectations of the scheme. *Disability and Society*, 33(5), 783–803. https://doi.org/10.1080/09687599.2018.1442321.

Makkawy, A. (2018). "Is that really our teacher professor person"? Working from the boundaries. In Jefress, M. (Ed.) *International Perspectives on Teaching with Disability: Overcoming Obstacles and Enriching Lives*, 1st Edition. Routledge (pp. 108–122). https://www.taylorfrancis.com/chapters/edit/10.4324/9781315099941-8/really-teacher-professor-person-working-boundaries-amin-makkawy

Malchiodi, C. A. (2005). Art therapy. In C. A. Malchiodi (Ed.), *Expressive Therapies* (pp. 16–45). Guilford Press.

Posner, M. I., & Patoine, B. (2009). How arts training improves attention and cognition. *Cerebrum*. The Dana Foundation (pp. 1–7). September 14, 2009. Available at: https://www.researchgate.net/publication/255655328_How_Arts_Training_Improves_Attention_and_Cognition.

Rogers, C. R. (1995). *On Becoming a Person: A Therapist's View of Psychotherapy*. Houghton Mifflin Harcourt.

Scior, K., Hamid, A., Hastings, R., Werner, S., Belton, C., Laniyan, A., Patel, M., & Kett, M. (2020). Intellectual disability stigma and initiatives to challenge it and promote inclusion around the globe. *Journal of Policy and Practice in Intellectual Disabilities*, 17(2), 165–175. Portico. https://doi.org/10.1111/jppi.12330.

Smith, S. (2021). What's in a word? Rephrasing and reframing disability. In Brown, N. (Ed.) *Lived Experiences of Ableism in Academia: Strategies for Inclusion in Higher Education* (pp. 73–90). Bristol University Press.

Ulman, E. (2001). Art therapy: Problems of definition. *American Journal of Art Therapy*, 40(1), 16.

United Nations Convention on the Rights of Persons with Disabilities, December 12, 2006, https://www.ohchr.org/en/hrbodies/crpd/pages/conventionrightspersonswithdisabilities.aspx.

Watson, J. (2016). Assumptions of decision-making capacity: The role supporter Attitudes play in the realisation of Article 12 for people with severe or profound intellectual disability. *Laws*, 5(1), 6. https://doi.org/10.3390/laws5010006.

Section 4

Connections

Chapter 12

Creating a Bridge between Clinical and Community Space

A Collaborative Project to Support Belonging for People with Learning Disabilities between Art Therapy and an Art Gallery

Shehnoor Ahmed

Positionality Statement

I (Shehnoor Ahmed) have written this chapter as a British Asian female without learning disabilities and a practising Art Psychotherapist. I have included the voices of Freddy (who requested his name to be changed for this chapter), a white male with learning disabilities who was a participant in the arts project, and Jo Bressloff, a white female without learning disabilities and a community artist and artist educator. Both Freddy and Jo have consented to their contribution being shared.

Introduction

In March 2023 Jo, Freddy and I met to discuss and share our reflections on 'Drawing Stories', a gallery-based therapeutic programme we'd all been part of. I wrote the words in this chapter; Jo and Freddy have contributed to this chapter through quotations taken from a recording we made when we met.

In this chapter I will consider how, as art therapists, we can actively support a person's engagement in the community, by reaching out and working collaboratively with external organisations through the example of 'Drawing Stories'. In this example, the partnership took place between a National Health Service (NHS) Community Learning Disability Service and Southampton City Art Gallery. A recovery-focused art-based intervention was offered in the gallery rather than in a clinical space. In this community space, the 'service user' became a 'participant' – the latter implying a more active engagement; and the facilitators and carers became 'fellow makers' – rather than 'helpers' – looking, learning and creating alongside one another.

Starting at the End

Before 'Drawing Stories', I knew Freddy as his art therapist. Towards the end of individual art therapy, Freddy drew an image of a beach. Freddy sits with

DOI: 10.4324/9781003350736-17

Figure 12.1 'Crossing the beach', a photograph of art made by Freddy.

Ash the Bear, his best friend, looking out across the sea to the buildings in the distance (Figure 12.1). When we first met, Freddy was living mostly in isolation from others, fearful of the world beyond his four walls. During therapy, which took place within a community NHS setting, we worked together to increase his confidence in leaving his home, supporting him to attend sessions in the art therapy room and then later, at the local gallery. By the end of his sessions Freddy had taken steps towards accessing day services, where (fast-forward several years) he was now happily settled. Freddy reflected on this time of transition:

> *I remember this picture. I was scared, really frightened, my head was exploding. In this picture I'm looking to the other side. I was thinking it's really scary. I don't want to do it. I didn't know how I would get there. But then I was thinking of being in the flat all on my own, with no one to talk to and how lonely I felt. I had to challenge myself, make myself do it because I didn't want to be on my own anymore.*

Freddy and I considered how his position on the beach was a daunting but hopeful one. He remembered how he first felt about participating in 'Drawing Stories' and how he felt following the session: "*I was really scared about going [to the art gallery] but then I did it and loved it. I loved using the charcoal!*"

Freddy's experience of loneliness is shared by over a third (36%) of people with learning disabilities (HF Trust, 2021). The UK Government's policy of austerity (2010–2019) has led to an erosion of local facilities (Power & Bartlett, 2015). All such lost provisions represent spaces and people that have the potential to increase a sense of connection and belonging. As Freddy has described: to find something that you really love and know that you can do it.

Background

The terms 'inclusion' and 'belonging' have led to much debate within the studies of marginalised groups. In the UK, since the 1990s, three models of inclusion have emerged:

- **Mainstreaming** was initially embraced by disability activists as a way of ensuring that people with learning disabilities had full and fair access to activities, social roles and relationships alongside non-disabled citizens (Bates et al., 2004) by being included in mainstream activities. This has resulted in mixed outcomes for people with learning disabilities struggling to meet high expectations (particularly around employment) leading to feelings of frustration and disappointment (Hall, 2010).
- Under the **differentiated** model, separate activities for people with learning disabilities are delivered within public services, enabling a greater degree of adaptation. It could be argued that this approach further alienates and stigmatises. However, Hall (2010) reframed this as gaining a sense of 'belonging' through being understood by those around you and moments of shared experience.
- Using an **individualised** approach, rather than 'one size fits all', personal budgets gave people greater choice and control over the services they accessed. For individuals requiring a higher level of personal support, funding can be used to access public spaces and services. This can mean that the responsibility to aid inclusion may fall on support workers, rather than public services (Weisel et al., 2002).

I have found it helpful to think of these three models as working alongside one another, rather than conflicting (Weisel et al., 2002). Used in combination, these models give a person greater flexibility in how they might choose to access public spaces and allow for services to take a broader approach to inclusion (Clegg and Bigby, 2017). As we will discuss further in this chapter, these differing approaches were considered whilst developing 'Drawing Stories'.

Art Therapy in Museums and Galleries

There are a growing number of art therapists taking their practice into museums and galleries. Objects can inspire creativity and personal connection (Holtum, 2020), while also being a space to see oneself as part of society rather than an NHS patient

(Colbert et al., 2013; Allan et al., 2015). Within Arts and Health research, there is strong evidence that participatory arts support mental health recovery, including promoting both positive emotions through enjoyment of the activity and belonging through a shared group identity (Stickley et al., 2018; Williams et al., 2020).

With my background in community arts, I was keen to explore how I could make use of the community's cultural resources as part of a therapeutic art-based intervention. From 2017 to 2019, I delivered several art therapy groups in the Southampton City Art Gallery, inviting participants to explore the gallery's collection, followed by personal art-making and reflection. For this, we hired private rooms in the building, which had a cost to our team. However, the location and the potential of its objects, in comparison to an NHS building on the edge of a trading estate (in an arguably less inspiring meeting room), made it an attractive venue for therapeutic interventions.

"I'm an artist too!"

Housed in the same building as the central library and the SeaCity Museum, Southampton City Art Gallery is located in the city centre with bus stops, a taxi rank and a bike park outside its entrance, giving numerous access options. There are accessible public spaces for those with physical disabilities, plenty of seating and a café for all-important refreshments. It is a building that holds objects, literature and artwork linked to the City's people and maritime history. It offers a space for quiet contemplation but also one that is social, hosting a variety of workshops and meet-ups. Upon entering the building, visitors are greeted by bright posters and colourful flyers advertising local events, connecting them with their community.

Its central location signifies the gallery as a space of importance, one that holds objects considered valuable by society. Chamberlain (2020) describes how participating in spaces such as these can give someone a greater sense of value, particularly those who have been marginalised by society. A common experience for people with learning disabilities, who speak of a lack of rights, independency, choice and inclusion.

My relationship with the gallery began with the delivery of two art therapy groups:

- 'Identity Group' for young people with learning disabilities (16 weeks) co-facilitated with psychology colleagues, with five members aged 21–30.
- 'Mindfulness & Art Therapy Group' for older women with learning disabilities (6 weeks) co-facilitated with occupational therapy colleagues, with 4–6 members.

These experiences gave me an insight into the gallery's potential for creating connection and belonging. Members of the Identity Group, inspired by the artworks, told us they wanted to spend more time making art. They also began to meet for coffee in town, expanding their contacts beyond the sessions. In the Mindfulness &

Art Therapy Group, there was a memorable connection between a disabled and non-disabled artist. During a mindful walkabout, the group came across an exhibiting artist. Jane, a group member, told them: *"I'm an artist too!"* Each week she brought her portfolio of paintings. Jane asked the other artist to wait a moment while she went back to the art room, retrieved her folder and presented it to her fellow artist.

From Visitor to Collaborator: 'Drawing Stories', 2019

Working in partnership to support inclusion requires sharing diverse knowledge, skills and resources (Zhvitiashvili, 2020). Kate Mitchell, the gallery education manager, wanted to build upon their outreach sessions in local day services by engaging people with learning disabilities in the gallery spaces. Following the success of the art therapy groups I'd co-led, we were keen to collaborate.

Partnered with Jo, a freelance arts educator working for the gallery, we developed a six-week course as part of their 'Lifelong Learning' adult education programme. Our course was funded by the local council's Lifelong Learning budget (arts educator costs and materials). Resources such as the learning space and organisational time were shared between the gallery and my NHS community service.

Using our combined skills in participatory arts and art therapy, we set the following shared objectives:

- Engagement in and expression through art.
- Learn and explore new art skills.
- Create an opportunity for connection and belonging.
- Increase confidence in accessing the art gallery.
- Promote the use of local resources to support wellbeing.

We are a bit more Flowie

The group was open to individuals accessing psychological therapies within my NHS service. All participants had a diagnosis of mild to moderate learning disabilities with some form of verbal communication. Those invited to attend the group had reached a point in their psychological therapy where they might gain confidence from accessing community spaces.

We ran two blocks of 'Drawing Stories' sessions (see Table 12.1). Out of the total 15 participants with learning disabilities, 11 had completed individual art

Table 12.1 'Drawing Stories' attendance per block

Drawing Stories Session Blocks	Block 1	Block 2
Number of sessions	6	8
Number of people with a learning disability	7	3
Number of support staff	3	3
Average attendance per session	64%	75%

therapy interventions, three had been rereferred to art therapy and one person had not taken part in art therapy previously.

Jo and I wished to be as inclusive as possible, though we were aware that we might be inviting people to take part who had few connections with peers, other than having learning disabilities. A frustration I heard often voiced in therapy by individuals with mild learning disabilities where they spoke of difficulties in finding a place in which they felt they belonged. Freddy, in his 50s, with mild learning disabilities, told Jo and I:

> I don't like being put in a box of just one thing. I don't like being in groups for just old people. I like to be with everybody of different ages. I prefer people who are younger than me anyway...my best friend is 25. We like the same music. But I do prefer being with people here [day service]. Staff understand us ... I feel safer.

For Freddy, 'the box' represented the age group and not learning disabilities. Often placed in the category of 'older adult', he wanted to be with people who like *"Justin Bieber and not Vera Lynn!"* Being with other people with learning disabilities helped Freddy to feel safe and understood. The group's internal diversity also creates an opportunity to find connections and friendship with people with similar likes and interests.

Freddy asked Jo: *"What is the difference to when you do children's workshops, to how do I put this, normal everyday adults, to us with problems?"* Jo replied:

> School workshops are quite structured sessions. When we have groups [for adults], like the one we had, they are much more open-ended. There is an opportunity to explore and experiment... and time to get to really know people. They are a lot less structured, like me really!

Freddy said:

> ...us type people with problems and learning disabilities we are a bit more 'flowie' if you like. We don't like being told do this or do that. Well, I know for me, I don't like being told what to do.

There were several members of the group who we knew would struggle to attend without their personal support worker. We were also aware of the difficulties of meeting a wide range of needs between two facilitators. In response to this, we invited participant's support workers to join us. To ensure that this did not take away opportunities for participants to act independently, we encouraged support workers to actively engage in sessions too. Freddy reflected on this and told us:

> I suppose if you need one, you need one. .... I didn't mind. Sometimes they would support other people too...but there are people here [at day service] who think

that they can't do things on their own. But the staff here just leave us to get on with it [in the art room] and they just do it themselves because there is no one else to do it for you.

It takes time to feel comfortable.

For each session the structure was as follows:

- Group check-in in the art room (education room)
- Walkabout/drawing in the gallery
- Back to the art room to put the kettle on!
- Art techniques introduced
- Themed art-making over tea and biscuits
- Group sharing and feedback

Sessions were two hours long, which provided ample time to move between the gallery and education room, with a break in-between. Participants, including carers, fed back that this was an ideal amount of time.

The opening check-in gave participants time to settle into the space. They were invited to speak about their journey to the gallery. We asked what they may have seen on the way, had they experienced any difficulties in getting here, and how they had felt about coming to the session. Some participants chose to share their wider concerns, such as problems they might be experiencing at home. As an art therapist, I used my skills and training to validate people's experiences, notice connections and contain more difficult thoughts and feelings.

Jo said:

The way that you introduced the Gallery sessions was really useful and helpful for me because, by asking all the participants how their journey had been that day and how we were feeling about joining the session. This was much more specific and easier to answer rather than just asking us to introduce ourselves.

When I asked Freddy what had helped him to feel comfortable in the session, he talked about the education room where the art-making took place, commenting positively on its three large tables: "*For me I like to choose a place, not just put everyone together. ... I'm always a bit worried of where I go. For me, personally, it takes time to feel comfortable.*"

I noticed that I used my skills to validate emotions and Jo's provided the security of a structured activity. The room itself, with its natural light and brightly coloured artworks hung from the ceiling, created an inviting space for participants to work in. All of these elements together provided a safe and containing space for participants.

The Waterfall

In Block 1, a visiting exhibition by Leonardo Da Vinci became a starting point for making. Inspired by the artist's use of drawing to capture his view of the world, the group was invited to explore a variety of drawing techniques and materials to draw their stories.

Kelly, a group member, drew a picture of herself standing next to a gushing waterfall. She then shared this with the group and spoke about a memory of living in Sweden for several months as a teenager during a youth camp in the 1980s. I heard Kelly speak fondly of her time at the camp and other places she lived or visited when younger. At the end of the session, Kelly's carer said that despite knowing her for many years she did not know about her travels. She had discovered something new. For Kelly, who often spoke of past turbulent relationships with carers, we observed a moment of connection and insight. Similar to evidence identified by Bourne et al. (2020), interactions such as these support the development of therapeutic relationships.

"It's Weird!"

In Block 2, Yinka Shonibare's curated exhibition challenged the group's notion of what art is. George, a group member, was intrigued by an Andy Holden sculpture, dripping with pastel-coloured plaster. He returned to the group each week telling us: *"It's weird"* and that looking at it made him happy.

It made me think of how connections can be experienced between a person and a piece of art. This was particularly significant for George whose learning disabilities and other aspects of his identity often positioned him on the fringes of society. In the gallery, there was permission to be and feel something different. The 'weird' or unusual was placed in a position of value; it was seen and celebrated.

"The best bit was drawing in the gallery"

Sketching in the gallery was introduced in Block 2. This enabled participants in the group who might struggle to engage in verbal discussions on artworks, to form a creative response. It also brought the group back together, after initially separating out into the gallery, as they naturally gravitated towards the benches in the centre of the room. During the feedback, many of the participants described 'being in the gallery' as the most enjoyable part of the session.

Jo said:

> Drawing in the gallery space was very valuable and provided a quiet time for us to connect with individually chosen artworks and to discuss them. It also inspired the workshop activities and helped to promote the feeling that the space is for everyone to use.

There also felt something important about the act of drawing in a public space; to be seen doing something that is skilful and respected by society (Figure 12.2).

Figure 12.2 'Drawing together', a photograph of participants drawing in the gallery space.

Discussion

Shifting the Balance

Working 'side-by-side' (Greenwood, 2017) shifts the power imbalance between therapist and 'patient' as they regain their sense of identity and agency, which is often lost within a biomedical model where people are 'diagnosed' and 'treated' by 'experts'. In the gallery space, we are learning together as participants and fellow makers.

James, a male trainee psychologist, sat side-by-side with Sam, a group member, who looked initially uncertain about participating. Similar in age; they made artwork alongside one another whilst chatting about films and video games. Sam shared at the end of the session that his favourite part of the workshop had been talking with James and expressed enthusiasm for returning the following week. I saw a meaningful connection made between them.

Another more active, power-shifting process is the giving and receiving of feedback in the therapeutic relationship (O'Farrell, 2017) which can help to 'feed identity'. This is especially important to a person who may have limited access to spaces to receive everyday feedback, such as in work or education. This two-way process had become an essential part of my therapeutic practice, particularly as O'Farrell had supervised me.

An image provides opportunity for feedback. At the end of the group, participants were invited to reflect on personal art-making and on the work of their peers. They noticed how it might evoke a feeling or memories, or express admiration in its makers' skills:

I like how their tile is so neat and tidy.

(group member)

You weren't afraid to use the paint. It makes me want to paint like that too.

(facilitator)

For carers, it modelled a way to engage in a person's art more meaningfully, rather than it just being 'good' or 'nice'. We modelled being curious and communicating the impression artwork made on us.

"It's got me out of my shell"

Following the art reflection, we invited the group to give verbal feedback on the session, asking participants: What did you enjoy about the session today? What could have been better? Their feedback was written down alongside our own reflections and grouped into the following themes:

1   Enjoyment
   "I enjoyed talking to the gallery staff.... I liked the tour."
   "I liked what I made. I am going to draw at home."
2   Supporting mental health
   "I liked looking at the artwork and having your own thoughts, but then reading more about it also. You can learn a lot about yourself."
   "Drawing better and getting new ideas. This helps with my anxiety and helps my head feel calmer."
3   Positive experiences
   "...I was nervous at the start of the session...I've never been here before... I've been inspired by the art...I didn't think it was going to look like this. It got me out of the house...It's the first time in a long time I've felt able to do this."
   "I feel more confident in getting a job."
4   Social connection
   "I liked being funny in the group."
   "I will miss the group, there's not been enough time."

Feedback on challenges was linked to miscommunication in travel access and a preference for a single location after a one-off visit to a different cultural venue in Block 1.

Closing the Feedback Loop

Jo and I were both excited and inspired by what participants brought to the group. Such as the use of art materials, interactions with the objects, fellow group members. At the end of the programme, each participant was sent a therapeutic letter, thus completing the feedback loop.

Ending at the Start

Returning to Freddy's image 'Crossing the beach' (Figure 12.3), he talked of a boat with people helping him to get to the other side. This could be a metaphor for our project. It remained separate from mainstream art workshops in the gallery, which many of our group would have struggled to access, but was included in a wider community adult learning programme. Taking both a differentiated and individualised approach enabled us to design a programme that each participant could engage with in a public venue which they may not have had access to previously.

A gallery is a 'democratic space' where people can freely meet with others (Power and Bartlett, 2018) outside of structured activities. It can be visited independently, with support or as part of a group. It is a space in which we can find our own way of connecting. It can also become, in time, a place of safety, through both its space and objects, which, Zhvitiashvili (2020) reflects, has the power to contain and validate people's stories and feelings.

Figure 12.3 'The Bridge', a photograph of a painting made by Freddy.

When Freddy spoke about his experience, he said:

getting there was a bit stressful. It's like being dropped in a town you don't know. It's not like going to your safe place. You've got to get to know the place. I look forward to going now. I've got used to it. ...

Jo asked: *"Would you be happy going on your own?"* Freddy replied: *"Not really. I don't really like going out on my own ... but yes, I would go with my carers."*

Freddy told us that he now goes to the gallery quite often with the day service art room leader. They take their sketchbooks and draw in the gallery. Freddy then proudly showed us a painting in progress in his day service art room (Figure 12.3). It is inspired by L. S. Lowry's 'The Canal Bridge', a painting depicting a historic industrial scene. I noticed that his painting was alive with people pouring in and out of the factory onto the streets, going about their everyday lives. Freddy reflected that previously his images only contained buildings, there are more people in his pictures these days. Together we linked this to his increased confidence in being in the company of others. Freddy spoke of friends and support at day services; he expressed pride in everything he has achieved. Freddy shared with us that he no longer feels that he is on his own.

Conclusion

This work evolved through partnership. Our project highlights how public spaces can play a valuable role in supporting inclusion and belonging and how this can be further strengthened by services working collaboratively.

The participants became artists (and were *seen* creating) in the gallery. They could explore and learn alongside others, including carers and facilitators, finding both inspiration and validation. At the end of sessions there was always a positive atmosphere, which I believe comes from a shared collective experience in which people feel connection. The approach in this chapter could also be explored in other public places such as parks, forests and gardens, where there might be objects, people and spaces to make a connection.

References

Access Southampton. 'Adult learning'. Available at: www.access-southampton.co.uk/adult-learning (Accessed: May 2023).

Allan, J., Barford, H., Horwood, F., Stevens, J., & Gerard, Tanti. (2015) ATIC: 'Developing a recovery-based art therapy practice'. *International Journal of Art Therapy* 20:1, 14–27. DOI:10.1080/17454832.968597.

Bates, P., & Davis, Fabian A. (2004). 'Social capital, social inclusion and services for people with learning disabilities'. *Disability and Society* 19:3, 195–207.

Bourne, J., Selman, M., & Hackett, S. (2020). 'Learning from support workers: Can a dramatherapy group offer a community provision to support changes in care for people with learning disabilities and mental health difficulties?'. *British Journal of Learning Disabilities* 48, 59–68. https://doi.org/10.1111/bld.12312

Chamberlain, M. (2020). 'Making space safe at modern art Oxford'. In A. Coles, & H. Jury (eds.), *Art Therapy in Museums and Galleries* (pp. 63–80). London: Jessica Kingsley.

Clegg, J., & Bigby, C. (2017). 'Debates about differentiation: Twenty-first century thinking about people with intellectual disabilities as distinct members of a disability group'. *Research and Practice in Intellectual and Developmental Disabilities* 4: 1, 80–87.

Colbert, S., Cooke, A., Camic, P., & Springham, N. (2013). 'The art-gallery as a resource for recovery for people who have experienced psychosis'. *The Arts in Psychotherapy* 40, 250–256.

Greenwood, H. (2017). 'The side-by-side approach in art therapy for psychosis. Deflation and empowerment within the therapeutic relationship'. In K. Killick (ed.), *Art Therapy for Psychosis* (pp. 135–153). Oxford: Routledge.

Hall, E. (2010). 'Spaces of social inclusion and belonging for people with intellectual disabilities'. *Journal of Intellectual Disability Review* 54:1, 48–57.

HF Trust (2021). *Loneliness and Isolation Report: 'Lockdown on Loneliness. Creating Connection for People with Learning Disabilities.'* HF Trust: Bristol. Available at: https://www.hft.org.uk/get-involved/lockdown-on-loneliness/

Holtum, S. (2020). 'Art Therapy in museums and galleries: Evidence and research'. In A. Coles, & H. Jury (eds.), *Art Therapy in Museums and Galleries* (pp. 26–43). London: Jessica Kingsley.

O'Farrell, K. (2017). 'Feedback feeds self-identity: Using art therapy to empower self identity in adults with learning disabilities'. *International Journal of Art Therapy* 20:2, 64–72.

Power, A., & Bartlett, R. (2015). 'Self-building safe havens in a post-service landscape: How adults with learning disabilities are reclaiming the welcoming communities agenda'. *Social and Cultural Geography* 19:3, 336–356. https://doi.org/10.1080/14649365.2015.1031686

Stickley, T., Wright, N., & Slade, M. (2018). 'The art of recovery: Outcomes from participatory arts activities for people using mental health services'. *Journal of Mental Health* 27(4): 367–373. DOI: 10.1080/09638237.2018.1437609.

Weisel, I., Bigby, C., Van Holsen, E., & Gleeson, B. (2022). 'Three modes of inclusion of people with intellectual disability in mainstream services: Mainstreaming, differentiation and individualism'. *Disability & Society.* 39(1), 40–61. https://doi.org/10.1080/09687599.2022.2060803

Williams, E., Genevieve, A. Dingle., Calligeros, R., Sharman, L., & Jolanda, J. (2020). 'Enhancing mental health recovery by joining arts-based groups: A role for the social cure approach'. *Arts & Health* 12:2, 169–181. DOI: 1080/17533015.2019.1624584.

Zhvitiashvili, N. (2020). 'From Isolation to relation: Reflections on the development of Museum-based art therapy in Russia'. In A. Coles, & H. Jury (eds.), *Art Therapy in Museums and Galleries* (pp. 82–107). London: Jessica Kingsley.

Chapter 13

Frames of Identity
Unveiling Life Stories of People with Down Syndrome through Art Therapy and Reminiscence

Tsz Yan Yana NG and Chi Kin Kwan

Positionality Statement

I, Tsz Yan Yana Ng, have authored this chapter as an Asian woman without learning disabilities, working as an Art Psychotherapist. When including the words of individuals with learning disabilities in my writing, I have utilized direct quotes. I have obtained explicit consent from the individuals I have written about, who have expressed their willingness for their words to be read by others. Throughout the collaborative process of writing, my co-author, Chi Kin Kwan, an Asian man and I worked closely together, sharing a common commitment to creating a comprehensive and engaging narrative. We maintained open communication and mutual respect, actively exchanging ideas, perspectives, and experiences. My co-author contributed his expertise in research and mental health, enriching the work with depth and insight.

Introduction

Talking therapies rely heavily on verbal communication, which poses a significant limitation for individuals with learning disabilities who struggle with verbal expression. However, art therapy offers an accessible approach, providing an alternative means of self-expression and communication through art-making. Despite a growing evidence base, largely from the United Kingdom (UK), the application of art therapy in China remains limited, and literature on the subject is scarce. Down syndrome is the most common genetic cause of learning disabilities, and people with this syndrome experience a certain degree of learning disability. Hence, this chapter aims to address several current gaps in the literature by exploring the utilization of a particular model of art therapy with individuals with Down syndrome in China. The practice-based evidence illustrated in this chapter shows that using reminiscence within an art-based approach can enhance the emotional well-being of individuals with Down syndrome.

Research indicates that individuals with learning disabilities often face challenges related to their emotions and developmental progress (Arthur, 2003). People with Down syndrome, in particular, face challenges related to speech intelligibility

DOI: 10.4324/9781003350736-18

and are likely to struggle with verbal communication, although they often possess strong visual thinking abilities (McGuire & Chicoine, 2021). When compared to their typically developing peers, children with learning disabilities are more likely to encounter a higher number of traumatic life events and have an increased risk of developing mental health difficulties which continue into adulthood (Hatton & Emerson, 2004; Emerson & Baines, 2011). The existing health services in China specifically tailored to this group are inadequate and lack a systematic approach, leading to insufficient attention to their experiences (Wong, 2011). Therefore, there is a need to support this population by enhancing their emotional well-being.

Additionally in this chapter, we wish to draw attention to the role of positive emotions in coping. Positive emotions have been shown to play an essential role in helping people cope with stressful life events (Shane et al., 2011; Moskowitz et al., 2011). Experiencing positive emotions can efficiently support individuals in moving on from challenging situations, taking a longer-term view of their problems, making plans, and achieving goals. Consequently, enhancing people's capacity to experience positive emotions has become an important topic for mental health practitioners.

Reminiscence Work and Art Therapy

Reminiscence is a process that can be structured or unstructured and involves remembering and re-experiencing past events and associated feelings. It goes beyond factual recall and can lead to conclusions about one's life and its meaning (Buchanan et al., 2002; Puyenbroeck & Maes, 2008). Reminiscence activities, also known as guided reminiscence, are structured and planned interventions to stimulate the process of reminiscence. They include a range of methods such as group reminiscence, individual life review therapy, a compilation of a scrapbook or photo album, autobiography, a reunion or pilgrimage to former homes, or a museum visit (Puyenbroeck & Maes, 2005).

The use of reminiscence interventions is well documented in literature with the general population, particularly with older adults. It can be a helpful method to improve the positive emotions of both young and older adults. When positive reminiscence is used as a constructive tool to gain perspective on the present, the frequency of positive reminiscence can increase levels of happiness (Bryant et al., 2005). For older adults, it can support revisiting and reframing significant past events, leading to enhanced meaning in life, especially for those experiencing depression (Bohlmeijer et al., 2008). Puyenbroeck and Maes (2008) emphasize the potential benefits of reminiscence work in strengthening self-identity and raising self-esteem for ageing individuals with learning disabilities. Stueber and Hassiotis (2012) consider reminiscence as a potentially valuable resource for older individuals with learning disabilities but caution readers that, to date, research with this population is limited.

Art therapy and reminiscence work have been combined in some forms of art therapy practice for older adults with dementia. For example, Stephenson (2006) emphasized that combining art therapy with reminiscence and book-making provides a valuable resource for discussing life review and end-of-life matters. The book serves as a symbol that bridges the creator's inner world with the external world, enabling the artist to express their thoughts and experiences to others (Stephenson, 2006).

Although reminiscence is relatively uncommon in the context of supporting people with Down syndrome or younger adults, we believe that it offers therapeutic potential through facilitating storytelling for this population, who may struggle with free recall of personal memories and expressing difficult emotions verbally. A solely verbal interaction would be insufficient due to these challenges, as well as the difficulty of expressing complex emotions associated with those memories. Therefore, structured approaches and additional support are necessary to promote reminiscing and enhance the retrieval of self-defining memories (OTT, 1993).

Our chapter proposes that integrating art therapy with reminiscence work can address the communication difficulties faced by individuals with Down syndrome. Instead of relying solely on verbal communication, art-making can serve as a form of expression, within the reminiscence intervention.

Setting up the Art-based Reminiscence Group

Four art-based reminiscence groups were run for Hong Kong Chinese adults with moderate Down syndrome and their carers to share their personal life experience through art-based reminiscence activities. The participants were recruited by an organization specializing in serving people with Down syndrome. Consent was obtained by this organization regarding participation in the groups and post-group interviews. Using photo album making, the group aimed to facilitate the narratives of individual personal histories.

The group ran weekly for six weeks. All sessions were facilitated by Yana and three other practitioners with art therapy training. Each group consists of six to eight pairs of individuals with Down syndrome (mixed gender in their 20s to 30s) and their caregivers. Each session lasted for two hours, and the groups took place at the service centres provided by the Hong Kong Down Syndrome Association.

The design of the groups followed three key requirements for working with individuals with learning disabilities: using a structured approach, involving caregivers, and utilizing creative approaches (Brooker & Duce, 2000; Puyenbroeck & Maes, 2008). The creation of life story books fulfilled these requirements by providing a structured framework for storytelling, involving caregivers in the process and employing a creative medium for expression and communication.

Firstly, a structured approach, such as guided reminiscence, was employed to help participants construct their life narratives. Creating a life story book allowed individuals with Down syndrome to develop a finished product on a theme. This provided a therapeutic means for those who had difficulty speaking or needed their thoughts recorded (Puyenbroeck & Maes, 2006). The life story book served as a personalized tool to initiate social interaction, explore dreams, and make plans for the future. Our group design combined the creation of the life story book with selected themes to provide a structured framework that was easier for group members to follow.

A balance was struck in the group design between maintaining creative elements (being less directive and offering choices) and providing structured directives (based on themes). During the initial 'meet and greet' session before the group officially began, all participants were invited to present the photos from their lives (life photos) that they had collected. They then collaborated to categorize the photos and develop corresponding themes. The therapist proposed several possible themes for the group's consideration, based on the photo-sorting process. Five themes were selected through voting: (1) school life, (2) family/friendship, (3) sports/hobby, (4) travel, and (5) performance/celebration/ceremony.

School life was prioritized as the focus of the first session, rather than family/ friendship, as it is considered a less intimidating theme that felt safer to explore in the beginning of the group. Themes with a focus on relationships, including family and friendship, were offered. Ceremony was also a theme with possibilities in triggering strong feelings of ending or loss. Therefore, other options such as performance and celebration were suggested to offer additional perspectives.

We involved carers in the groups to foster social interaction and connection. Including carers meant they had the opportunity to share family life stories, strengthening the bond between carers and individuals. Engaging in life story work allows for exploration of each other's identities and can lead to moments of profound intimacy, promoting mutual understanding and personal growth (Hewitt, 2000; Meininger, 2005).

Our groups focused on offering various sensory and creative experiences for individuals with Down syndrome. Because the group aimed to create a life story book, a wide range of 2D materials with different sensory qualities were prepared, such as feathers, finger paint, and foam stickers. The group usually started with a theme, followed by a warm-up art activity to encourage playfulness and freedom. Participants were invited to select materials based on their association with the theme. This encouraged them to make their own choices and to connect their feelings with the sensory qualities of different materials. After art-making with the photo album, all participants would get back together to share their artwork and talk about the stories of the photos selected with the group.

Evaluation of the Art-based Reminiscence Group

The evaluation followed a social constructionist approach. After the art-based reminiscence groups ended, a convenience sampling method was used to invite two groups of participants to attend a post-group feedback session. With their consent, I (Yana) facilitated two sessions at the service centre with which they were familiar. The groups consisted of three and five participants. I informed them about the session's objectives and invited them to share their significant group experiences in a semi-structured format (see Table 13.1) with questions, which were informed by the literature as well as the authors' experience, to guide the discussion.

Table 13.1 Questions used to structure the feedback groups

Participant	Question
For both (carers and young people with Down syndrome)	Can you recall any particular moments from the group that still resonate with you?
For both	What have you learned during your participation in the group?
For both	What aspects of the group did you like the most? The least?
For individuals with Down syndrome	Prior to this group, did you have any opportunities to discuss similar topics or experiences?
For caregivers	Did the group inspire you in any way?
For both	If another group similar to this were offered, would you be willing to: • provide suggestions to improve future groups? • express your interest in joining another group like this?
For both	Is there anything else you would like to share, or any other comments you would like to provide?

Each post-group feedback session lasted around 45 minutes. An inductive six-phase thematic analysis method (Braun & Clarke, 2006) was used to analyze the data. The interview discussions were first recorded and then transcribed. Patterns relevant to the research question were identified through line-by-line coding. Possible themes related to this chapter's objectives were recorded and are reported in this chapter. Additionally, group observations that I (Yana) made in the sessions were incorporated into the analysis.

Results

This section presents an overview of the findings from the chapter arranged thematically, highlighting the effect of involving carers in the groups and the positive outcomes observed.

Improved Communication and Bonding between Participants with Down Syndrome and Their Carers

We found that involving carers in the groups may facilitate a powerful experience for both the participants with Down syndrome and their carers. The groups helped explore identities and enhance the relationship between the participant with Down syndrome and the carer. Based on the feedback from the feedback sessions, the groups offered a precious chance to take out and look at the photos that had been stored and long forgotten. Carers reported the experience of searching photo albums and revisiting those past memories to be powerful and emotional. One participant with Down syndrome shared, "*I enjoyed listening to the stories about the photos (from her carer), and it was fun to look at my younger self.*"

Evoked a Positive Attitude

Bringing life photos to the group provided a chance for carers and the cared-for to reminisce about shared past memories. Some of the life photos and stories had long been forgotten. In the group, led by Yana, they brought up memories of close family friends, happy family times visiting theme parks, traveling to different countries during different seasons, and tasting various cuisines. Although some photos were more relatable, as they were taken when the participants with Down syndrome were older, others were taken when they were younger. The carers helped share the memories of the trips, and these instances of positive reminiscence showed a positive effect too: "*The family trip photos in the past reminded us some of the great moments we had. It made us want to plan a family trip again.*"

Provided a Chance to Express and to be Understood Through Verbal and Non-verbal Means

Several interviewees with Down syndrome said that reviewing photos of different stages of their life in a group setting was a unique experience. It allowed their stories to be heard. One interviewee with Down syndrome said, "*No one would talk to and listen to me about all this.*" Several other interviewees and their carers agreed.

The use of art therapy provided a valuable means for participants to express themselves non-verbally and explore their subjective point of view. For example, the group session emphasized the non-judgemental and playful ways of using the art materials. In the group (run by Yana), I observed that in the last two sessions of the group, a participant with Down syndrome began cutting out her portrait from a performance photo and incorporating text and craft materials to create collages that reflected her positive self-perception. The use of creative means offered a different way of thinking that complements the emphasis on the subjective and emotional needs of reminiscence work (Pounsett et al., 2006). This creative and flexible approach to art media allowed participants to express the way they viewed themselves within the context of specific themes, enhancing their self-expression and strengthening their self-identity.

Opening up to Difficult and Sensitive Topic around Aging and Loss

Revisiting past memories made them compare their current well-being to their past well-being, which made them think about the uncertainties of their future. A powerful conversation came up in a group session when the participant with Down syndrome and the carer shared how things had changed over time, and the carer worried she wouldn't be around to care for the participant forever. The participant with Down syndrome was also able to respond and communicate her worries about losing her carer. The group facilitator addressed the theme and explored the issue with the participant and the carer, sharing psychoeducation about life and death. The carer shared that she now tries to enjoy 'living in the moment' and the time they spend together. The group provided a safe space for participants to openly share difficult thoughts and worries which would otherwise be avoided or unaddressed.

Our Learning

Throughout the group experience, we gained valuable insights that shaped our approach, leading to a greater sense of safety and promoting interaction among participants.

Make a Careful Selection of Themes to Foster Safety

By thoughtfully choosing and adjusting the themes, we were able to encourage participants to open up about sensitive topics that they might have found overwhelming. This approach provided a safe space for individuals with Down syndrome and their carers to explore these topics, while containing strong emotions.

In our sessions, we found that the process of collectively reviewing photos and creating individual photo albums facilitated sharing among participants. After reviewing the photos together, each participant had dedicated time to create their own album. At the end of each session, participants were encouraged to look at each other's artwork, fostering verbal and non-verbal communication through discussion and shared visual experiences.

One theme that proved particularly powerful was the celebration and performance theme, which we chose for our final session. This theme allowed us to consolidate the group's journey of loss and gains and focus on the strengths of the participants with Down syndrome. Despite the experiences of loss and worries that were shared throughout the group, we intentionally emphasized positive memories by celebrating the participants' accomplishments. This approach elicited enthusiastic responses from the group, as they reminisced about past performances and competitions, expressing how much they enjoyed being part of those experiences and feeling proud of their achievements.

Be Sensitive to Personal Photos as Art Materials

We learned to be sensitive to personal photos as part of 'art materials' when working with participants with Down syndrome. While facilitating the photo album-making process, we discovered that some participants began using photos as art materials, cutting out specific parts to create collages. To accommodate this creative expression, we made copies of the photos, ensuring that participants could freely use them in their artwork as they desired. This flexible approach allowed participants to explore different ways of using photos and encouraged their non-verbal expression, without damaging or losing the original photograph.

Provide Options for Sensory Qualities of Art Materials

We also found that providing options for different sensory qualities of art materials further facilitated non-verbal communication and connected participants' feelings. In one session focused on the theme of endings and good wishes, a participant chose a purple feather to add to her photo album. She shared that the softness and colour of the feather made her feel *'good'* and *'happy,'* representing the blessing she bestowed upon herself and her family. Through art-making, participants with Down syndrome were able to recall, record, and share their memories in a subjective way, overcoming the challenges of verbal communication and expression.

Ensuring Participants Have Their Own Voices, Whilst Valuing Carers

During our group sessions, we observed that carers sometimes assumed a caregiving role by assisting individuals with Down syndrome in their art-making process. Although carers played a vital role in helping participants understand their life stories during group discussions, we recognized the importance of ensuring that each participant had their own voice in their artwork. To address this, we allocated dedicated time and space for individual art-making, allowing both carers and individuals with Down syndrome to develop their own artistic journeys. To facilitate collaboration, we utilized a photo album with disc-bound pages, enabling participants and their carers to work on separate pages and later assemble them, fostering group sharing and discussion of their respective images.

Response Art

I had several roles in this work. I ran one of the art-based reminiscence groups, conducted the focus groups, and led the analysis. I used response art to help me with processing or making sense of all of these roles (see Figure 13.1). Here's what I wrote after I made 'Interwoven Hearts':

> *I was attracted to the softness and vibrant colours and the user-friendliness of the pipe cleaners, as they reminded me of some of the childlike and genuine qualities of the participants with Down syndrome in the group. The process of weaving is to twist and entwine fibres together so they are purposefully entangled. I chose weaving to put a small bunch of pipe cleaners together, like the way the group experience was formed by the participation of each member and like the process of interviewing, gathering their comments, and putting the whole experience in writing to form a narrative.*
>
> *The weaving process was like an exploration of the pipe cleaners. Unlike weaving with string, pipe cleaners are pliable and can be manipulated to form 3D shapes, and no glue is needed. Due to the unique qualities of pipe cleaners, the process led to the building of a sphere with two ends. Each end has a shape that resembles the other and looks like a hand, a sun, or a flower. There are*

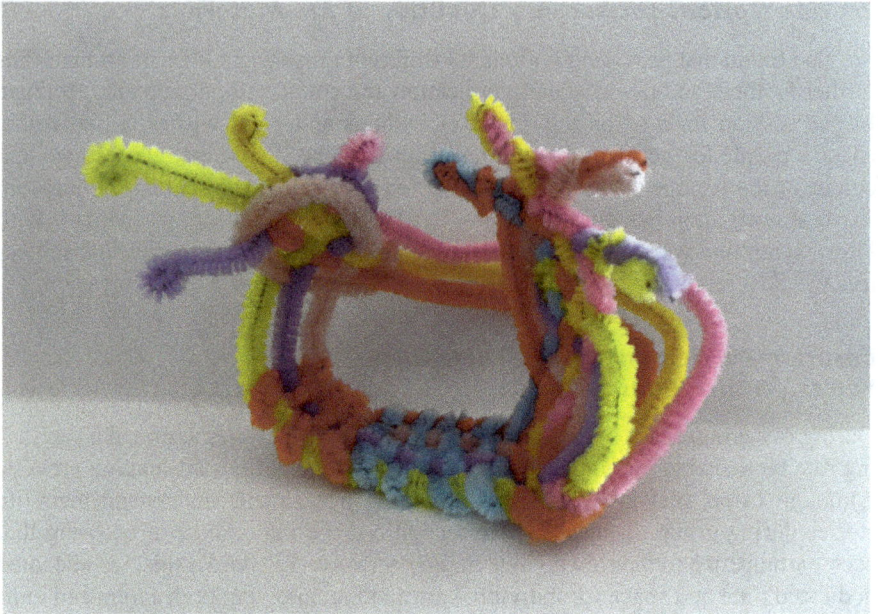

Figure 13.1 'Interwoven Hearts' photograph of artwork made by Yana.

two paths that connect the two shapes. The first path was woven and involved a repetitive process which felt orderly, leading to a more complex- looking outcome. It led to the making of another path that had three pipe cleaners and had some flexibility to be played with. This may mirror the two means of communication offered in the group: one was the conversation on an intellectual level, and the other was the intuitive expression with art materials and the drawing in the photo albums. When the two paths met, all pipe cleaners merged into some messier but playful and unique patterns on both ends. In the group, both means enabled a more holistic connection between the participants with Down syndrome and their carers.

For me, the art-making process also evoked other memories related to the group and thoughts about the whole process. I did this art in my studio. I got a pile of pipe cleaners and only one of them was black, oddly standing out from a colourful bunch of rainbow pipe cleaners. As I finished the artwork and reflected on the colours I picked, I realised the artwork was quite childlike and reminded me of the materials I got when preparing art materials for the group. I noticed the feathers, pre-cut foam shapes, and the coloured corrugated cardboard that is packaged by local craft shops did not come with a full range of colours but mostly bright colours. On reflection, I wish I had been more careful with the colour selection of certain craft materials and had included darker colours in some of the materials, as a wider range of colour choices could facilitate a fuller emotional expression.

During a supervision with my art therapist supervisor, it was noted that the outcome of my response art was unique and distinct from other artwork I'd created using other materials such as fabrics, acrylic, or clay. This uniqueness may be attributed to the new approach applied in the group project, which also represented a novel experience in my clinical practice. This innovative approach led to several unique discoveries in understanding the potential of incorporating different therapeutic approaches and settings to facilitate both verbal and non-verbal expression among individuals with Down syndrome.

Conclusion

Empowering individuals with Down syndrome through reminiscence work requires structured approaches that promote the development of self-defining memories. Utilizing art as a primary means of communication can significantly benefit these individuals, enhancing positive emotions and self-expression. Integrating art therapy with reminiscence work through life story books involving caregivers fosters identity and raises self-esteem. This chapter demonstrated how the participants connect with themselves on a deeper level. Through artistic expression, they explored their memories, emotions, and personal experiences, leading to a greater understanding of their own identities. The process not only empowers the individuals but also strengthens the bond between them and their caregivers. Engaging in art therapy and reminiscing on life stories together creates a shared experience that fosters mutual understanding, empathy, and appreciation within the carer and the cared-for relationship. This enhanced connection and mutual empowerment promote the emotional growth of both parties.

Recognizing the power of artistic expression and the involvement of caregivers, this intervention holds the potential to support the lives of individuals with Down syndrome. By further researching and fully harnessing the benefits of art therapy for individuals with learning disabilities, we may unlock even greater possibilities for enhancing emotional well-being and enriching relationships in this population.

Acknowledgement

Yana wishes to thank her art therapy supervisor, Sally Weston, for her support as she helped review the chapter and discussed it with Yana during the process.

References

Arthur, A. R. (2003). The emotional lives of people with learning disability. *British Journal of Learning Disabilities, 31*(1), 25–30.

Bohlmeijer, E. T., Westerhof, G. J., & Emmerik-de Jong, M. (2008). The effects of integrative reminiscence on meaning in life: Results of a quasi-experimental study. *Aging and Mental Health, 12*(5), 639–646.

Braun, V., & Clarke, V. (2006). Using thematic analysis in psychology. *Qualitative Research in Psychology, 3*(2), 77–101. https://doi.org/10.1191/1478088706qp063oa

Brooker, D., & Duce, L. (2000). Wellbeing and activity in dementia: A comparison of group reminiscence therapy, structured goal-directed group activity and unstructured time. *Aging & Mental Health, 4*(4), 354–358.

Bryant, F. B., Smart, C. M., & King, S. P. (2005). Using the past to enhance the present: Boosting happiness through positive reminiscence. *Journal of Happiness Studies, 6*(3), 227–260.

Emerson, E. & Baines, S. (2011). Health inequalities and people with learning disabilities in the UK. *Tizard Learning Disability Review*, Emerald Group Publishing Limited, *16*(1), 42–48. https://doi.org/10.5042/tldr.2011.0008

Hatton, C., & Emerson, E. (2004). The relationship between life events and psychopathology amongst children with intellectual disabilities. *Mental Handicap Research, 17*(2), 109–117. https://doi.org/10.1111/j.1360–2322.2004.00188.x.

Hewitt, H. (2000). A life story approach for people with profound learning disabilities. *British Journal of Nursing, 9*(2), 90–95.

McGuire, D., & Chicoine, B. (2021). *Mental Wellness in Adults with Down Syndrome: A Guide to Emotional and Behavioral Strengths and Challenges* (2nd ed.). Brookes Publishing.

Meininger, H. P. (2005). Narrative ethics in nursing for persons with intellectual disabilities. *Nursing Philosophy, 6*(2), 106–118.

Moskowitz, J., Hult, J., Duncan, L., et al. (2011) A positive affect intervention for people experiencing health-related stress: Development and non-randomized pilot test. *Journal of Health Psychology, 17*(5), 676–692. https://doi.org/10.1177/1359105311425275

Ott, R. L. (1993). Enhancing validation through milestoning with sensory reminiscence. *Journal of Gerontological Social Work, 20*(1–2), 147–159.

Pounsett, H., Parker, K., Hawtin, A., & Collins, S. (2006). Examination of the changes that take place during an art therapy intervention. *International Journal of Art Therapy, 11*(2), 79–101. https://doi.org/10.1080/17454830600980325

Puyenbroeck, J. V., & Maes, B. (2005). Reminiscence in ageing people with intellectual disabilities: An exploratory study. *The British Journal of Development Disabilities, 51*(100), 3–16.

Puyenbroeck, J. V., & Maes, B. (2006). Program development of reminiscence group work for ageing people with intellectual disabilities. *Journal of Intellectual & Developmental Disability, 31*(3), 139–147. https://doi.org/10.1080/13668250600862988

Puyenbroeck, J. V., & Maes, B. (2008). A review of critical, person-centred and clinical approaches to reminiscence work for people with intellectual disabilities. *International Journal of Disability, Development and Education, 55*(1), 43–60. https://doi.org/10.1080/10349120701827979

Stephenson, R. C. (2006). Promoting self-expression through art therapy. *Generations, 30*(1), 24–26.

Stueber, K., & Hassiotis, A. (2012). Reminiscence therapy for older service users. *Learning Disability Practice, 15*(2), 12–16. https://doi.org/10.7748/ldp2012.03.15.2.12.c8965

Wong, C. W. (2011). Adults with intellectual disabilities living in Hong Kong's residential care facilities: A descriptive analysis of health and disease patterns by sex, age, and presence of Down syndrome. *Journal of Policy and Practice in Intellectual Disabilities, 8*(4), 231–238. https://doi.org/10.1111/j.1741-1130.2011.00318.x

How Do We Hear the Voice Behind the Smile? Group Art Therapy Coming Out of a Coronavirus Pandemic Lockdown

Siobhán Burns, Hazel Meakin and Connie Newcombe

Positionality Statement

The writers Siobhán Burns and Hazel Meakin are white female Art Psychotherapists without learning disabilities working in the National Health Service (NHS) in England. Co-author Dr Connie Newcombe is a white female without learning disabilities working as a Clinical Psychologist in the same healthcare service. When we have included the words of people with learning disabilities in our writing, we have used direct quotes. The people we have written about gave their permission for us to use their words and they let us know that they were happy for other people to read their words. They have chosen their own pseudonyms to protect their identity.

Introduction

This chapter discusses an art therapy group provided in a National Health Service (NHS), Community Learning Disability Team in the aftermath of a lockdown as a result of the COVID-19 pandemic, where people were asked by the UK government to stay at home and their travel was restricted. The group was delivered as restrictions in England were lifting and people tried to resume their everyday lives. Our aim was to provide a restorative experience and a safe place for people with learning disabilities to process some of their thoughts, feelings, and memories in connection with lockdown. In the group, people also reflected on multiple complex losses that may have been triggered by their experiences during the coronavirus pandemic. Our work as art therapists in the Community Learning Disability Team has taught us that the voices of people with learning disabilities are often not heard and frequently dismissed, leading to chronic disempowerment. We also present both quantitative and qualitative data collected for evaluation purposes during the therapy which focuses on mental health and three people's experience of the group.

Lockdown in England

When the coronavirus pandemic began at the end of 2019, no one anticipated the total number of COVID deaths or the changes society would experience in

DOI: 10.4324/9781003350736-19

response. Governments across the world responded differently, with some countries choosing to 'lockdown' movement of populations to try to contain the spread of the virus.

As COVID-19 cases increased in the UK, people waited to see how the British government would respond. From March-June 2020, England experienced a national lockdown with all non-essential businesses closing. People were instructed to stay at home and only leave their homes for essential purposes, such as buying food or accessing essential healthcare. Non-urgent healthcare appointments were cancelled, schools were closed, and people were instructed to leave a minimum distance of two metres between each other when passing on the street or queuing in shops. This was the first lockdown in England.

Three further lockdowns occurred in the next nine months, up to March 2021, with a range of different rules to try to manage infections but keep society functioning, as a new variant of coronavirus emerged. For much of the rest of 2021, there was a staged easing of restrictions, to support schools and businesses to re-open, as the population learned to live with coronavirus (House of Commons, 2021).

By December 2023, almost a quarter of a million COVID-19-related deaths were recorded in the UK (Gov.UK, 2023) with the global estimate at almost 7 million (Worldometer, 2024). In addition to loss of life, it seems impossible to quantify the overall impact of COVID-19; the loss of loved ones, the long-term impact of COVID-19 on people's physical and mental health, the impact of enforced isolation, as well as the disruption to normal life including education, health services, and businesses.

The Impact of the Coronavirus Pandemic on People with Learning Disabilities in Britain, Inequities, and the Psychological Impact

There has been a disproportionate impact of the pandemic on people with learning disabilities. Not only were existing barriers to accessing healthcare exacerbated during COVID-19 (Mencap, 2020), but the death rate for people with learning disabilities was up to six times higher than the general population (Public Health England, 2020).

Another example of significant health inequalities for people with learning disabilities was the higher risk of receiving an inappropriate 'Do Not Attempt Cardiopulmonary Resuscitation' (DNACPR) during the early phases of the coronavirus pandemic, which could potentially deny this group of people lifesaving treatment (White et al., 2022). Some individuals reported being told by doctors, that if they required the use of a ventilator, this would be denied (Clegg, 2021). These messages have an impact on the internal lives of people with learning disabilities and can affect their relationship with themselves, with others and with their trust in society.

The combination of England's lockdown policy with additional guidance for people with health vulnerabilities needing to clinically shield resulted in extended periods of isolation for many people with learning disabilities. Although not intended as an oppressive measure, this involved closing off spaces so that people were unheard and unseen. The Mencap report *Left Behind and Locked Down* (2022) highlighted how isolation during the pandemic impacted people's lives and care, and this took away spaces to hear the voice of people with learning disabilities. As restrictions were lifted, and services reopened, the potential of an art therapy group was significant in addressing increased isolation and beginning to build lost confidence in the world outside people's homes, which for many of us had become unfamiliar and frightening.

Adapting Art Therapy Practice in the Coronavirus Pandemic

All healthcare professionals were forced by the coronavirus pandemic to rapidly adapt practice to continue to meet the clinical needs of the populations they served. Largely this meant finding ways to observe social distancing but continue to deliver clinical sessions and also to make use of online technology to assist in continuing to provide clinical care (Zubala & Hackett, 2020). Art therapists quickly adapted to new ways of working, though remote consultations (e.g. over the phone or video call) did not always meet the needs of people with learning disabilities (Power, Dolby & Thorne, 2021).

In our Community Learning Disability Service, the team was predominantly working from home during lockdown and the support focused more on the systems around people with learning disabilities, so their voices were often not heard directly. Video call art therapy sessions were offered where service users had access and support to use technology. For others, we made doorstep deliveries of art materials or sent resources by post. Often, we felt restricted, hoping that somehow the limited informal support we offered at a distance to carers and families might filter down as reassurance or encouragement to the people in receipt of services.

When we were able to return to offering some face-to-face appointments, strict guidelines had to be followed which impacted the delivery of art therapy. One of the ways we supported people with learning disabilities to prepare for these new ways of working was through reasonable adjustments, in the form of writing social stories (Gray, 1991). This was an easy-read statement in written and picture form explaining how to follow the COVID guidelines in an art therapy session. These sometimes included photos of the therapists with and without face coverings so that clients would not be alarmed if we looked different from usual.

The Aim of the Art Therapy Group, a Space to Be Seen and Heard

Running an art therapy group as soon as restrictions eased was an act of trying to restore some of what had been lost in the pandemic, to restore spaces where people can be seen and heard. We also acknowledged that for many people with learning disabilities, historic and ongoing losses and trauma are a significant part of their life experience that can be seen as multilayered or a spectrum of loss (Power, Harrison, Hackett and Carr, 2023). For people with learning disabilities who communicate differently and who are often reliant on other people for daily living, voice is complex. Being able to express anything other than satisfaction or contentment can be risky if you are dependent on the goodwill or compassion of others to meet your daily needs. When compassion or empathy is in short supply and carers' and professionals' resources are stretched, a smile may be a protective defence against painful feelings rather than an authentic expression of joy (Sinason, 2010, 2020). In the art therapy group, we worked to provide a safe enough space for people to be vulnerable and bring all the parts of their experiences.

Loss and Trauma for People with Learning Disabilities

The link between learning disabilities and trauma is well established. People with learning disabilities are more likely to experience trauma than the general population (McNally, Taggart, and Shevlin, 2021). We aimed to make our art therapy group trauma informed so that it could be an accessible space for people with learning disabilities to start to process their difficult experiences and give voice to painful losses. We can all respond differently to the same event, and if it is a traumatic response, we may continue to be affected a long time after the event or events have happened. At the time of offering the group, we were experiencing a global pandemic which has been described as traumatic (Sanchez-Gomez et al., 2021).

The Voice behind the Smile, Eliciting and Amplifying People's Voices in the Group

In designing the group, we were aware of the overwhelming tendency of many people with learning disabilities to acquiesce, to agree, to be all right and say 'yes' when asked a question. We tried to encourage people to feel safe enough to consider alternatives if this was helpful. We were aware that smiling and being 'all right' was a useful mask in some situations but can be damaging if it excludes the possibility of people being able to express a more complex range of responses.

As non-learning disabled art therapists, we cannot assume understanding and consent from a nod or a smile. For people with learning disabilities, saying 'No' may be met with surprise. This could provoke further questions, further explanations, a querying of whether the decision to say 'No' is an informed one or whether the individual really has capacity to make that particular decision at that particular time. Saying 'No' when it is more helpful to say 'Yes' could become a 'behaviour of concern' if it is persistent. Words such as 'difficult', 'stubborn' or 'challenging' may be used, and there are consequences to these labels so perhaps 'Yes' is easier, safer and, not surprisingly, heard more often. This is movingly articulated by Adam in *Art Therapy & Learning Disabilities: Don't guess my happiness!* (O'Farrell, 2012, P. 1).

Being in a group with other people who have learning disabilities can allow people to share experiences of frustration about the lack of control they experience over their own lives when life-changing decisions are made by others in their best interests. We were mindful of creating opportunities for genuine choice in the group (e.g. in the use of art-making) while recognising the limitations of choice and the number of decisions made solely by the facilitators (e.g. the group members were informed rather than consulted about the venue, length of sessions and length of the group rather than this being collaboratively designed).

Intersecting Losses: Before, During and After the Pandemic

Loss and powerlessness have been identified as common themes in working with people with learning disabilities (O'Farrell, 2012). The pandemic was identified as a societal trauma involving bereavement and loss (Kaubisch et al., 2022). There was loss of structure and routine, loss of predictability, loss of health, loss of connections and loss of life. The new experience of loss also brings up previous losses that may not have been able to be fully recognised, acknowledged or thought about at the time (O'Riordan et al., 2022). The bereavement experience of group members prior to the pandemic included loss of parents, a sister, the loss of a baby for one group member and for another a recent loss of a family member through suicide. For some, there had also been loss of contact with family members and friends during lockdown.

Planning and Structuring the Group

The group was offered to people who were referred to art therapy or clinical Psychology and who were considered to have had a difficult or isolated experience in lockdown. Each person came to an individual assessment meeting to discuss the group with two art therapists.

Four people accepted a space in the art therapy group after the initial assessment meeting, although one person did not continue after the first session due to experiencing high anxiety around health issues. Detailed risk assessments were completed to comply with NHS Trust and UK Government guidelines around COVID-19 and were discussed in the initial assessments.

The group had 12 weekly art therapy sessions, each lasting for 90 minutes. Sessions were co-facilitated, usually by two art therapists, but a third art therapist and a trainee clinical psychologist also supported facilitation as needed (e.g. where one therapist was on sick leave due to COVID).

The sessions began with welcoming the group members and taking time to check-in with how people were feeling. Visual resources such as pictures of faces showing different emotions were used to support the check-in. People often expressed feeling happy in the check-in, as if it were a default position of what was expected. A numerical scale with pictures of a sad and happy face at either end was sometimes helpful for people to think about their current mood or how they had felt during the week. The one-to-ten scale opened up the possibility of understanding mood or emotions as more nuanced and people were able to consider their mood on a scale rather than just as being 'happy' or 'sad'. This was followed by art-making or a more structured activity such as creating self-sooth boxes with support offered from the art therapists. There was time at the end of the group for discussion of people's experiences of using the materials including any thoughts or feelings people had noticed during the session. Several themes were explored, which we will discuss in the following sections.

Themes which Emerged in the Art Therapy Group

Identity

In the first session, group members were asked to make self-portraits or to create an image which described something about themselves that they wanted to share with the group. Michael, who had restricted mobility and came to the group in a wheelchair, made an image of himself playing football. Christine, who was in her 60s and had short silver hair, used collage materials to depict herself with long hair made of wool. This theme highlighted people's desire to be seen as more than their age or disability.

Shared Image Making

In the second and third sessions, group members worked collaboratively on a shared image around the theme of gardens and the outside spaces that had been important during the lockdown (Figure 14.1). Each group member decided on an individual aspect of the image that they wanted to work on. For Tracy and Christine, this involved choosing to colour pictures of animals visiting the garden. Michael took the lead in bringing the different elements of the image together, and the result was a large colourful image in multimedia which was collectively owned and appreciated by the group. Each group member was given a laminated photo of the group image to add to their individual folders of art produced in the group.

This activity helped to foster a positive group dynamic. People could see their contributions as representing their own voice, and at the same time, working together on a shared image was a way to create connections.

Making Connections, Sending Out Shoots

The respectful and supportive group dynamic was a recurring theme in the group. Turn taking and the expectation that each group member would have time to talk and be listened to was part of the inherent structure of the group. A gentle and open curiosity to everything the group members shared either verbally or through art-making was modelled by the art therapists with follow-up questions prompting

Figure 14.1 Group collage.

group members to explore further the issues that they shared with the group. Christine said this allowed her space to talk about living in a home environment where people are *'always falling out'*. She had expressed dissatisfaction with her living arrangements over a sustained period, and it took literally years for any changes to be made. Staying with family during lockdown offered a break from these difficult dynamics; however, return to normality for Christine meant returning to living with another person she felt incompatible with. Christine's comment: *'Things happen, whether we like them or not'* illustrates an insight into the ongoing disempowerment she felt regarding the choices in her life.

In the group, people listened and took an interest in the work of others. Shared feelings of pride in what each member had created were expressed and acknowledged by other group members. Absences were noticed and missed, and people asked facilitators to let the other members of the group know when they would return.

In one of the early group sessions, we asked group members if they would like to plant flower bulbs which would be stored in plant pots over the winter and returned to the group members by the end of the group. Planting the bulbs could be seen as act of hope for the future. When they were returned to the group, there was genuine delight that the bulbs which were a selection of hyacinths, daffodils and tulips had grown and transformed into plants. We could see the green shoots which had emerged along with some longer stems and we hoped that the group members would be able to see their plants flower at home after the group had ended.

Recognising Loss

It Was Important to Create Spaces for Expression of Loss as well as Hope

Some art-based activities enabled people to voice painful losses. One way that loss emerged was in response to a *Personal Universe* activity. Group members made models depicting the important relationships in their lives. This involved putting themselves at the centre of an image and identifying people close and important to them and also people who were significant but more distant. This activity can help people to notice if they would like some people to be closer or want more space from others. It can highlight where a person feels supported and where there are difficulties.

During this activity, group members noted that people who have died are very much part of our personal universe, and it gave space for people to include them in a less direct way. Michael, who had lost his mother several years ago but had struggled to talk about it, was able to notice and express that even though his mother was no longer here, she was a very significant part of his life. This seemed a supportive development in the process of his grieving.

A theme later in the group involved making images thinking about absent friends and remembering special people. Christine made an image of a church interior in memory of a relative who had died. Both the image and the conversation about the layout of the picture seemed to create space for her to identify feelings in relation to her loss. The image also resonated with other members of the group. Tracy was able to talk about attending the funeral of her child and talked in detail about the painful experience of the journey to and from the ceremony. Previously she had denied any experience of loss, perhaps feeling too vulnerable or unsafe in the group, or not knowing how to begin.

Plant Pots as Containers

The theme of 'containing' (Bion, 1962) was introduced through a group activity of making pots to hold the plants (grown from bulbs) out of modelling materials. We provided an assortment of different three-dimensional media. Group members were particularly interested in comparing the feel of plasticine, play dough and clay, bringing awareness to the tactile experience. This activity may have offered a way to hold or contain experiences without relying on verbal communication. The sensory experience of exploring modelling materials aligns with a 'bottom-up' approach to trauma treatment (Van der Kolk, 2015). This can help to explore and regulate traumatic experiences in a safe way, through tactile discovery which relies on sensory processing, rather than on words (Porges, 2017; Ogden, Minton & Pain, 2006).

Empowerment and Finding a Voice

Disempowerment is often part of the lived experience of people with learning disabilities (Bull and O'Farrell, 2012). This was intensified during the pandemic. By the end of the group, we saw that art therapy had supported some members to feel more empowered. Tracy said that she wanted to speak for herself. Previously at review meetings, she had allowed her husband to speak for her as her carer and her own progress had been considered through the lens of her husband's opinions. She said, *"I have got a tongue in my head too"*. Tracy demonstrated her increased confidence in finding and using her own voice. She also shared her feeling of increased confidence with the group members and described an occasion where she had spoken in public at church. This was recognised and celebrated in the group.

Capturing Voices Using Data

We used two paper-based outcome measures: (1) Hospital Anxiety and Depression Scale (HADS; Zigmond & Snaith, 1983; Dagnan et al, 2008) which is a self-report measure. It has the following subscales: anxiety and depression. (2) Moss Psychiatric Assessment Schedule – Intellectual Disability (Moss-PAS ID; Beail et al., 2015) which is an informant-based measure which means that questions were answered by a carer or professional who knows the individual well. It has the following subscales: anxiety, depression, hypomania and mania, obsessive-compulsive, psychosis, unspecified, autism. These outcome measures were administered by a clinical psychologist, pre- and post-intervention. Verbal feedback from group members was gathered about people's experience during a session mid-way through the group and at the end of the group as well as in follow-up meetings with individuals a year after the group ended. This more informal feedback was carried out by two art therapists who facilitated the majority of the sessions.

Pre- and Post-Group Measures

Four individuals consented to completing the pre-group measures and only two were able to prioritise completing the post-group measures six months after completing the pre-group measures. The HADS (anxiety and depression) mean total scores decreased after the group [mean total score reduced from pre- 10.5 ($n = 4$) to post-group 7.5 ($n = 2$)].

For the Moss-PAD ID, due to the limited data set, statistical significance has not been calculated as this would not be meaningful. The two members of the group who completed pre- and post-group Moss-PAD ID measures showed improvements on specific subscales. For example, Michael's scores reduced below the clinical threshold (to a non-clinical level) on subscales for 'anxiety' and 'psychosis', showing measurable improvement. Christine also had reduced scores to below the clinical threshold for the 'anxiety' and 'depression' subscales. Individuals moving from a clinical threshold to a non-clinical threshold for specific symptom subscales indicates that some group participants experienced helpful post-group mental health symptom reduction.

Qualitative Feedback

People were asked about their experience of the group during a session mid-way through the group with one of the art therapists taking the lead in asking the questions while the other therapist made notes. The questions and responses show how a standardised questionnaire would not elicit the voices of the group members in the way that a more conversational style can. It shows it is important to be able to adapt the way the questions are asked to enable people with learning disabilities to express their voice (Finley & Lyons, 2001).

Christine

Christine said:　"*I've really, really enjoyed it. I would like to come back to another group.*"

Art therapist:　What have you liked about it?

Christine:　"*Yes*"

Art therapist:　Have you liked talking to people or making art?

Christine:　"*Yes*"

Art therapist:　What did you think about the size of the group?

　　　　　　　"*I liked a small amount of people, about four*"

We asked which activities people had enjoyed, which included creating self-portraits, making a group picture, planting flower bulbs, making a coping skills poster, decorating a self-soothe box, making bowls from clay. Christine said: "*I think I've liked them all*".

Christine also talked about enjoying the group as "*people are kind to each other with no falling out*". She compared this to her experience of conflict at her supported living home which she found extremely difficult.

Tracy

Tracy said:

> *I really enjoyed the group and I'd like to come back. I liked having time for myself. I liked meeting everyone as well, I liked colouring and planting bulbs, I've never grown anything before, I didn't know I could do that.*

Michael

Michael said:　"*I think its been good*"

Art therapist:　Is there anything in particular you have liked?

　　　　　　　"*planting bulbs*"

Art therapist:	Is there anything you'd have liked to be different?
	"I enjoyed it all!"
Art therapist:	What about the size of the group?
	"I would like more people ... about seven"
	We asked about the experience of having different facilitators of the group.
Michael said:	*"It was nice to meet different people".*

Although we asked for change suggestions for future groups or anything people would have liked to be different about the group, we did not gather any ideas for change.

Revisiting the Group Members to Write this Chapter

We arranged to meet with Christine, Tracey, and Michael to discuss the possibility of writing this chapter and each agreed to the two authors visiting them individually at their homes to talk to them about what they remembered about the group and ask their consent to write about this. We wanted to hear their thoughts and feelings as they reflected on the group over a year later. We used a combination of voice recording and note taking and extracted comments specific to the art therapy group.

Christine

Art Therapist:	Can you remember what you liked or didn't like?
Christine:	*"It was just a lovely group"*
	Art Therapist asked about the size of the group.
Christine (described liking a small group):	*"If you have a lot of people in the group, they can't hear themselves talk"*

Tracy

Art Therapist:	What can you remember about the group?
Tracy:	*"Making a picture of me, a wooden template, wool hair"*
	"Making boxes, treasure, smelly things, sweets, teddy bear for softness"
	"Cutting out pictures to stick on the box"
	"A group picture, a hedgehog, squirrel"
	"At the beginning of the group we introduced ourselves, saying our names"
Art therapist:	Was there anything you liked or didn't like?
Tracy:	*"I enjoyed all the groups, helps with isolation"*
	"I talked about losing someone, lost a baby. I remember Christine's drawing of a church to remember a relative".

Michael

Art therapist: Can you remember what you liked?
Michael: *"It was good, the people, I can't remember their names"*
Art therapist: Can you remember anything you did?
Michael: *"Planting the bulbs, painting, drawing"*
                  "Is there another group?"

Conclusion

The story of the art therapy group coming out of the COVID lockdown has drawn our attention to the potential of art therapy groups to support empowerment and hear the unheard voice. At a time when people with learning disabilities were less visible, the group was a space where people were seen and heard. People were able to be heard more fully as they started to bring and share the parts of themselves that were hidden behind the mask of contentment or the 'handicapped smile' (Sinason, 2010). Michael was able to acknowledge the painful loss of his mother, Tracey shared the trauma of loss of a child, and Christine shared her frustration at not having choice and control over her living arrangements. O'Driscoll states "disability therapists, by understanding their clients' experiences, are in a privileged position to give voice to their needs" (O'Driscoll, 2022). This is something we are passionate about. The inequalities highlighted by the coronavirus pandemic reminded us of the continuing need to acknowledge the oppression of people with learning disabilities. As art therapists who do not have learning disabilities, we will inevitably have blind spots and what we cannot see impacts therapy spaces. We hope this awareness enables an openness to deepen our capacity to listen and hear. We hope the space of the art therapy group went some way towards enabling the voice of people who too often find it difficult to be heard.

References

Beail, N., Mitchell, K., Vlissides, N., & Jackson T. (2015). Concordance of the Mini-Psychiatric Assessment Schedule for Adults who have Developmental Disabilities (PAS-ADD) and the Brief Symptom Inventory. *Journal of Intellectual Disability Research, 59*(2), 170–175. https://doi.org/10.1111/jir.12073

Bion, W. R. (1962). *Learning from Experience*. London: Karnac Books.

Bull, S., & O'Farrell, K. (Eds.) (2012). *Art Therapy and Learning Disabilities: Don't Guess my Happiness*. London & New York: Routledge.

Dagnan, D., Jahoda, A., McDowell, K., Masson, J., Banks, P., & Hare, D. (2008). The Psychometric Properties of the Hospital Anxiety and Depression Scale Adapted for use with People with Intellectual Disabilities. *Journal of Intellectual Disability Research, 52*(2), 942–949. https://doi.org/10.1111/j.1365-2788.2008.01053.x

Finley, W. M. L., & Lyons, E. (2001). Methodological Issues in Interviewing and Using Self-Report Questionnaires with People with Mental Retardation. *Psychological Assessment, 13*, 319–335. https://doi.org/10.1037/1040-3590.13.3.319

GOV.UK. (2023). *Coronovirus (COVID-19) in the UK* (last updated 14 December 2023).

McNally. P Taggart, L., & Shevlin, M. (2021). Trauma Experiences of People with an Intellectual Disability and their Implications: A Scoping Review. *Journal of Applied Research in Intellectual Disabilities, 34* (4), 927–949. https://doi.org/10.1111/jar.12872

Mencap. (2020). *My Health, My Life: Barriers to Healthcare for People with a Learning Disability during the Pandemic. Health Report. Mencap.* Online Resource. Available at: https://www.mencap.org.uk/get-involved/campaign-mencap/treat-me-well/barriers-healthcare-people-learning-disability-during

Mencap. (2022). *Left Behind and Locked Down - New Figures from Mencap Highlight how Social Care has been 'Ravaged by the Pandemic'.* 21 March 2022. Online Resource. Available at: https://www.mencap.org.uk/press-release/left-behind-and-locked-down-new-figures-mencap-highlight-how-social-care-has-been

O'Driscoll, D. (2022). *Community Living Valerie Sinason – a Prime Mover in Psychotherapy for People with Learning Disabilities.* Charity C L Initiatives Ltd.

Ogden, P., & Minton K. Pain, C. (2006). *Trauma and the Body: A Sensorimotor Approach to Psychotherapy.* W.W Norton & Company.

O'Riordan, D., Conway, E., Dodd, P. & Guerin, S. (2024). Adapting Complicated Grief Therapy for Use With People With Intellectual Disabilities: An Action Research Study. *Journal of Applied Research in Intellectual Disabilities*, *37*, e13296. https://doi.org/10.1111/jar.13296

Porges, S. (2017). *The Pocket Guide to the Polyvagal Theory: The Transformative Power of Feeling Safe.* W.W. Norton & Company.

Power, N., Harrison, T., Hackett, S.H., & Carr, C. (2023). *Art Therapy as a Treatment for Adults with Learning Disabilities Who Are Experiencing Mental Distress: A Configurative Systematic Review with Narrative Synthesis.* Available at: https://www.sciencedirect.com/science/article/piiS0197455623000953

Power, N., Dolby, R., & Thorne, D. (2021). 'Reflecting or Frozen?' The Impact of Covid-19 on Art Therapists Working with People with a Learning Disability. *International Journal of Art Therapy*, 26(3), 84–95. https://doi.org/10.1080/17454832.2020.1871388

Sinason, V. (2010). *Mental Handicap and the Human Condition: An Analytic Approach to Intellectual Disability.* Revised edition. Free Association Books.

Sinason, V. (2020). *The Truth about Trauma and Dissocation: Everything you Didn't Want to Know and Were Afraid to Ask.* Confer Books.

Van Der Kolk, B. (2015). *The Body Keeps the Score.* Penguin Books. https://www.worldometers.info/coronavirus/ Coronavirus Death Toll and Trends Feb2024

White, A., Sheehan, R., Ding, J., Roberts, C., Magill, N., Keagan-Bull, R., Carter, B., Ruane, M., Xiang, X., Chauhan, U., Tuffrey-Wijne, I., & Strydom, A., (2022). *Learning from Lives and Deaths - People with a Learning Disability and Autistic People (LeDeR) Report for 2021 (LeDeR 2021).* Autism and Learning Disability Partnership, King's College. Online Resource. Available at: https://www.kcl.ac.uk/ioppn/assets/fans-dept/leder-main-report-hyperlinked.pdf

Worldometer. (2024). *COVID-19 Coronavirus Pandemic.* Online Resource. Available at: https://www.worldometers.info/coronavirus/

Zigmond, A. S., & Snaith, R. P. (1983). The Hospital Anxiety and Depression Scale. *Acta Psychiatrica Scandinavica*, *67*(6), 361–370. https://doi.org/10.1111/j.1600-0447.1983.tb09716.x

Zubala, A., & Hackett, S. (2020). Online art Therapy Practice and Client Safety: A UK-wide Survey in Times of COVID-19. *International Journal of Art Therapy*, *25*(4), 161–171. https://doi.org/10.1080/17454832.2020.1845221

Chapter 15

Revising the Rules of Social Interaction

Stories of Power, Inclusion, and Why I Don't Have a Mustache

Sandra Hewitt-Parsons

Positionality Statement

I (Sandra Hewitt-Parsons) am a Canadian registered Art Therapist (RCAT). I also identify as a white cis-gender woman with complex disabilities. I have worked with people with learning and complex disabilities for over ten years. I'm very grateful to the people I have written about in this chapter for allowing me to tell our story. Their artwork is used with permission.

Introduction

"You're just like me!"

Brandon, who was one of the participants at our community art studio that day, was quite astonished at his discovery. He acknowledged this revelation by gleefully exclaiming the words above.

Unfortunately, I was on a roll. And, since I was on a roll at that moment, I was speaking before my brain got a chance to really process what was said.

"Mmmmmm...well, I don't know", I said, dramatically squinting while scrutinizing him carefully, *"...I don't have a mustache."*

Laughter erupted from the personal support workers behind me. But Brandon didn't change his expression. He didn't speak. He didn't need to. The look in his eyes spoke volumes.

Deeply ashamed of myself at that moment, I wished I could take back my words. I wished I could wave a magic wand and rewind to just seconds ago when we talked, laughed, and respected each other. I knew what he was thinking. I knew how he was feeling. I *knew*.

And I should have known better.

A deficit-oriented disability perspective can completely shut down a desire for genuine connection (Nario-Redmond et al., 2019; Robey et al., 2006). Despite progress in the last few decades, dominant social groups can still think of disability as "less than" (Brown, 2019). As a society, we may not often discriminate against people with disabilities on a conscious level; however, implicit attitudes toward disability are slow to change (Colorafi et al., 2021; Redley et al., 2012; Van

DOI: 10.4324/9781003350736-20

Aswegen & Shevlin, 2019). These implicit attitudes can result in deficit-oriented responses to disability, including pity, patronizing interactions, and avoidance (Reber et al., 2022). These responses can reinforce the privileged perspective of ableism while creating feelings of vulnerability, frustration, and anger among those of us who identify with the diverse disability community (Ingham, 2018; Reber et al., 2022). Of this diversity, people with learning disabilities are particularly vulnerable (Abbott & McConkey, 2006).

Unspoken rules based on a traditional social hierarchy tend to govern how we interact in society (Brown, 2019). Rather than engaging with people based on a traditional power dynamic framework, appreciating community members with disabilities can be accomplished from a social justice perspective. One way to introduce this perspective is through open art studio groups (Miller, 20200; Timm-Bottos, 2006). These inclusive studios encourage people of different backgrounds, cultures, and abilities to work creatively with various art materials. In these "third spaces" (Timm-Bottos & Reilly, 2015b, p. 1), participants are encouraged to express themselves honestly in a safe and supportive environment. This authenticity can result in better communication and increased understanding between individuals with disabilities and other participants. Social interaction within an open art studio space can lead to a strengthened sense of self and improved relationships with others (Timm-Bottos, 2006).

This chapter will explore these "rules" of social interaction through a disability lens by drawing on my experiences as an art therapist with a disability at the local community art studio. After my introduction and a summary of the Art Hives movement, this chapter will continue in three sections. The first section will examine the pros and cons of community inclusion, with diverse participants from my small town in the studio. The second section will take a closer look at studio interactions between participants with a learning disability and those who care for these participants. The third section will unpack interactions between participants with a learning disability and myself as a disabled art therapist.

My Background

I am a person with a disability. I also believe that societal norms have physically, economically, and educationally disabled individuals with limitations. Therefore, the terms "person with a disability" and "disabled" will be used interchangeably throughout this chapter. In addition, I will use the term "ableist" to describe traditional values and attitudes that disable those of us with impairments. No offense to the reader is intended.

I was not disabled from birth; rather, my disability resulted from a massive childhood stroke at eight years of age.

This time and place are relevant to my story. The late 1970s to early 1980s were the beginning of positive change for disability. In Canada, we were beginning to transition from institutions and segregation to community living. But not everyone in my community was comfortable with that.

In those days, my disability was rarely, if ever, discussed. The medical experts at the time believed that talking about my traumatic head injury would only confuse and upset me. There also seemed to be a general belief among the wider community that to acknowledge disability was to admit weakness. To mention my limitations would only invite pitying stares and patronizing responses.

My family insisted that I was just as good as anyone else. Though it didn't stop some people from treating me like I didn't belong, I had to pretend to be just like everyone else to fit in. I must have done an exceptional job at this pretense. In high school, I can easily remember teachers and other students commenting *"You don't act like someone with a disability"* and *"I don't see you as disabled"*. Rather than openly talking about disability, I realize now that these were the statements that really confused me. I'll speak more on that later in this chapter.

It's never been easy to look back at my childhood when I was denying a huge part of myself. I didn't want to have a disability if disability was pitiable. It's a little silly to think of now because my physical impairment is obvious. However, I felt I had to construct an identity out of bits and pieces of characteristics valued by my community. As a result, my complex struggles related to my disability (including challenges with the physical environment and with learning) became my shameful secrets.

The turning point for me came after I moved away from home. At university, I met other people with disabilities. These people spoke of issues that were like my own. It took some time, but I slowly began to realize that the world wouldn't end if I admitted that I needed help. By the time I decided to apply for an art therapy master's, I was working with people with a diversity of mental and physical challenges. These people were trying to integrate their disabilities as part of who they were as individuals.

I first heard of Art Hives (Timm-Bottos, 2006; Timm-Bottos & Reilly, 2014) while I was an art therapy student. This network is a social justice initiative to unite people through artmaking. Starting in 2007 in Albuquerque, New Mexico by Janis Timm-Bottos, the Art Hives network is now an international movement with growing numbers of studios in North America and elsewhere worldwide.

This was a turning point in my life – my perfect way to introduce a social justice-informed, diversity-oriented framework in my home community!

Description of the Art Hives

Timm-Bottos states that the Art Hive model is founded in a hybridized collaboration of art therapy, art education, science, critical studies, and the creative arts (2016). This network brings together people of all cultures, ethnicities, social status, and abilities to connect through art. The Art Hive movement is grounded in relational theory (Allport, 1954; Winnicott, 1971). It is designed to be a liminal space where traditional rules of society do not apply but where magic can happen. Participants are known by their first names and not extraneous titles, diagnoses, or labels. In an Art Hive, traditional power dynamics are cast aside in favor of engaging authentically with one another. This kind of relational exchange allows us to define ourselves as real people through interaction experience. In this space, peers from the diverse participant group learn from each other; therefore, no one person is seen as a consistent group leader. In this way, new skills can be shared, alternate perspectives can be discovered, and new knowledge can be uncovered.

Growing up with a disability, I have experienced the negative impact of ableist power dynamics and cultural bias in my small community. I knew the pain of being unable to express who I was and having to hide part of myself like it was something to be ashamed of. With this experience, I knew that creating an Art Hives studio was just what my area needed.

With community partners providing the space, community members providing donations of art supplies, and the local university providing undergraduate volunteers, I opened the region's first community art studio in the fall of 2013. As an art therapy student, I was enthusiastic. I was fully prepared to deconstruct assumptions and provide learning opportunities brought about by new experiences in social engagement. Little did I know that my education in social interactions had only just begun!

Us vs Them – Inclusivity and the whole Community

First set up in pop-up studios at various places around town, a permanent location for the community art studio was soon established in the local arts center. Promotions and invitations went out on social media, community bulletin boards, and by word of mouth to everyone I knew.

The first few drop-in groups included professional artists, students interested in art therapy, families, seniors, and people with various disabilities. They went exceedingly well, with group members meeting, engaging, and interacting with each other.

Over the next few weeks, however, certain participants stopped coming.

For some people, this was understandable. The seniors had their own art groups, professional artists had their own art practices to run, and families had other fall and winter activities in which to participate.

A few participants with no disabilities admitted feeling a little uncomfortable in the sharing of the art space. They didn't know what to say or how to interact meaningfully with learning-disabled participants. They didn't want to offend or upset these group members. Though they believed in what we were trying to achieve, this awkwardness soon resulted in these participants avoiding the studio.

Others seemed to have stronger opinions. I remember one particularly upset individual telling me that they thought this studio was for "everyone", but instead, it was "that kind" of art class. To remedy this, a few participants asked the visual arts coordinator of the arts center to help them create a separate art studio group, to be held weekly after our "inclusive" event.

Some participants with learning disabilities felt uncomfortable too. Many of these group members were people I had worked with one-on-one. Though they knew me, these participants did not know other people at the studio. There was a lack of familiarity and trust among many individuals with disabilities toward those without disabilities. These disabled participants did not want to do or say anything that would reinforce potentially stereotypical attitudes held by some of those without disabilities. These group members would often fall silent, congregating in their own little corner and allowing much of the conversation to be led by individuals with no disabilities.

Participants seemed to enjoy themselves in the first few sessions of this inclusive program. But the word "inclusion" is not precisely or consistently defined in contemporary public policies (Griffo, 2014; Yuval-Davis, Anthias, & Kofman, 2005). Perhaps it was initially popular because of the novelty of a free open art studio. Perhaps I had ensured participation by those who had a similar understanding of "inclusion" with the understanding that there would be diverse groups there. Whatever the case, as numbers dwindled, it seemed like the "us" versus "them" gap was reinforced as a recognition of difference was once again established. Inclusion was all but forgotten as community social norms tried to re-assert themselves.

Social norms (Allen et al., 2021) are traditional perspectives interwoven through the cultural fabric of everyday experience. These perspectives are so prevalent that we may not even think about them until we are forced to. If somebody from another culture shares the space with us, our interactions can become explicitly mindful as we wonder what customs are shared, what customs are different, and how the newcomers will interpret our interactions.

As children, new experiences act as opportunities to learn about the world. Open community spaces are ideal if this type of learning is taking place (Timm-Bottos, 2006). We also rely on the perspectives of our family, friends, and other respected group members to establish social norms in shaping our view of the world.

As adults, these norms are often heavily relied upon because novel experiences in interacting with others are lacking. When assumptions based on these social norms are relied on exclusively, privileged group members can deem individuals as "other" (and often "less than") because of differences. This is when open community spaces can be the most rejecting (Hall, 2004; Wiesel & Bigby, 2014).

Despite such a promising start, there were times when our community art studio felt like a very uncomfortable place to be. At the first year's end, no one really felt like they belonged to a unified group. I certainly did not want these awkward encounters and local power dynamics to translate into hurt feelings and rejection. After speaking with community partners, volunteers, and several regular participants, it was decided that we would revise our goals and strategy for the next year.

Still Us vs Them – Participants and their Support Workers

As I transitioned to a practicing art therapist, my volunteers and I focused on making people feel welcome in year two of the community art studio. Though no one was turned away from the studio, I was particularly intent on encouraging the return of some of the people with learning disabilities and their personal support workers. These individuals were regular participants in our first year. Despite some uncomfortable moments at the program's onset, these participants really benefitted from interacting with each other in that first year.

Though the literature is divided on providing groups focused on inclusion for people with disabilities alone (Abbott & McConkey, 2006; Clement & Bigby, 2009), such groups can still have positive benefits. Many people with learning disabilities in my community lived independently but with limited contact with individuals outside the home. Most of the studio participants were at least familiar with one another and looked forward to socializing every week. Needed support and unique behavior were anticipated and not judged by strangers for what they would consider "abnormal". As a result, participants could feel free just to be themselves.

Social inclusion, meaningful interaction, and having a voice were still important goals for the group. Again, our community studio was an ideal place to accomplish these goals (Hall, 2010). Acknowledging and celebrating participants' diversity eventually led to an increased sense of empathy and an improved self-image. This acknowledgment also generated feelings of connection and belonging to the group. This resulted in a space that felt safer and more welcoming. It was hoped that participants would develop authentic, long-term friendships in the studio. Group members could build positive social skills by rehearsing them with each other in this revised "third space" (Timm-Bottos & Reilly, 2015, p. 1). Choice and control over materials to use, subjects to create, and even whether to make art each week felt empowering to many participants.

Figure 15.1 shows a painting by one of the community art studio participants.

At long last, this group was beginning to come together in the way I had envisioned. It was much better than the first year, at least. However, I still noticed uncomfortable moments between some participants and their support workers.

In year one, participants with disabilities would often separate from the main group in a passive presence and not actively interact with the individuals surrounding them. In year two, there seemed to be three types of relationships between disabled participants and their support workers:

1   many participants were building respectful and reciprocal relational bonds
2   some participants were engaging within a relational power dynamic
3   other participants were not engaging at all

Some group members made art alongside their support workers, reinforcing their relationship as they worked concurrently. The participants engaged in meaningful and authentic conversations with their workers; the conversations often expanded to include other group members sitting nearby. These interactions validated participants, making them feel seen, heard, and valued in the group.

Unequal power dynamics were at play between other disabled group members and their support workers. These participants made art while their support workers adopted a directing role. Dictating the types of art that were acceptable, the workers

Figure 15.1 Painting made by community art studio participant (used with permission.)

encouraged group members to create *"good art"* (or subjects based on positive emotions, like rainbows and kittens), while establishing that *"bad art"* (or subjects based on the group member's questionable or negative emotions) was off-limits. As a result of these directions, many participants felt angered and frustrated in a struggle for control over their own artwork.

A few participants had only limited contact with their support workers in the studio. These participants sat in one part of the room while their support workers sat in their own corner, engaging with their phones or magazines. Many of these participants became upset when their support workers seemed to ignore them. Some of these group members were eventually included in ongoing conversations, but others refused to make any more art or engage with anyone else in the space.

The community art studio was intended to enable people from all walks of life to meet, interact, and build meaningful relationships. This was accomplished for a lot of participants.

However, Jackman-Galvin and Partridge (2022) argue that it is hard to discard traditional institutionalized culture and resulting power differentials when interacting with people with intellectual disabilities. This was evident as support workers made executive decisions about what constituted "good art" for participants. Their perception of "bad art" seemed to violate idealized but biased notions of what a person with learning disabilities should be. Because their choices of concepts to create were limited to "happy" subjects, group members didn't always feel heard or understood for personal lived experience. As adults, they didn't want to be treated like children who must always be happy. They resisted when someone attempted to control their thoughts, questions, and ideas.

Other support workers declined to take part in these sessions. A few workers went further in dismissing the artwork, calling it *"silly"* and *"kindergarten art"*. These comments seemed to further alienate and "other" some of the group members with learning disabilities. If their support workers judged these activities to be "kindergarten-like", these adult participants wanted to distance themselves from artmaking.

Significant relationships remained key to feeling appreciated and included. Implicit attitudes based on social norms and traditional power dynamics disrupted these connections. Something needed to change to make everyone feel like they belonged to the group.

With the help of volunteers, we changed the physical layout of our safe space. No longer having separate tables and chairs all around the room, we arranged the seating areas into one long table. We encouraged the support workers who previously sat by themselves to join the larger group. These workers were surprised as they didn't consider this studio a relationship-building event for everyone. Rather, they assumed it was an "arts and crafts class" for participants with learning disabilities. Some of the workers resisted, saying that they couldn't draw. I reminded them that making art was a choice, not a requirement. Though self-determinism also extended to the personal support workers, relationship building required them to engage with those around them. Being present in the space and witnessing another's expression are keys to feeling valued and connected.

We also arranged discussions with the support workers who judged participants' creations as "good art" or "bad art". Based on the Art Hives model, the community art studio encouraged people to express their authentic selves and authentic emotions through artmaking. Though they perceived their role as supportive, these support workers were actually limiting participants' expressions by only allowing artwork that would reinforce traditional perspectives. We encouraged these workers to see the artwork as an invitation to discuss the participants' thoughts and feelings. In prohibiting creative works that didn't meet their criteria for "happy", many of these participants' experiences, ideas, and questions were being ignored. Authentic engagement over the art would ensure meaningful interaction.

With the above changes, I feel that we were successful in building stronger relationships among the group. In the years that followed, the volunteers and I would sometimes introduce sessions with unstructured spontaneous directives (such as scribble conversations, crayon tag, and picture stories) to initiate authentic conversation. These additional activities enhanced feelings of belonging to the group while supporting the development of a unique sense of self for individual participants (Kramer, 2000).

This conclusion marks the perfect place for the story of my experiences within the community art studio to end. In fact, it would end here, if I were talking about these social interactions as a neutral observer. But there was still one more unspoken rule for me to encounter. This rule involved interactions between participants who were learning disabled and myself as a disabled art therapist.

Us, Them, and me – Participants and me

I discovered this important rule when Brandon announced to the group:

"You're just like me!"

My response was fast and flippant. To everyone else, my response may have been funny. But I knew Brandon didn't find it very humorous. Immediately after the words escaped my mouth, I could truly understand why he wasn't laughing.

As I mentioned earlier in this chapter, I was not born with a disability. After my traumatic head injury, after a stay in the hospital and a lot of rehabilitation, I was sent back to my community. Physically, I was more or less "normalized" – I could walk (with a brace) and talk (stumbling over my words). Mentally, however, I was nowhere near prepared to resume community life. No one had ever talked to me about what it meant to be disabled and about the kind of discrimination that I would likely encounter. I don't suppose that anyone thought of this at the time, since professionals who were disability "experts" didn't have disabilities themselves. With limited support in my small community, I was left to my own devices. To fit in, I would have to navigate the uncharted social dynamics of small-town life while pretending I wasn't different than everyone else.

Of course, I was different. Though I was only eight years old, I soon realized that my social status had changed. No longer popular amongst the other third graders, my peers would tease me mercilessly about my gait, my metal leg brace, my "bad" arm, and my slurred words.

When I would become upset, they would retort *"Sandra can't take a joke!"*

Years later, as I stood there speechless and staring at Brandon's face, I wished I knew what to say to make this right again. Suddenly, one of the support workers spoke up from behind me. Though she meant well, her words validated what I had feared all along:

"Don't feel bad...Brandon can't take a joke..."

What had I become?

Did I think I was part of the dominant social group? Had I internalized ableist belief so much over the years that I was becoming one of them?

Paolo Freire (2005) said that when we fight oppression, we risk turning into our oppressors if we haven't had exposure to any other type of empowerment. As a disabled child and inspired by all these "jokes" at my expense, I quickly discovered that humor was a powerful defense mechanism. Humor diffused tension and deflected attention. Over the years, I developed a keen wit that would efficiently shut down taunts and jeers. Looking back, I cringe when I remember that I may have become just as merciless as those who teased me. There was one particular incident with some poor kid who asked me *"Hey...what's wrong with your hand?"* I wasted no time in replying *"There's nothing wrong with my hand...what's wrong with your nose?"*

Affirming my disability in university made me feel empowered. In retrospect, however, I recognize I did not fully embrace this identity. Cognitively, I knew what disability was. I knew I had a disability. But emotionally, disability was never discussed and never integrated into my sense of self.

When it came to the emotional side of disability, I was a mess. After all these years of avoiding and ignoring, I was still raw and vulnerable. Therefore, I was only really comfortable with the concept at arm's length. I felt safest in my neutrality, watching the privileged "us" interact with a marginalized "them" from afar. Even when I helped support clients with disability integration, I didn't stop to think that I could have used the same support. After all, I was not a typical person with a disability...was I? I had a higher education (didn't most people with disabilities face barriers to education?). I was married (weren't most people with disabilities single?). I may have faced barriers to employment, but I built a private practice all by myself (weren't most people with disabilities unemployed or under-employed?).

Brandon had succeeded in hitting a nerve with his accurate observation. While Brandon had been trying for meaningful connection by acknowledging our similarities, I had shut him down with my well-honed deficit-oriented defenses. At the time, I didn't know how to articulate these overwhelming feelings in the form of a proper apology. To move on from here, however, I realized that I would have to apologize. To do that, I would have to come to terms with my own limitations and privileges.

Discussion (or why I don't have a Mustache)

Inclusion does not have a consistent definition across the literature. However, this term has become integral to government, healthcare, and education policies. Despite continued advocacy on paper, not much is known about how much is followed up in practice (Browne & Millar, 2016). This is further complicated when we try to apply traditional rules of social interaction to inclusive encounters with diverse populations.

Sometimes people feel safer among a group of other individuals with similar backgrounds, cultures, age range, and other factors. These similarities can increase social solidarity, reinforcing the sense of belonging to the group. It can be perceived as threatening when people of diverse cultures attempt to join this group. Though some authors suggest that inclusion isn't meaningful unless we identify people to exclude (Abrams & Hogg, 2005; Fiske, 2004), experiential learning can't take place in homogenous spaces (Timm-Bottos, 2006). The Art Hives model promotes diverse communities by providing safe places to interact.

Interaction within smaller marginalized groups is, in some ways, more beneficial than interactions with the community at large. However, shaking institutionalized culture and resulting power dynamics can be hard. Social norms dictate certain relationships between those in power and those who are dependent. Traditionally, people employed as caretakers are perceived to be in charge of people who need support. This power differential can sometimes result in a loss of voice and meaningful connection with learning-disabled individuals. The Art Hives model dismisses traditional ways of thinking, promoting instead an exploration and greater understanding of disabled individuals' perspectives.

Social interaction is not always as simple as "us" and "them". Though ableist perspectives tend to generalize the entire population, each individual with disabilities faces a unique array of abilities and limitations. The World Health Organization (2002) defines disability as an umbrella term, covering a wide spectrum of physical, cognitive, intellectual, developmental, sensory, and otherwise neurodiverse challenges. But because disability itself is diverse, building a sense of unified community is difficult.

For this reason, power dynamics are also sometimes enacted between members of the disability population itself. Deal (2003) proposes a disability hierarchy that categorizes disability according to types that society finds easier (or harder) to tolerate. The more privileges (such as education, employment) that the person with disabilities can access, the higher they are in the hierarchy. It's also easier for them to pass as members of dominant society. People with disabilities at the top of the hierarchy may resist associating with those who find it more challenging to pass as part of the dominant group. This may be because of stigma, access to resources, and the dominant culture's assumption of global limitations (Deal, 2003).

Until that day in the community art studio, Rosemarie Garland-Thomson would point out that I was still "in the closet" (2016). Growing up, I had to dismiss my disability to fit in with the rest of the local ableist culture. After years of this pretense and internalizing this ableism that surrounded me, I realized that I had even fooled myself. I knew I was disabled. I could rattle on about disability culture and disability pride. But I was keeping myself separated. After all these years, I didn't fully accept my part of our shared social identity. Traditional social norms had established themselves so firmly in my own perspectives that I wasn't thinking about the end goal of the Art Hives network. Changing the rules of social interaction was part of my motivation to create a local community art studio in the first place.

Why I don't have a Mustache (and other People do)

Though many group members interpreted my quick retort as a joke, there is some truth to it. Traditional society is built on worth, comparison, and interactions based on power dynamics. In our community art studio, participants were encouraged to see other individuals based on their own merits, not labels or stereotypical categories. This doesn't mean ignoring differences or only accepting people based on similarities. Acknowledging and accepting diversity is crucial in developing a unique sense of self, as well as generating a sense of belonging among group members.

Diversity does not equal "less than" or "more than". Disabilities show us the diversity of the human body. Some of us may be limited in our abilities, but safe, supportive spaces allow us to be interdependent as we build community together.

This is the reason it's important that I don't have a mustache. Facial hair, skin color, gender identity, ethnicity, and ability are all examples of the various facets that make up our individual identities. This kind of diversity is accepted, reinforcing the fact that you can be different yet still belong. Diversity due to disability is slower to be accepted when interacting in an ableist framework. It's hard to change our way of thinking from implicit attitudes and homogenous exclusion. But I think we made progress in the six years of our community open art studio.

Not that this progress happened overnight. Brandon was quite upset with me for some time. It also took a while for me to establish a disability consciousness and to accept the vulnerability that came with this part of my identity. Gradually, through little interactions and through artmaking, Brandon's trust in me was slowly rebuilt. I saw Brandon again at the community art studio in the last weeks of 2019, this time with a new personal support worker. He waved me over and introduced me.

"Brian, this is Sandra...she's just like me! But she doesn't have a mustache."

To the obvious confusion on the part of Brian, we both laughed. Time and experience in the studio convinced Brandon that I respected and valued him as a community member. As Timm-Bottos suggests, time and experience were the secrets to successful social interactions in the liminal space of our community art studio. In addition, a willingness to suspend traditional social norms in favor of attempting to understand other perspectives was crucial in building authentic relationships.

Conclusion

The Art Hive model advocates for spaces that feel safe to ensure individuals feel free to be themselves. Participants must be ready to unlearn assumptions based on social norms. It takes courage to question ingrained beliefs and revise foundational values. When traditional, outside-world norms don't apply, participants must be open to possibilities. This is incredibly hard to do since implicit assumptions can be mistaken for common sense thinking.

The community art studio ran from June 2013 to just before the pandemic in January 2020. I learned so much in those six years. To truly feel included, individuals need acknowledgment, acceptance, authentic interaction, and being witnessed by fellow community members. It was unfortunate that we couldn't get everyone in the community involved in our art studio. However, working among group members with learning disabilities was an important learning experience in itself.

Inclusion is a slow process. This is especially true if an individual is inflexible in their thinking. Learning can be uncomfortable. But this is what makes the liminal space of the community art studio so magical. A person cannot be judged on one identity facet – such as disability – alone. We should be seen and appreciated for the complex intersectional beings we are. When we are willing to reach beyond traditional social norms, we can change from seeing only limitations to imagining potential.

Acknowledgment

I acknowledge that the lands on which my research is conducted are situated in the traditional territories of diverse Indigenous groups, and I acknowledge with respect the diverse histories and cultures of the Beothuk, Mi'kmaq, Innu, and Inuit of Newfoundland and Labrador.

References

Abbott, S., & McConkey, R. (2006). The barriers to social inclusion as perceived by people with intellectual disabilities. *Journal of Intellectual Disabilities, 10*(3), 275–287. https://doi.org/10.1177/1744629506067618

Abrams, D. & Hogg, M. A. (2005). A social psychological framework for understanding social inclusion and exclusion. In Abrams, D., Hogg, M. A., & Marques, J. M. (Eds) *The Social Psychology of Inclusion and Exclusion* (pp. 1–23). Psychology Press: New York.

Allen, K., Kern, M. L., Rosek, C. S., McInerney, D. M., & Slavich, G. M. (2021). Belonging: A review of conceptual issues, an integrative framework, and directions for future research. *Australian Journal of Psychology, 73*(1), 87–102. https://doi.org/10.1080/00049530.2021.1883409

Allport, G. W. (1954). The effect of contact. In *The Nature of Prejudice* (pp. 261–282). Addison-Wesley Publishing Company: Reading, MA.

Brown, J. M. (2019). Relational equality and disability injustice. *Journal of Moral Philosophy, 16*(3), 37–357. https://doi.org/10.1163/17455243-20180008

Browne, M., & Millar, M. (2016). A rights-based conceptual framework for the social inclusion of children and young persons with an intellectual disability. *Disability & Society, 31*(8), 1064–1080. https://doi.org/10.1080/09687599.2016.1232190

Clement, T., & Bigby, C. (2009). Breaking out of a distinct social space: Reflections on supporting community participation for people with severe and profound intellectual disability. *Journal of Applied Research in Intellectual Disabilities, 22*(3), 264–275. https://doi.org/10.1111/j.1468-3148.2008.00458.x

Colorafi, K., Cupples, L., Kallman, D., & Kennedy, J. (2021). Disability stories: Personal perspectives of people with disabilities on navigating the U.S. health system. *Disability & Society, 38*(9), 1585–1607. https://doi.org/10.1080/09687599.2021.2004879

Deal, M. (2003). Disabled people's attitudes toward other impairment groups: A hierarchy of impairments. *Disability & Society, 18*(7), 897–910. https://doi.org/10.1080/0968759032000127317

Fiske, S. T. (2004). Stereotyping, prejudice, and discrimination: Social biases. In *Social Beings: A Core Motives to Social Psychology* (pp. 419–470). Wiley: United States of America.

Freire, P. (2005). Chapter 1. In *Pedagogy of the Oppressed* (30th anniversary ed., pp. 43–69). Continuum: New York & London.

Garland-Thomson, R. (2016). Becoming disabled. *The New York Times.* Ection SR, Page 1. https://www.nytimes.com/2016/08/21/opinion/sunday/becoming-disabled.html

Griffo, G. (2014). Models of disability, ideas of justice, and the challenge of full participation. *Modern Italy, 19*(2), 147–159. https://dx.doi.org/l0.1080/13532944.2014.910502

Hall, E. (2004). Social geographies of learning disability: Narratives of exclusion and inclusion. *Area, 36*(3), 298–306. https://doi.org/10.1111/j.0004-0894.2004.00227.x

Ingham, E. (2018). The (physically) wounded healer: The impact of a physical disability on training and development as a counseling therapist: A case study. *The European Journal of Counselling Psychology, 7*(1), 31–46. https://doi.org/10.5964/ejcop.v7i1.131

Jackman-Galvin, V., & Partridge, M. (2022). Relationships and power: An exploration of person-centredness in an intellectual disability service in Ireland. *Health & Social Care in the Community, 30*(6), e6294–e6302. https://doi.org/10.1111/hsc.14068

Kramer, E. (2000). The art therapist's third hand: Reflections on art, art therapy and society at large. In L. A. Gerity (Ed.), *Art as Therapy: Collected Papers*. Jessica Kingsley. Miller, 47–72.

Nario-Redmond, M. R., Kemerling, A. A., & Silverman, A. (2019). Hostile, benevolent and ambivalent ableism: Contemporary manifestations. *Journal of Social Issues, 75*(3), 726–756. https://doi.org/10.1111/josi.12337

Reber, L., Kreschmer, J. M., James, T. G., Junior, J. D., DeShong, G. L., Parker, S., & Meade, M. A. (2022). Ableism and contours of the attitudinal environment as identified by adults with long-term physical disabilities: A qualitative study. *International Journal of Environmental Research and Public Health, 19*(12), 7469–7491.

Redley, M., Banks, C., Foody, K., & Holland, A. (2012). Healthcare for men and women with learning disabilities: Understanding inequalities in access. *Disability & Society, 27*(6), 747–759. https://doi.org/10.1080/09687599.2012.673080

Robey, K. L., Beckley, L., & Kirschner, M. (2006). Implicit infantilizing attitudes about disability. *Journal of Developmental and Physical Disabilities, 18*(4), 441–453. https:// doi. org/10.1007/s10882-006-9027-3

Timm-Bottos, J. (2006). Constructing creative community: Reviving health and justice through community arts. *The Canadian Art Therapy Association Journal, 19*(2), 12–26. https://doi.org/10.1080/08322473.2006.11432285

Timm-Bottos, J., & Reilly, R. C. (2015). Learning in third spaces: Community art studio as storefront university classroom. *American Journal of Community Psychology, 55*(1–2), 102–114. https://doi.org/10.1007/s10464-014-9688-5

Timm-Bottos, J. (2016). Beyond counseling and psychotherapy, there is a field. I'll meet you there. *Art Therapy, 33*(3), 160–162. https://doi.org/10.1080/07421656.2016.1199248

Van Aswegen, J., & Shevlin, M. (2019). Disabling discourses and ableist assumptions: Reimaging social justice through education for disabled people through a critical discourse analysis approach. *Policy Futures in Education, 17*(5),634–656. https://doi.org/10.1177/1478210318817420

Wiesel, I., & Bigby, C. (2014). Being recognized and becoming known: Encounters between people with and without intellectual disabilities. *Environment and Planning A: Economy and Space, 46*(7OP), 1754–1769. https://doi.org/10.1068/a46251

Winnicott, D. W. (1971). *Playing and Reality*. Tavistock Publications.

World Health Organization. (2002). *ICF Beginner's Guide: Towards a Common Language for Functioning, Disability, and Health*. https://www.who.int/publications/m/item/icf-beginner-s-guide-towards-a-common-language-for-functioning-disability-and-health

Yuval-Davis, N., Anthias, F., & Kofman, E. (2005). Secure borders and safe haven and the gendered politics of belonging: Beyond social cohesion. *Ethnic and Racial Studies, 28*(3), 513–535. https://doi.org/10.1080/0141987042000337867

Conclusion

Chapter 16

Bridging Practice and Research

Art Therapy with Children and Adults with Learning Disabilities

Simon Hackett and Nicki Power

Introduction

As we conclude this book, we want to draw together the diverse approaches and experiences of art therapy described across the previous chapters. We've chosen to do this in a structured way to build a bridge between clinical practice and research. As active researchers in the field of art therapy with people with learning disabilities, we want to grow the evidence base through supporting clinicians to enhance their research skills by fostering their innate curiosity and providing a framework to grow their confidence in evaluating practice and exploring interventions.

This chapter begins with a review of the types of evidence that can support our evolving profession. It then provides a summary of the art therapy practice that has been described by each of the chapter authors to give an overview of the approaches used. This does not represent a systematic approach to reporting on art therapy used in general, but we hope to provide a helpful summary, a snapshot, of the components of art therapy interventions reported in the previous chapters. In our discussion, we also frame the strengths in this volume, the areas which brought us joy as editors and where we think a future collected edition could offer further insight. Finally, we offer a manifesto to inspire art therapists and people with learning disabilities to continue to advocate for personal, community, and societal change using art therapy.

Building Our Evidence Base in Art Therapy with People with Learning Disabilities

Traditionally, the hierarchy of evidence (Murad et al., 2016) provides a framework which locates research in terms of robustness and reliability. This hierarchy places systematic reviews and meta-analyses at the pinnacle due to their comprehensive synthesis of multiple data sources to answer a specific question. Randomised Control Trials are also viewed as high-quality evidence. In these studies, comparison is made between two different conditions, one being the intervention, and bias is minimised due to random allocation to treatment and blinded study procedures (Hackett et al., 2020). Conversely, at the base of the hierarchy of evidence sit

DOI: 10.4324/9781003350736-22

expert opinion and case reports, which are deemed to offer important insight but lack generalisability and reliability.

However, building an evidence base requires both resources (financial, physical, time, human, technological) and expertise (knowledge, skills, social). Since art therapy is an emerging profession (Harpazi et al., 2023), which involves diverse training, regulation, and practice, we must recognise that building our research capacity will take time, motivation, and international, as well as local, collaboration.

The components of evidence-based practice in medicine are, at their very best, a conscientious, explicit, and judicious use of current best evidence (Sackett et al., 1996). Best practice is considered in clinical decision making as the integration of clinical expertise, seeking patient or client preferences and drawing on other types of similar evidence in external fields. However, it can take an average of 17 years for evidence to change practice and only 1 in 5 evidence-based interventions make it to routine clinical practice (Rubin, 2023).

Art Therapy Practice-Based Guidelines

Art therapy practice with adults and children with learning disabilities is varied, with some attempts being made to reach a professional agreement on what constitutes 'good practice' (Hackett et al., 2017). Using consensus methods, art therapists in the UK established guidelines for their practice (Hackett et al., 2017). Here clinical expertise, with service user consultation, was harnessed to set a framework to support the delivery of consistent care, which is safe and ethical, efficiently uses limited resources, and provides a structure to evaluate outcomes and quality. While the guidelines can be used by clinicians to support their own accountability, they can also empower people with learning disabilities or their families in knowing what to expect from an art therapist.

The guidelines are as follows:

- *Working relationship:* build a positive working alliance which includes developing an understanding of the person's strengths and preferences.
- *Communication:* pay attention to all aspects of communication, including written, visual, and spoken information.
- *Support networks:* actively work with the people who support the person with learning disabilities in their day-to-day life.
- *Managing risks and vulnerability:* be aware of a person's vulnerabilities, and ensure any concerns are acted upon at the earliest opportunity.
- *Therapy agreements:* dynamically manage therapy arrangements, including gaining consent for treatment, negotiating a therapy contract, and agreeing the scope of information sharing.
- *Assessment, formulation, and therapeutic goals:* undertake a full assessment leading to a clinical formulation that develops understanding of the person's strengths.
- *Work creatively and flexibly:* implement adaptive ways of working that support the person to fully engage in the therapeutic intervention.

- *Work psychotherapeutically:* apply up-to-date knowledge of developmental and mental health problems and use psychologically informed approaches to guide practice.
- *Monitor progress:* take steps to assess your work, which could include evaluating changes alongside gathering feedback from the person about their experience of therapy and whether it is helping.
- *Professional responsibilities and self-care:* take responsibility for having supportive professional structures in place that will develop and sustain your safe practice.

This guidance, while specific to clinical art therapy practice with children and adults with learning disabilities, also reflects the Code of Conduct which regulates all art therapy practice in the UK (Health & Care Professions Council, 2023).

Literature Reviews of Art Therapy with People with Learning Disabilities

More recently, researchers and practitioners in the field of art therapy have sought to consolidate existing evidence through conducting systemic reviews. This empirical approach to knowledge synthesis is seen as the foundation of intervention development (Skivington et al., 2021). This type of review supports readers to understand what works, for whom, and in what circumstances. Through consolidating the evidence in a systematic way, areas of strengths and gaps in research are identified. Appraisal of the literature is used to assess quality so that readers can make a judgement on reliability and trustworthiness of the data.

For children with learning disabilities, a wide-ranging systematic literature review which included art therapy, highlighted the adaptability of interventions and the high value placed upon the therapy by participants (Martínez-Vérez et al., 2024). Providing therapy in specific time periods, for example, during primary education, was considered as having an important contribution to developing social skills; however, most published studies included in this review took place in 'clinical settings' (Martínez-Vérez et al., 2024). Further to this, art therapy was considered to be efficacious in supporting improvements for children in the areas of behaviour, communication, and cognitive and emotional skills (Martínez-Vérez et al., 2024).

For adults with learning disabilities experiencing mental distress, a systematic literature review (Power et al., 2023) included 68 publications globally, spanning 40 years of practice and research. For individual art therapy interventions, the duration of treatment was most likely to be 13 months, with the most common length of art therapy sessions being 60 mins, and the frequency being weekly. For group work, the most common length of therapy was six months, within a range of 2 to 15 months, and group sessions being more likely to be provided for 90 mins once per week (Power et al., 2023). Qualified art therapists predominantly led either individual or group work with involvement of trainee art therapists and a range of other practitioners from artists to psychologists. This review highlighted the broad variation in practice across location, time and clinical setting, with limited systematic testing of interventions which seemed to offer promising outcomes. It identified that outcomes were largely behavioural and were not resource orientated. The experiences of this population were not often gathered, though when asked in an accessible format, people with learning disabilities provided meaningful feedback on art therapy.

In a scoping literature review, that does not exclude research papers based upon low research quality standards or publication type, a very low number of papers, comparatively, were returned in database searches of the published literature (Harpazi et al., 2023). Literature searches of English language publications covering a period of 31 years (1990–2021), including MA and PhDs, yielded just 169 written works on art therapy with people with learning disabilities (following removal of duplicates), with 39 included in the final review (Harpazi et al., 2023). The UK was the primary source of most publications (22/39) with the US following this (12/39), and five publications from Switzerland, Greece, Thailand, Italy, and China (Harpazi et al., 2023). Interestingly, the editors of this book (Hackett & Power) were authors of 7/39 (3%) of the publications within the last nine-year time period of the searches. The year with the most publications on the topic, 2017, coincided with a special edition on 'Art therapy with people who have learning disabilities' in the *International Journal of Art Therapy* (Hackett, 2017). We can conclude from this that, whilst we strongly propose the importance of this work and the need to develop an understanding of the approach and its benefits, there are only a few people globally making this a focus of their attention. Yet, there is a clear indication across a wide range of research studies of psychosocial group interventions with people who have learning disabilities that inclusion of a creative element is one factor that can improve outcomes (Bourne et al., 2022).

Making the Complex Simple – Reporting what we do in Art Therapy

Why is art therapy called an 'intervention'? Well, in fact, art therapy is considered to be a 'complex intervention' (Power et al., 2023). The level of complexity in 'interventions' increases with number of components and the interactions between them, the range of expertise, skill, techniques required by those delivering it, the groups of people and the context they are in. Additionally, the level of flexibility and tailoring of the intervention in response to specific needs and circumstances increases complexity and replicability (Skivington et al., 2021). As can be seen in the descriptions of art therapy practice included in this book, we see multiple components described, a wide range of skills and expertise demonstrated by art therapists who utilise applied theories, techniques, and adapt their communication styles to adjust to the needs of the people they work with. Therapists often seek to act upon and attune, in a considered way, with the person they are working with to make adjustments. Art therapists routinely tailor their approaches to meet the specific needs of the adults and children they work with.

Letting people know what is involved in art therapy's complex mix of interpersonal, physical and sensory, contextual, process orientated, theory based, adaptable and flexible approaches is important. Agreed international standards on better reporting of interventions (Hoffmann et al., 2014), the Template for Intervention Description and Replication (TIDieR) checklist, provide consistency, structure, and guidance. We encouraged our chapter authors, included in this book, to share information in this format so that their work and approaches could be clearly communicated and understood. By answering some simple questions, 'why, what, how, where, when?' (Hoffmann et al., 2014), we can gain insights into similarities and differences in art therapy practice, both for comparison and consideration of how approaches can be replicated in different contexts. We encourage all reports of art therapy practice and research more generally, in whatever form they might take, to include and describe this basic information in reports of interventions in practice.

A Summary of Art Therapy Interventions

What was the Intervention?

Out of the 15 chapters included describing art therapy practice, we can see that the majority are delivered for groups (10/14) (see Table 16.1), with a much higher number of interventions being reported for adults (12/14). The interventions described range from art-based workshops, led by an Art Therapist with the purpose of supporting people with learning disabilities to engage in advanced care planning (Chapter 5) and a life story journaling group (Chapter 6), to individual therapy in support of people who have experienced trauma (Chapters 3, 4, 9, and 10), art therapy groups (Chapters 7, 12, 13, and 14), art-based groups (Chapters 8 and 11), and open art groups/studios (Chapters 2 and 15).

It is interesting that the accessibility of art therapy is indicated through the length of session time being provided, ranging from 60 mins to 180 mins. We know that art therapists adapt and adjust the time that children and adults are in sessions according to their needs. However, routine provision of long session times suggests that people remain motivated and engaged throughout. Furthermore, we see that motivation and engagement are often sustained over a course of therapy, routinely provided as weekly sessions, with planned breaks.

There is a strong indication that work with an art therapist can achieve short-term and focused outcomes (Chapter 5) but that therapeutic relationships can also be sustained over a number of years (Chapter 10) with people who have highly complex needs and require higher levels of support, for example in long-term care settings.

In addition, the range of adaptability of art therapy means that children and adults with high communication needs can access therapy and address personally challenging issues related to mental health, trauma, and experiences of marginalisation (Chapters 3, 4, and 9).

Table 16.1 Summary of interventions included in 'Art Therapy with People with Learning Disabilities: Authentic Voices in Clinical Practice and Research'.

Chapter/ Author	Page	City, Country	What type of intervention?	Individual (Ind) or Group (Grp-size)	Who was it for?	Who provided it and who helped?	Session Time?	How often was it?	How long was it?	Where did it happen?	Funding?
1 Royster	p00	Chicago, USA	Open Art Studio	Grp	Children	Art Therapist Students	90 mins.	Weekly	10+ wks. / Rolling programme	School	Education/ Grant
2 Benton, Batt & Sage	p00	Bristol, UK	Art Therapy	Ind	Adults	Art Therapist	60 mins.	Weekly	3 yrs.	Community Centre	NHS
3 Liz, Joey	p00	Coventry, UK	Art Therapy	Ind	Adult	Art Therapist	75 mins.	Weekly	6 yrs.	NHS Community Team	NHS
4 Jerwood et al.	p00	Birmingham, UK	Art-Based Workshop	Grp (3–10)	Adults	Art Therapist Practitioner co-facilitator Support Staff	120 mins.	Weekly	3 wks.	Online and Community Venue	Charity
5 Rossi	p00	Melbourne, Australia	Life Story Journaling	Grp	Adults	Art Therapist	60 mins.	Weekly	2 yrs. / Rolling programme	Day Centre	Day Centre
6 King	p00	Manchester, UK	Art Group	Grp (5–6)	Children	Art Therapist Trainee	60 mins.	Weekly	2 yrs. / Rolling programme	School	Education
7 Gentle & Calhoun	p00	New South Wales, Australia	Art Group	Grp	Adults	Art Therapist Researcher Support Staff	180 mins	Weekly	1 yr.	Art Studio	NGO
8 Harrison & Lizzy	p00	Newcastle upon Tyne, UK	Art Therapy/ Supported Advocacy	Ind	Adult	Art Psychotherapist	60 mins.	Weekly	2 yrs.	NHS Community Team	NHS

		Location	Approach	Format	Population	Facilitator	Duration	Frequency	Length	Setting	Funding
9 Koizumi	p00	London, UK	Art Therapy	Ind	Adult	Art Psychotherapist Nursing staff	60 mins.	Yrs. 1–2, twice weekly Yrs. 3–5, weekly Yrs. 6 monthly	6 yrs.	NHS Secure Care	NHS
10 Rose	p00	Sydney, Australia	Art-Based Group	Grp (20–25)	Adult	Art Psychotherapist Artist Teacher	120 mins.	Weekly	10+ wks. / Rolling programme	Arts Centre	-
11 Ahmed	p00	Southampton, UK	Art Therapy	Grp (3–7)	Adults	Art Therapist Artist Educator Support Staff	120 mins.	Weekly	10 wks.	Gallery	NHS/ Grant
12 Ng & Kwan	p00	Hong Kong, China	Art-Based Group	Grp (12–16)	Adults Carers	Art Therapist Practitioner	120 mins.	Weekly	6 wks.	Down Syndrome Association Centres	Resources Group
13 Meakin, Burns & Newcombe	p00	Rotherham, UK	Art Therapy	Grp (3–4)	Adults	Art Therapist/s	90 mins.	Weekly	12 wks.	NHS Community Team	NHS
14 Hewitt-Parsons	p00	Newfoundland, Canada	Community Open Art Studio	Grp	Adults	Art Therapist Students	180 mins.	Weekly	14+ wks. / Rolling programme	Arts Centre	Voluntary/ Grant

Who Provided the Intervention?

Art therapists have led and delivered all of the interventions described, but it is also important to recognise the collegiality and multi-disciplinary approaches demonstrated across a range of interventions. Specifically, art therapists report working closely with the support of other practitioners, teachers of teaching assistants, artists, volunteers, trainee clinical psychologists, researchers, support workers, and carers. Collectively, this approach allows for attention to be shared and the varied needs of individuals to be addressed, particularly within group settings.

Where Were Sessions Held?

Versatile contexts and venues for art therapy to take place in are also reported, including schools, art studios, performing arts centres, gallery spaces, community and day centres, and National Health Service (NHS) venues in the community and in hospitals, with a recent example of an online group (Chapter 5).

Art therapists are engaging with local communities to deliver accessible interventions to a broad range of individuals. They are seeking out collaborative partnerships (Chapters 2, 5, 8, 12, and 15) and demonstrating how the arts can be used to challenge the status quo in their community and to confront issues of social justice locally which are reflected globally.

Who Funded the Intervention?

Funding is certainly not consistent for art therapy; perhaps the more consistent examples of funded provision are due to employment of art therapists/art psychotherapists in some UK NHS hospitals and community teams. However, this is not included as standard in the provision of services for people with learning disabilities in the UK and there is no indication of this provision being funded consistently nationwide. There are some examples of funding in educational and state provision of day services. It is also important to highlight charitable and volunteer organisations providing or commissioning art therapy.

Discussion

It is possible to conclude from the summary and overview of art therapy practice that in all its potential forms, art therapy provides a wide range of approaches and formats for delivering therapy. Key messages are the widely indicated accessibility of art therapy, either for individuals or groups, promoting engagement and motivation to sustain attention, relationships, and helping manage responses to difficult and challenging personal issues, circumstances, and societal injustices. The skills of art therapists in being able to adapt practice and tailor it to the needs of groups and individuals are central. This includes an ability to lead other practitioners in contributing to the safe, engaging, and interactive processes that are shown to offer beneficial experiences and outcomes for children and adults with a learning disability.

There is a need for ongoing advocacy for accessible therapies and approaches for people with learning disabilities. The importance of finding and amplifying diverse voices within the field has been an explicit aim within this book.

Whilst we recognise and endorse the need for the further development of an evidence base for art therapy, as a flexible and adaptable approach, we also wish to highlight some barriers to this. Traditionally, (a) people with learning disabilities have been excluded from research, (b) national and international funding for research has not prioritised the health and mental health of people with learning disabilities, (c) methods for assessing the effectiveness of psychosocial interventions are not always accessible to people with learning disabilities and thus, exclude their participation, and (d) due to patchy provision of art therapy, because of lack of funding (sometimes a lack of evidence base is cited as the reason for this), there is low capacity for recruitment of people to participate in studies. In addition, the countries that are producing and publishing the majority of reports of practice and research have established publicly funded healthcare systems and research infrastructure, i.e. the UK. However, this also highlights a huge global gap in the delivery of art therapy, the reporting on its practice development, and an ability to make progress on building a diverse and culturally sensitive evidence base that can crosscut international healthcare systems and varying national contexts.

This cycle of low priority and low levels of funding for art therapy also maintains a situation where there are lower levels of research being carried out and the studies that are undertaken are assessed as being lower quality, for example, due to including small numbers of participants.

In many ways, this is a disservice to people with learning disabilities, where access to accessible psychological therapies could be highly beneficial to people's health and wellbeing. Not least, we also highlight examples of creative methods and art therapy reported in this book to help in personal decision making and planning, processing traumatic events, building friendships and social networks, advocating against unjust treatment, and empowering the voices of people with learning disabilities to 'self-advocate' and participate fully in society. Based upon this 'evidence', we believe that greater attention and greater resources should be directed towards people with learning disabilities across their life course to support increased access to arts therapies internationally.

Next Steps in Practice & Research (A Manifesto)

To build on the work we have presented in this volume, it is essential to recognise the challenges we encountered as editors.

Firstly, there is a notable need for greater representation of art therapy with certain groups, namely, children and young people, individuals with severe, profound, and multiple learning disabilities, and racially minoritised groups (or the global majority).

Secondly, some practice contexts need further investigation, particularly online practices to widen access further (Zubala & Hackett, 2020; Zubala et al., 2021), as well as work set within physical health, mental health, inpatient and secure care (forensic).

When we launched the competitive process of seeking chapter contributions, we sought global representation. However, it was the 'global north' that responded and has been included. Future volumes which include contributions from diverse regions, including Africa, South America, and Europe, would enhance the global representation in art therapy practice and research.

Furthermore, the significance of leadership roles for art therapists within health, social care, and other contexts cannot be overlooked, as strategic, operational, and advanced clinical leadership all play vital roles in the success of therapeutic practices, service delivery, and effective healthcare provision.

Conclusion

Art therapy is highly valued by many people with learning disabilities that have experienced it. This includes the many co-authors with learning disabilities who have contributed to the reporting and description of practice held within this book. We advocate 'doing with' and not 'doing to' in recognition of the labelling and stigma that has been and is still being experienced by many people (Power et al., 2022). We see co-production as being central to the progression of art therapy practice with people with learning disabilities.

References

Bourne, J., Harrison, T. L., Wigham, S., Morison, C. J., & Hackett, S. (2022). A systematic review of community psychosocial group interventions for adults with intellectual disabilities and mental health conditions. *Journal of Applied Research in Intellectual Disabilities,* 35(1): 3–23. https://doi.org/10.1111/jar.12919.

Hackett, S. (2017). Editorial. *International Journal of Art Therapy*, 22(2): 45–45. https://doi.org/10.1080/17454832.2017.1323686.

Hackett, Ashby L., Parker, K., Goody, S., & Power, N. (2017). UK art therapy practice-based guidelines for children and adults with learning disabilities. *International Journal of Art Therapy*, 22(2): 84–94. https://doi.org/10.1080/17454832.2017.1319870.

Hackett, S., Zubala, A., Aafjes-van Doorn, K., Chadwick, T., Harrison, T. L., Bourne, J., Freeston, M., Jahoda, A., Taylor, J. L., & Ariti, C. (2020). A randomised controlled feasibility study of interpersonal art psychotherapy for the treatment of aggression in people with intellectual disabilities in secure care. *Pilot and Feasibility Studies*, 6, 1–14.

Hackett, S. S., Ashby, L., Parker, K., Goody, S., & Power, N. (2017). UK art therapy practice-based guidelines for children and adults with learning disabilities. *International Journal of Art Therapy*, 22(2): 84–94. https://doi.org/10.1080/17454832.2017.1319870.

Harpazi, S., Regev, D., & Snir, S. (2023). What does the literature teach us about research, theory, and the practice of art therapy for individuals with intellectual developmental disabilities? A scoping review. *The Arts in Psychotherapy*, 82: 101988. https://doi.org/10.1016/j.aip.2022.101988.

Health & Care Professions Council. (2023). *The Standards of Proficiency for Arts Therapists*. The standards of proficiency for arts therapists. https://www.hcpc-uk.org/standards/standards-of-proficiency/arts-therapists/.

Hoffmann, T. C., Glasziou, P. P., Boutron, I., Milne, R., Perera, R., Moher, D., Altman, D. G., Barbour, V., Macdonald, H., Johnston, M., Lamb, S. E., Dixon-Woods, M., McCulloch, P., Wyatt, J. C., Chan, A.-W., & Michie, S. (2014). Better reporting of interventions: template for intervention description and replication (TIDieR) checklist and guide. *British Medical Journal*, 348: g1687. https://doi.org/10.1136/bmj.g1687.

Martínez-Vérez, V., Gil-Ruíz, P., & Domínguez-Lloria, S. (2024). Interventions through art therapy and music therapy in Autism spectrum disorder, ADHD, language disorders, and learning disabilities in Pediatric-aged children: A systematic review. *Children (Basel)*, 11(6): 706. https://doi.org/10.3390/children11060706.

Murad, M. H., Asi, N., Alsawas, M., & Alahdab, F. (2016). New evidence pyramid. *Evidence Based Medicine*, 21(4): 125–127. https://doi.org/10.1136/ebmed-2016-110401.

Power, N., Harrison, T. L., Hackett, S., & Carr, C. (2023). Art therapy as a treatment for adults with learning disabilities who are experiencing mental distress: A configurative systematic review with narrative synthesis. *The Arts in Psychotherapy*, 86: 102088. https://doi.org/https://doi.org/10.1016/j.aip.2023.102088.

Power, N., Millard, E., The Lawnmowers Independent Theater Company, A., Artists, a., & Carr, C. (2022). Un-Labelling the language: Exploring labels, Jargon and power through participatory arts research with arts therapists and people with learning disabilities. *Voices: A World Forum for Music Therapy*, 22(3). https://doi.org/10.15845/voices.v22i3.3391.

Rubin, R. (2023). It takes an average of 17 years for evidence to change practice-the Burgeoning field of implementation science seeks to speed things up. *Journal of the American Medical Association*, 329(16): 1333–1336. https://doi.org/10.1001/jama.2023.4387.

Sackett, D. L., Rosenberg, W. M., Gray, J. A., Haynes, R. B., & Richardson, W. S. (1996). Evidence based medicine: what it is and what it isn't. *British Medical Journal*, 312(7023): 71–72. https://doi.org/10.1136/bmj.312.7023.71.

Skivington, K., Matthews, L., Simpson, S. A., Craig, P., Baird, J., Blazeby, J. M., Boyd, K. A., Craig, N., French, D. P., McIntosh, E., Petticrew, M., Rycroft-Malone, J., White, M., & Moore, L. (2021). Framework for the development and evaluation of complex interventions: gap analysis, workshop and consultation-informed update. *Health Technology Assessment*, 25(57): 1–132. https://doi.org/10.3310/hta25570.

Zubala, A., & Hackett, S. (2020). Online art therapy practice and client safety: a UK-wide survey in times of COVID-19. *International Journal of Art Therapy*, 25(4): 161–171. https://doi.org/10.1080/17454832.2020.1845221.

Zubala, A., Kennell, N., & Hackett, S. (2021). Art therapy in the digital world: An integrative review of current practice and future directions. *Frontiers in Psychology*, 12: 595536. https://doi.org/10.3389/fpsyg.2021.600070.

Index

For Product Safety Concerns and Information please contact our EU
representative GPSR@taylorandfrancis.com
Taylor & Francis Verlag GmbH, Kaufingerstraße 24, 80331 München, Germany

www.ingramcontent.com/pod-product-compliance
Lightning Source LLC
Chambersburg PA
CBHW052002270326
41929CB00015B/2755

9 781032 396507